The Philosophical Baby

The Philosophical Baby

WHAT CHILDREN'S MINDS TELL US ABOUT

TRUTH, LOVE, AND THE MEANING OF LIFE

✳

Alison Gopnik

FARRAR, STRAUS AND GIROUX

New York

FARRAR, STRAUS AND GIROUX
18 West 18th Street, New York 10011

Library of Congress Cataloging-in-Publication Data
Gopnik, Alison.
    The philosophical baby : what children's minds tell us about truth, love,
and the meaning of life / Alison Gopnik.
        p. cm.
    Includes bibliographical references and index.
    ISBN-13: 978-0-374-23196-5 (hardcover : alk. paper)
    ISBN-10: 0-374-23196-6 (hardcover : alk. paper)
    1. Cognition in children. 2. Human information processing in children.
3. Perception in children. I. Title.

BF723.C5G675 2009
155.4'13—dc22

                                                            2008049226

Designed by Gretchen Achilles

www.fsgbooks.com

3   5   7   9   10   8   6   4

TO BLAKE, MY PHILOSOPHICAL BABY BROTHER,

WITH PROFOUND GRATITUDE FOR THE TRUTH AND LOVE

HE HAS ALWAYS GIVEN ME

Contents

✳

2. Imaginary Companions: How Does Fiction Tell the Truth?   47

3. Escaping Plato's Cave: How Children, Scientists, and Computers Discover the Truth   74

4. What Is It Like to Be a Baby? Consciousness and Attention   106

5. Who Am I? Memory, Self, and the Babbling Stream   133

6. Heraclitus' River and the Romanian Orphans: How Does Our Early Life Shape Our Later Life?   164

7. Learning to Love: Attachment and Identity   179

The Philosophical Baby

Introduction

*

A one-month-old stares at her mother's face with fixed, brow-wrinkling concentration, and suddenly produces a beatific smile. Surely she must see her mother and feel love, but what are seeing and feeling like for her? What is it like to be a baby? A two-year-old offers a hungry-looking stranger a half-chewed lollipop. Could a child this young already feel empathy and be altruistic? A three-year-old announces that she will come to dinner only if a place is laid for the Babies, the tiny purple-haired twins who live in her pocket and eat flowers for breakfast. How could she believe so profoundly in something that is just a figment of her own imagination? And how could she dream up such remarkable creatures? A five-year-old discovers, with the help of a goldfish, that death is irreversible. How could a child who can't yet read or add uncover deep, hard truths about mortality? The one-month-old turns into the two-year-old and then the three-year-old and the five-year-old and eventually, miraculously, turns into a mother with children of her own. How could all these utterly different creatures be the same person? All of us once were children and most of us will become parents—we have all asked these sorts of questions.

Childhood is a profound part of the human condition. But it is also a largely unexamined part of that condition—so taken for granted that most of the time we hardly notice it at all. Childhood is a universal fact, but when we do think about it, it is almost always in individual first-person terms: What should I do, now, about *my* child? What did *my* parents do that led *me* to be the way I am? Most books about children are like this, from memoirs and novels to the ubiquitous parenting advice books. But childhood is not just a particular plot complication of Irish autobiographies or a particular problem to be solved by American self-help programs. It is not even just something that all human beings share. It is, I'll argue, what makes all human beings human.

When we start to think about childhood more deeply, we realize that this universal, apparently simple fact is riddled with complexities and contradictions. Children are, at once, deeply familiar and profoundly alien. Sometimes we feel that they are just like us—and sometimes they seem to live in a completely different world. Their minds seem drastically limited; they know so much less than we do. And yet long before they can read or write they have extraordinary powers of imagination and creativity, and long before they go to school they have remarkable learning abilities. Their experience of the world sometimes seems narrow and concrete; at other times it looks far more wide-ranging than adult experience. It seems that our experiences as children were crucial in shaping who we are. And yet we all know that the path from child to adult is circuitous and complex, and that the world is full of saints with terrible parents and neurotics with loving ones.

The younger children are, the more mysterious they are. We can more or less remember what it was like to be five or six, and we can talk with school-age children on a reasonably equal basis. But babies and toddlers are utterly foreign territory. Babies can't walk or talk, and even toddlers, well, toddle, and yet science, and indeed common sense, tells us that in those early years they are learning more than they ever will again. It may be hard to see just how the child is father to the man. Yet it is even more difficult to trace the link between the "I" writing this page and the seven-pound bundle of fifty years ago, all eyes and forehead, or even the later thirty-pound whirlwind of tangled sentences, intense emotions, and wild pretend play. We don't even have a good name for this age range. This book will focus on children under five and I'll sometimes use the word "babies" to talk about anybody younger than three. For me "babies" means that particularly adorable combination of chubby cheeks and funny pronunciation, though I recognize that many three-year-olds themselves would reject the description vigorously.

New scientific research and philosophical thinking have both illuminated and deepened the mystery. In the last thirty years, there's been a revolution in our scientific understanding of babies and young children. We used to think that babies and young children were irrational, egocentric, and amoral. Their thinking and experience were concrete, immediate, and limited. In fact, psychologists and neuroscientists have discovered that babies not only learn more, but imagine more, care more, and experience more than we would ever have thought possible. In some ways, young children are actually smarter, more imaginative, more caring, and even more conscious than adults are.

This scientific revolution has led philosophers to take babies seriously for the first time. Children are both profound and puzzling, and this combination is the classic territory of philosophy. Yet you could read 2,500 years of philosophy and find almost nothing about children. A Martian who tried to figure us out by studying Earthling philosophy could easily conclude that human beings reproduce by asexual cloning. The index of the thousands of pages in the 1967 *Encyclopedia of Philosophy* had no references to babies, infants, families, parents, mothers, or fathers, and only four to children at all. (There are hundreds of references to angels and the morning star.)

Very recently, however, this has begun to change. Philosophers have started to pay attention to babies and even to learn from them. The current *Encyclopedia of Philosophy* includes articles that are actually about babies, with titles such as "Infant Cognition" and "The Child's Theory of Mind." I talk at the American Philosophical Association as well as the Society for Research in Child Development, and philosophers argue about when babies understand the minds of others, how they learn about the world, and whether they are capable of empathy. A few even sit precariously on little chairs in preschools and do experiments with children. Thinking about babies and young children can help answer fundamental questions about imagination, truth, consciousness, identity, love, and morality in a new way. In this book I'll argue for a new view of these fundamental philosophical ideas, based on babies, and a new view of babies, based on these philosophical ideas.

HOW CHILDREN CHANGE THE WORLD

There's one big, general idea behind all the specific experiments and arguments in this book. More than any other creature, human beings are able to change. We change the world around us, other people, and ourselves. Children, and childhood, help explain how we change. And the fact that we change explains why children are the way they are—and even why childhood exists at all.

Ultimately, the new scientific explanations of childhood are rooted in evolutionary theory. But studying children leads to a very different picture of how evolution shapes our lives than the traditional picture of "evolutionary psychology." Some psychologists and philosophers argue that most of what is significant about human nature is determined by our genes—an innate hardwired system that makes us who we are. We're endowed with a set of fixed and distinct abilities, designed to suit the needs of our prehistoric ancestors 200,000 years ago in the Pleistocene. Not surprisingly, this view discounts the importance of childhood. The picture is that a "good enough" childhood environment may be necessary to let the innate aspects of human nature unfold. But beyond that, childhood won't have much influence because most of what is important about human nature in general, and individual character in particular, is in place at birth.

But this view doesn't capture our lives as we actually live them and as they change and develop over time. We at least feel as if we actively create our lives, changing our world and our selves. This view also can't explain the radical historical changes in human life. If our nature is determined by our genes, you would think that we would be the same now as we were in the Pleistocene. The puzzling fact about human beings is that our capacity for change, both in our own lives and through history, is the most distinctive and unchanging thing about us. Is there a way of explaining this flexibility and creativity, this ability to alter our individual and collective fate, without resorting to mysticism?

The answer, unexpectedly, comes from very young children—and it leads to a very different kind of evolutionary psychology. The great evolutionary advantage of human beings is their ability to escape from the constraints of evolution. We can learn about our environment, we can imagine different environments, and we can turn those imagined environments into reality. And as an intensely social species, other people are the most important part of our environment. So we are particularly likely to learn about people and to use that knowledge to change the way other people behave, and the way we behave ourselves. The result is that human beings, as a central part of their evolutionary endowment, and as the deepest part of their human nature, are engaged in a constant cycle of change. We change our surroundings and our surroundings change us. We alter other people's behavior, their behavior alters ours.

We begin with the capacity to learn more effectively and more flexibly about our environment than any other species. This knowledge lets us imagine new environments, even radically new environments, and act to change the existing ones. Then we can learn about the unexpected features of the new environment that we have created, and so change that environment once again and so on. What neuroscientists call plasticity—the ability to change in the light of experience—is the key to human nature at every level from brains to minds to societies.

Learning is a key part of the process, but the human capacity for change goes beyond just learning. Learning is about the way the world changes our mind, but our minds can also change the world. Developing a new theory about the world allows us to imagine other ways the world might be. Understanding other people and ourselves lets us imagine new ways of being human. At the same time, to change our world, our selves, and our society we have to think about what we ought to be like, as well as what we actually are like. This book is about how children develop minds that change the world.

Psychologists, philosophers, neuroscientists, and computer

scientists are beginning to carefully and precisely identify some of the underlying mechanisms that give us this distinctively human capacity for change—the aspects of our nature that allow nurture and culture to take place. We even are starting to develop rigorous mathematical accounts of some of those mechanisms. We'll see that this new research and thinking, much of it done just in the past few years, has given us a new understanding of how the biological computers in our skulls actually produce human freedom and flexibility.

If I look around at the ordinary things in front of me as I write this—the electric lamp, the right-angle-constructed table, the brightly glazed symmetrical ceramic cup, the glowing computer screen—almost nothing resembles anything I would have seen in the Pleistocene. All of these objects were once imaginary—they are things that human beings themselves have created. And I myself, a woman cognitive scientist writing about the philosophy of children, could not have existed in the Pleistocene either. I am also a creation of the human imagination, and so are you.

HOW CHILDHOOD CHANGES THE WORLD

The very fact of childhood—our long protected period of immaturity—plays a crucial role in this human ability to change the world and ourselves. Children aren't just defective adults, primitive grown-ups gradually attaining our perfection and complexity. Instead, children and adults are different forms of *Homo sapiens*. They have very different, though equally complex and powerful, minds, brains, and forms of consciousness, designed to serve different evolutionary functions. Human development is more like metamorphosis, like caterpillars becoming butterflies, than like simple growth—though it may seem that children are the vibrant, wandering butterflies who transform into caterpillars inching along the grown-up path.

What *is* childhood? It's a distinctive developmental period in which young human beings are uniquely dependent on adults. Childhood literally couldn't exist without caregivers. Why do we go through a period of childhood at all? Human beings have a much more extended period of immaturity and dependence, a much longer childhood, than other species, and this period of immaturity has become longer as human history has gone on (as we parents of twenty-somethings may recognize with a sigh). Why make babies so helpless for so long, and why make adults invest so much time and energy in caring for them?

This protracted period of immaturity is intimately tied up with the human capacity for change. Our human capacities for imagination and learning have great advantages; they allow us to adapt to more different environments than any other species and to change our own environments in a way that no other animal can. But they also have one great disadvantage—learning takes time. You don't want to be stuck exploring all the new possible ways to hunt deer when you haven't eaten for two days, or learning all the accumulated cultural wisdom about saber-toothed tigers when one is chasing you. It would be a good idea for me to spend a week exploring all the capabilities of my new computer, as my teenage son would, but with the saber-toothed tigers of grant deadlines and classes breathing down my neck, I'll just go on relying on the old routines.

An animal that depends on the accumulated knowledge of past generations has to have some time to acquire that knowledge. An animal that depends on imagination has to have some time to exercise it. Childhood is that time. Children are protected from the usual exigencies of adult life; they don't need to hunt deer or ward off saber-toothed tigers, let alone write grant proposals or teach classes—all of that is done for them. All they need to do is learn. When we're children we're devoted to learning about our world and imagining all the other ways that world could be. When we become adults we put all that we've learned and imagined to use.

There's a kind of evolutionary division of labor between children and adults. Children are the R&D department of the human species—the blue-sky guys, the brainstormers. Adults are production and marketing. They make the discoveries, we implement them. They think up a million new ideas, mostly useless, and we take the three or four good ones and make them real.

If we focus on adult abilities, long-term planning, swift and automatic execution, rapid skillful reaction to the deer and the tigers and the deadlines, then babies and young children will indeed look pretty pathetic. But if we focus on our distinctive capacities for change, especially imagination and learning, then it's the adults who look slow. The caterpillars and butterflies do different things well.

This basic division of labor between children and adults is reflected in their minds, their brains, their everyday activities, and even their conscious experience. Babies' brains seem to have special qualities that make them especially well suited for imagination and learning. Babies' brains are actually more highly connected than adult brains; more neural pathways are available to babies than adults. As we grow older and experience more, our brains "prune out" the weaker, less used pathways and strengthen the ones that are used more often. If you looked at a map of the baby's brain it would look like old Paris, with lots of winding, interconnected little streets. In the adult brain those little streets have been replaced by fewer but more efficient neural boulevards, capable of much more traffic. Young brains are also much more plastic and flexible—they change much more easily. But they are much less efficient; they don't work as quickly or effectively.

There are even more specific brain changes that play a particularly important role in the metamorphosis from childhood to adulthood. They involve the prefrontal cortex, a part of the brain that is uniquely well developed in human beings, and that neuroscientists often argue is the seat of distinctively human abilities. Scientists have located sophisticated capacities for thinking, planning, and control in the prefrontal area. For example, through a tragic combination of error and arrogance, psychiatric patients in the fifties were subjected to prefrontal lobotomies—operations that removed this part of their brains. Although these patients remained superficially functional, they had largely lost the ability to make decisions, to control their impulses, and to act intelligently.

The prefrontal cortex is one of the last parts of the brain to mature. The wiring of this part of the cortex, the process of pruning out some connections and strengthening others, may not be complete until the mid-twenties (another sigh from parents of twenty-somethings). Recently neuroscientists have discovered that all of the brain is more plastic and changeable, even in adulthood, than we ever thought before. Still, some parts, the visual system, for example, seem to take their adult form in the first few months of life. Others, like the prefrontal cortex, and the connections between the prefrontal area and other parts of the brain, mature much more slowly. They continue to change through adolescence and beyond. The visual cortex is much the same at six months and sixty, while the prefrontal area takes on its final form only in adulthood.

You might think this means that children are defective adults, that they lack the parts of the brain that are most crucial for rational adult thought. But you could equally say that, when it comes to imagination and learning, prefrontal immaturity allows children to be superadults. The prefrontal cortex is especially involved in "inhibition." It actually helps shut down other parts of the brain, limiting and focusing experience, action, and thought. This process is crucial for the complex thinking, planning, and acting that adults engage in. To execute a complex plan, for example, you have to perform just the actions that are dictated by that plan, and not all the other possible actions. And you have to pay attention to just the events that are relevant to your plan and not all the others. Anyone who tries to persuade a three-year-old to get dressed for preschool will develop an appreciation of inhibition. It would be so much easier if he didn't stop to explore every speck of dust on the floor, pull out all the drawers in turn, and take off his socks just after you've put them on.

But, as we'll see, inhibition has a downside if you are primarily interested in imagination and learning. To be imaginative, you want to consider as many possibilities as you can, even wild and unprecedented ones (maybe the dresser would work better without all those drawers). In learning, you want to remain open to anything that may turn out to be the truth (maybe that speck of dust holds the secret of the universe). The lack of strong prefrontal control may actually be a benefit of childhood.

In another sense the prefrontal cortex is the *most* active part of the brain during childhood, it constantly changes throughout those years, and its final form depends heavily on childhood experience. The powers of imagination and learning during childhood provide us with the information that we adults use to plan and control our behavior intelligently. In fact, there is some evidence that high IQ is correlated with later maturing and more plastic frontal lobes. Keeping your mind open longer may be part of what makes you smarter.

Those different brains and minds mean that adults and children also spend their days differently—we work, babies play. Play is the signature of childhood. It's a living, visible manifestation of imagination and learning in action. It's also the most visible sign of the paradoxically useful uselessness of immaturity. By definition, play—the baby nesting blocks and pushing the buttons of a busy box, the toddler pretending to be everything from a mermaid to a ninja—has no obvious point or goal or function. It does nothing to advance the basic evolutionary goals of mating and predation, fleeing and fighting. And yet these useless actions—and the adult equivalents we squeeze into our workday—are distinctively, characteristically human and deeply valuable. Plays are play, and so are novels, paintings, and songs.

All these differences between children and adults suggest that children's consciousness, the texture of their everyday experience of the world, must be very different from ours. Children's brains and minds are radically different from ours, so their experience must be too. These differences are not just a source of idle wonder. We can actually use what we know about children's minds and brains to explore their consciousness. We can use the tools of psychology, neuroscience, and philosophy to understand the inner lives of children. In turn, understanding children's consciousness gives us a new perspective on our everyday adult consciousness and on what it means to be human.

These differences also raise intriguing questions about identity. Babies and adults are radically different creatures with different minds, brains, and experiences. But from another perspective we adults are just the final product of childhood. Our brains are the brains that were shaped by experience, our lives are the lives that began as babies, our consciousness is the consciousness that reaches back to childhood. The Greek philosopher Heraclitus said that no man ever steps in the same river twice because neither the river nor the man is the same. Thinking about children and childhood makes it vivid that our lives, and our history as a species, are that sort of ever-changing perpetually flowing river.

All the processes of change, imagination, and learning ultimately depend on love. Human caregivers love their babies in a particularly intense and significant way. That love is one of the engines of human change. Parental love isn't just a primitive and primordial instinct, continuous with the nurturing behavior of other animals (though certainly there are such continuities). Instead, our extended life as parents also plays a deep role in the emergence of the most sophisticated and characteristically human capacities. Our protracted immaturity is possible only because we can rely on the love of the people who take care of us. We can learn from the discoveries of earlier generations because those same loving caregivers invest in teaching us. It isn't just that without mothering humans would lack nurturance, warmth, and emotional security. They would also lack culture, history, morality, science, and literature.

A ROAD MAP

In the first three chapters of this book, I'll explore the philosophical thinking and psychological research behind our new understanding of imagination and learning. Even the youngest babies know a great deal about how the world works. And yet toddlers spend most of their waking hours in wild pretend worlds, politely drinking imaginary tea and ferociously battling imaginary tigers. Why? In chapter 1, I'll explain how knowledge and imagination are intertwined. Children use their knowledge to construct alternate universes—different ways the world might be.

Children also know a great deal about how people work. This lets them imagine new ways that people, including themselves, might think or act. In chapter 2, I'll explain how those abilities lead children to create imaginary friends—and lead grown-ups to create plays and novels. Imagining how they could be different actually lets children, and adults, become different. We can turn ourselves into our imaginary alter egos.

In chapter 3, I'll show where knowledge and imagination come from. Philosophers of science and computer scientists have developed new ideas about how learning and imagination are possible—ideas that have actually been used to design computers that can learn and imagine. These ideas can also explain how children learn and imagine as much as they do. I'll show that babies, like scientists, use statistics and experiments to learn about the world. But they also have a particularly powerful and distinctively human way of learning: they have caregivers who teach them. These kinds of learning allow us to constantly change our view of the world and of the possibilities it offers.

In the next two chapters I'll talk about consciousness. Is the way we see the world as adults the way we always have and always will see the world? Or could consciousness itself change? What is it like to be a baby? There are two very different aspects of consciousness in grown-ups. First there is our external consciousness—our vivid awareness of the world outside us, the blue of the sky, the song of the birds. In chapter 4, I'll describe new studies of babies' minds and brains, and especially babies' attention. Babies attend to the world in a very different way than we do, and this kind of attention is related to their extraordinary learning abilities. I'll argue that babies are actually more conscious than we are, more vividly aware of everything that goes on around them.

We also experience internal consciousness. This is the stream of thoughts, feelings, and plans that seem to run past that inner "I" who is also the inner "eye"—the internal observer, autobiographer, and executive we call our self. In chapter 5, I'll argue that this internal consciousness may be quite different for babies and toddlers, and adults. Babies experience the past and the future, memory and desire, very differently than we do. They don't seem to have the same kind of inner observer, and they remember the past and plan for the future in very different ways. A single unified self is something we create—not something we are given.

In the next three chapters, I'll consider what these new ideas can tell us about another set of questions—questions about identity, love, and morality. These are often the most urgent questions for us as parents of our children, and indeed as children of our parents. In chapter 6, I'll talk about the relation between our lives as children and our lives as adults. How do the experiences and actions of childhood shape our later experiences and actions? How does our childhood make us who we are? In chapter 7, I'll focus on a particular part of this question. Where does the love between parents and children come from? How does it shape our adult loves and lives? I'll argue that we aren't simply determined by either our genes or our mothers. Instead, our childhood experiences guide the way we create our own lives.

In chapter 8, I'll explain what children tell us about our moral lives. Babies and young children are not the amoral creatures we once thought. Even the youngest babies have striking capacities for empathy and altruism. And even toddlers know that rules should be followed but that they can be changed. These two capacities,

capacities for love and law, for caring about others and following the rules, allow our characteristically human combination of moral depth and flexibility. They explain how we can change our laws and rules to suit new circumstances without falling into moral relativism.

Finally, in chapter 9, I'll talk about the spiritual significance of babies—about babies and the meaning of life. For most parents, raising children is one of the most significant, meaningful, and profound experiences of their lives. Is this just an evolutionary illusion, a trick to make us keep on reproducing? I'll argue that it's the real thing, that children really do put us in touch with truth, beauty, and meaning.

Nothing in this book will help parents get their children to sleep or send them to a good college or guarantee them a happy adult life. But I hope it will help parents, and people who aren't parents too, to appreciate the richness and significance of childhood in a new way. Even the most mundane facts of three-year-old life—the extravagant pretend play, the insatiable curiosity that makes them get into just about everything, and the intuitive sympathy for others—tell us what it means to be human. Philosophy and science can help us understand how our children think and feel and experience the world—and how we do too.

I.

Possible Worlds

WHY DO CHILDREN PRETEND?

✳

Human beings don't live in the real world. The real world is what actually happened in the past, is happening now, and will happen in the future. But we don't just live in this single world. Instead, we live in a universe of many possible worlds, all the ways the world could be in the future and also all the ways the world could have been in the past, or might be in the present. These possible worlds are what we call dreams and plans, fictions and hypotheses. They are the products of hope and imagination. Philosophers, more drily, call them "counterfactuals."

Counterfactuals are the woulda-coulda-shouldas of life, all the things that might happen in the future, but haven't yet, or that could have happened in the past, but didn't quite. Human beings care deeply about those possible worlds—as deeply as they care about the real actual world. On the surface counterfactual thinking seems like a very sophisticated and philosophically puzzling ability. How can we think about things that aren't there? And why should we think this way instead of restricting ourselves to the actual world? It seems obvious that understanding the real world would give us an evolutionary edge, but what good do we get from imaginary worlds?

We can start to answer these questions by looking at young children. Is counterfactual thought present only in sophisticated grown-ups? Or can young children think about possibilities too? The conventional wisdom, echoed in the theories of both Sigmund Freud and Jean Piaget, is that babies and young children are limited to the here and now—their immediate sensations and perceptions and experience. Even when young children pretend or imagine they can't distinguish between reality and fantasy: their fantasies, in this view, are just another kind of immediate experience. Counterfactual thought requires a more demanding ability to understand the relation between reality and all the alternatives to that reality.

Cognitive scientists have discovered that this conventional picture is wrong. We've found out that even very young children can already consider possibilities, distinguish them from reality, and even use them to change the world. They can imagine different ways the world might be in the future and use them to create plans. They can imagine different ways the world might have been in the past, and reflect on past possibilities. And, most dramatically, they can create completely imaginary worlds, wild fictions, and striking pretenses. These crazy imaginary worlds are a familiar part of childhood—every parent of a three-year-old has exclaimed, "What an imagination!" But the new research profoundly changes the way we think about those worlds.

In the past ten years we've not only discovered that children have these imaginative powers—we've actually begun to understand how these powers are possible. We are developing a science of the imagination. How could children's minds and brains be constructed to allow them to imagine this dazzling array of alternate universes?

The answer is surprising. Conventional wisdom suggests that knowledge and imagination, science and fantasy, are deeply different from one another—even opposites. But the new ideas I'll outline show that exactly the same abilities that let children learn so much about the world also allow them to change the world—to bring new worlds into existence—and to imagine alternative worlds that may never exist at all. Children's brains create causal theories of the world, maps of how the world works. And these theories allow children to envisage new possibilities, and to imagine and pretend that the world is different.

THE POWER OF COUNTERFACTUALS

Psychologists have found that counterfactual thinking is absolutely pervasive in our everyday life and deeply affects our judgments, our decisions, and our emotions. You would think that what really matters is what actually happens, not what you imagine might have happened in the past or could happen in the future. This is particularly true of counterfactuals about the past—what might have happened but didn't—the woulda-coulda-shouldas of life. Yet the woulda-coulda-shouldas have a deep impact on experience.

In one experiment, the Nobel Prize–winning psychologist Daniel Kahneman and his colleagues asked people to imagine the following sort of scenario. Mr. Tees and Mr. Crane are both in a taxi to the airport, desperate to catch their respective planes, which are both scheduled to take off at 6:00. But traffic is impossibly snarled and the minutes tick by. Finally, at 6:30 they arrive at the airport. It turns out that Mr. Tees's flight left at 6:00 as planned but Mr. Crane's flight was delayed till 6:25 and Mr. Crane sees it take off as he arrives. Who is more upset?

Just about everyone agrees that Mr. Crane, who just missed his flight, will be much more unhappy. But why? They both missed their flights. It seems that what is making Mr. Crane unhappy is not the actual world but the counterfactual worlds, the ones in which the taxi arrived just that much earlier or the plane was delayed just a few minutes more.

You needn't turn to artificial scenarios like this one to see the effects of counterfactuals. Consider the medalists in the Olympics. Who is happier, the bronze medalist or the silver? You'd think that objectively the silver medalist, who, after all, has actually done better, would be happier. But the relevant counterfactuals are very different for the two. For the bronze medalist the relevant alternative was to finish out of the medals altogether—a fate she has just escaped. For the silver medalist, the relevant alternative was to get the gold medal—a fate she has just missed. And, in fact, when psychologists took clips of the medals ceremonies and analyzed the facial expressions of the athletes, it turned out that the bronze medalists really do look happier than the silver medalists. The difference in what might have been outweighs the difference in what is.

Like Mr. Crane at the airport, or the silver medalist, people are most unhappy when a desirable outcome seems to be just out of reach, or to have just been missed. As Neil Young adapted John Greenleaf Whittier: "The saddest words of tongue and pen are these four words, 'it might have been.'"

Why do we humans worry so much about counterfactuals, when, by definition, they are things that didn't actually happen? Why are these imaginary worlds just as important to us as the real ones? Surely "it is, and it's awful" should be sadder words than "it might have been."

The evolutionary answer is that counterfactuals let us change the future. Because we can consider alternative ways the world might be, we can actually act on the world and intervene to turn it into one or the other of these possibilities. Whenever we act, even in a small way, we are changing the course of history, nudging the world down one path rather than another. Of course, making one possibility come true means that all the other alternative possibilities we considered won't come true—they become counterfactuals. But being able to think about those possibilities is crucial to our evolutionary success. Counterfactual thinking lets us make new plans, invent new tools, and create new environments. Human beings are constantly imagining what would happen if they cracked nuts or wove baskets or made political decisions in a new way, and the sum total of all those visions is a different world.

Counterfactuals about the past, and the characteristically human emotions that go with them, seem to be the price we pay for counterfactuals about the future. Because we are responsible for the future, we can feel guilty about the past; because we can hope, we can also regret; because we can make plans, we can be disappointed. The other side of being able to consider all the possible futures, all the things that could go differently, is that you can't escape considering all the possible pasts, all the things that could have gone differently.

COUNTERFACTUALS IN CHILDREN: PLANNING THE FUTURE

Can children think counterfactually? The most evolutionarily fundamental kind of counterfactual thinking comes when we make plans for the future—when we consider alternative possibilities and pick the one we think will be most desirable. How can we tell if a very young baby can do this? In my lab, we showed the baby the sort of post with stacking rings that is a standard baby toy. But I had taped over the hole in one of the rings. How would the baby respond to this apparently similar but actually recalcitrant ring? When we brought a fifteen-month-old into the lab he would use a kind of trial-and-error method to solve the problem. He would stack some of the rings, look carefully at the taped-over one—and then try it on the post. And then try it on the post again, harder. And try it on the post one more time. Then he would look up puzzled, try one of the other rings again—and then again try the taped-over one. Basically, young babies would keep at this until they gave up.

But as they got older and learned more about how the world worked, babies would behave entirely differently. An eighteen-month-old would stack all the other rings and then hold up the trick ring with a "Who do you think you're kidding?" look and refuse even to try it. Or she would immediately pick the trick ring up and dramatically throw it across the room, and then calmly stack the rest. Or, equally dramatically, she would hold it up to the post and shout "No!" or "Uh-oh!" These babies didn't have to actually see what the ring would do—they could imagine what would happen if you put it on the post, and act accordingly.

In another experiment we saw whether babies could discover a new use for an object—if they could, in a simple way, invent a new tool. I put a desirable toy out of the babies' reach and placed a toy rake beside it. As with the ring, fifteen-month-olds sometimes did pick up the rake, but they couldn't figure out how to use it as a tool. They pushed the toy from side to side or even, frustratingly, farther away from them, till they either accidentally got it or gave up. But older babies looked at the rake and paused thoughtfully. You could almost see the wheels spinning. Then they produced a triumphant smile and often a certain look of smugness.

You could almost see the lightbulb switching on. Then they put the rake in just the right position over the toy and triumphantly used it to bring the toy toward them. Again they seemed able to mentally anticipate—to imagine—all the possible ways the rake could affect the toy and then chose just the right possibility.

Simple trial and error, trying different actions until one succeeds, is actually often a very effective way of getting along in the world. But anticipating future possibilities lets us plan in this other more insightful way—using our heads instead of our hands. The older babies seemed to be anticipating the possible future in which the ring or the rake would fail and avoiding that future. Other studies have shown that this isn't just a difference between fifteen- and eighteen-month-olds. Even younger babies can solve problems insightfully if they have the right kinds of information.

This ability to solve problems insightfully seems to be particularly human. There is a little evidence that chimpanzees, and even some very smart birds like crows, can do this occasionally. But even chimpanzees and crows, and certainly other animals, overwhelmingly rely on either instinct or trial and error to get along in the world. And, in fact, instinct and trial and error are often very effective and intelligent strategies. It is extremely impressive to see a bird putting together the complex set of instinctive behaviors that allows it to build a nest, or a chimpanzee using trial and error to gradually zero in on the right strategy to open a box with elaborate locks. But they are different from the strategies that babies and very young children use. Anthropologists agree that using tools and making plans, both abilities that depend on anticipating future possibilities, played a large role in the evolutionary success of *Homo sapiens*. And we can see these abilities emerging even in babies who can't talk yet.

RECONSTRUCTING THE PAST

In these experiments babies seem to be able to imagine alternative possibilities in the future. Can children also imagine past counterfactuals, different ways the world might have been? We have to infer babies' counterfactual thinking from what they do, but we can explicitly ask older children counterfactual woulda-coulda-shoulda questions. Until recently psychologists claimed that children were quite bad at thinking about possibilities. Children are indeed quite bad at producing counterfactuals about subjects they know little about, but when they understand the subject matter even two- and three-year-olds turn out to be adept at generating alternative worlds.

The English psychologist Paul Harris probably knows more than anyone about young children's imaginative abilities. Harris is tall, thin, reserved, and very English, and worked for many years at Oxford University. His work, like the work of the great Oxford writer Lewis Carroll, is a peculiarly English combination of the strictest logic applied to the wildest fantasy.

Harris told children a familiar English countryside story. Then he asked them about future and past counterfactuals. Naughty Ducky is wearing muddy boots and is about to walk into the kitchen. "What would happen to the floor if Ducky walked through the kitchen? Would it be clean or dirty?" "What would have happened to the floor if Ducky had cleaned his boots first? Would it be clean or dirty?" Even young three-year-olds say that the floor would have been spared if only Ducky had cleaned his boots.

In my lab, David Sobel and I designed a set of storytelling cards—cartoon pictures that told the right story if you put them in order. We showed children a sequence of pictures, say a girl going to a cookie jar, opening the jar, looking inside, finding cookies, and looking happy. But we also had a set of several other pictures, including the girl finding that there were no cookies, and the girl looking sad and hungry. We showed the children the cards in the right sequence and asked them to tell the story. Then we said, "But how about if the girl had been sad at the end instead?" and changed the last card, so that the girl looked sad instead of happy. "What would have had to happen then?" Three-year-olds consistently changed the earlier pictures to fit the hypothetical ending—they replaced the picture of the full cookie jar with the picture of the empty one. These very young children could imagine and reason about an alternative past.

IMAGINING THE POSSIBLE

We can also see evidence for counterfactual thinking in children's play. Babies start pretending when they are as young as eighteen months old or even younger. Pretending involves a kind of present counterfactual thinking—imagining the way things might be different. Even babies who can't talk yet, and are barely walking, can still pretend. A one-and-a-half-year-old baby may fastidiously comb her hair with a pencil, or rest her head on a pillow dramatically pretending to be asleep, giggling all the while. A little later babies start to treat objects as if they were something else. Toddlers turn everything from blocks to shoes to bowls of cereal into means of transportation by the simple expedient of saying "brrm-brrm" and pushing them along the floor. Or they may carefully, tenderly, put three little toy sheep to bed.

We take this for granted when we choose toys for these young children. The toddler sections of toy stores are full of toys that encourage children to pretend: the farmhouse, the gas station, the zoo—even the toy ATM and cell phone. But it's not that two-year-olds pretend because we give them dolls; instead we give them dolls because they love to pretend. Even without toys toddlers are just as likely to turn common objects—food, pebbles, grass, you, themselves—into something else. And even in cultures where pretend play is discouraged, rather than cultivated, like Mr. Gradgrind's school in Dickens's *Hard Times*, children continue to do it anyway. ("No child left behind" testing policies seem to be echoing Mr. Gradgrind, replacing dress-up corners and pretend play with reading drills in preschools.)

As soon as babies can talk they immediately talk about the possible as well as the real. As a graduate student at Oxford I recorded all the words that nine babies used when they first began to talk. These babies, who were still just using single words, at the very start of language, would use them to talk about possibilities as well as actualities. There was not only the ubiquitous "brrm-brrm," but "apple" when pretending to eat a ball, or "night-night" when putting a doll to bed. One particularly charming red-haired toddler had a beloved teddy bear, and his mother had knitted two long scarves, like the ones Dr. Who wears in the British TV series, a small one for the bear and a larger one for Jonathan. Jonathan one day put his teddy bear's scarf around his neck and, with enormous grins and giggles, announced his new identity: "Jonathan Bear!"

In fact, learning language gives children a whole powerful new way to imagine. Even young babies who can't talk yet have some ability to anticipate and imagine the future. But being able to talk gives you a particularly powerful way to put old ideas together in new ways, and to talk about things that aren't there. Consider the power of "no," one of the very first words that children learn. When parents think about "no" they immediately think of the terrible two-year-old absolutely refusing to do something. And children do use "no" that way. But they also use "no" to tell themselves not to do something, like the child who said "no" holding the taped-up ring over the post. And they use "no" to say that some-thing isn't true. When Jonathan's equally charming mom teased him by saying that the swimming pool was full of orange juice, he immediately said, "No juice!" Other less obvious words have some of the same power. Take "uh-oh." This hardly counts as a word for grown-ups but it's one of the most common words that young chil-dren use. And "uh-oh," like "no," is a word about what could have happened. Babies use it when they try to do something and fail—"uh-oh" contrasts the ideal with the unfortunate real.

Being able to say "no" and "uh-oh" immediately puts you in the world of the counterfactual and the possible—the road not taken, the possibility that isn't real. And we discovered that, in fact, babies start talking about unreal possibilities at the same time that they start to use tools in an insightful way. Being able to talk about pos-sibilities helps you to imagine them.

By the time they are two or three children quite characteristi-cally spend much of their waking hours in a world of imaginary creatures, possible universes, and assumed identities. Walk into any day-care center and you will be surrounded by small princesses and superheroes in overalls who politely serve you nonexistent tea and warn you away from nonexistent monsters. And these children are adept at playing out the consequences of their counterfactual pretend premises. Paul Harris found that even two-year-olds will tell you that if an imaginary teddy is drinking imaginary tea, then if he spills it the imaginary floor will require imaginary mopping-up. (As with Ducky, toddlers seem particularly taken with the pos-sibilities involved in making a terrible mess.) Children were quite specific about their counterfactuals. If the teddy spills tea you'll need a mop, but if he spills baby powder you'll need a broom.

In the past, this imaginative play has been taken to be evidence of children's cognitive limitations rather than evidence of their cognitive powers. Earlier psychologists, including both Freud and Piaget, claimed that make-believe was a sign that young children are unable to discriminate between fiction and truth, pretense and reality, fantasy and fact. Of course, if you saw an adult doing the same things that preschoolers do—if, for example, someone with wild hair and a sparkly cloak around her shoulders announced to you that she was queen of the fairies—you would probably conclude that she *was* confused about reality and fantasy, and that she should probably make sure she got back on her meds. However, neither Freud nor Piaget investigated this question systematically.

More recently, cognitive scientists have carefully explored what children know about imagination and pretense. It turns out that even two- and three-year-olds are extremely good at distinguishing imagination and pretense from reality. One of the most distinctive things about even the earliest pretend play is the fact that it's accompanied by giggles. It's the giggles, the knowing look, the dramatic exaggeration, that signal that this is not to be taken seriously. In fact, there turns out to be a consistent set of signals—giggles, exaggerated gestures, theatrical and melodramatic facial expressions—that indicate that actions are "just pretend." And, after all, even the youngest children don't actually try to eat the pretend cookies or even try to actually talk to Mom on the pretend cell phone.

Preschool children spend hours pretending, but they *know* that they are pretending. The psychologist Jacqui Woolley did an experiment where children pretended that there was a pencil in one box, and actually saw a pencil in another box. Then the boxes were closed. An assistant came into the room, looking for a pencil, and asked the children which box she should open. Three-year-olds said quite clearly that she should look in the box with the real pencil, not the pretend one. In much the same way three-year-olds say that everyone can see and touch a real dog but not an imaginary one, and that you can turn an imaginary dog, but not a real one, into a cat just by thinking about it.

Children may seem confused because they are such expressive and emotional pretenders. They can have real emotional reactions to entirely imaginary scenarios. Rather than asking children to imagine pencils in the box, Paul Harris asked them to imagine a monster in the box. Children again said very clearly that really there was no monster in the box, and that they would not see one if they opened the box—they were just imagining it. Nevertheless, when the experimenter left the room many children gingerly moved away from the box.

In this respect, however, children don't seem to be that different from adults. The psychologist Paul Rozin asked adults to fill a bottle with water from the tap, write "cyanide" on a label, and affix it to the bottle. Although they knew perfectly well that they were only pretending that the water was poisonous, they still wouldn't drink it. I am perfectly capable of being scared silly by Hannibal Lecter although I have absolutely no doubt of his fictional status.

Children's emotions are more intense and more difficult to control than adult emotions, whether the causes of those emotions are real or not. To a worried parent, it may seem that the child trembling under the covers must believe that there really is a monster in the closet. But the scientific studies show that this is not because children don't understand the difference between fiction and fact. They are just more moved by both than grown-ups.

IMAGINATION AND CAUSATION

We know that even very young children constantly think about future, past, and present possible worlds. And we know that this ability gives us distinctive evolutionary advantages. How do human minds, even the very youngest human minds, manage to produce counterfactuals? How can we think about the possible worlds that might exist in the future or could have existed in the past, when those worlds don't actually exist now? Even more important, our evolutionary advantage comes because we can not only imagine possibilities but also act on them—we can turn them into reality. But how do we know which possibilities will come true in what circumstances? And how do we decide just what we have to do to make them real?

Part of the answer is that our ability to imagine possible worlds is closely tied to our ability to think causally. Causal knowledge is itself an ancient philosophical puzzle. The great Scottish philosopher David Hume thought we could never really know that one event caused another—all we could know was that one event tended to follow another. What makes causal knowledge more than just one damned thing after another? The modern philosopher David Lewis was the first to point out the close link between causal knowledge and counterfactual thinking, and many philosophers have followed this idea up since then.

Once you know how one thing is causally connected to another you can predict what will happen to one thing if you act to change another—you can see what a difference making things different will make. You can also imagine what would have happened if you had acted in a certain way, even though you didn't. Once I know that smoking causes cancer I can imagine possible worlds in which my actions cause people to stop smoking, and conclude that in those worlds they will be less likely to become ill. I can take a wide variety of actions, from advertising to legislation to inventing nicotine patches, to get people to stop smoking, and I can accurately predict just how these actions will change the world. I can make a world with less cancer than the world had before. And

I can also look backwards and calculate how many lives would have been saved if the tobacco industry had not resisted those changes in the past.

Causal understanding lets you deliberately do things that will change the world in a particular way. We might simply have had the ability to track the world as it unfolded around us. But, in fact, we have the ability to intervene in the world, as well, to actually make things happen. Intervening deliberately in the world isn't the same as just predicting what will happen next. When we intervene we envision a particular possible future we would like to bring about and our action actually changes the world to make that future real.

Of course, other animals, or people in some situations, may act on the world effectively without necessarily understanding the world in a causal way. Like the fifteen-month-olds and the ring, or like the chimpanzees, you may just hit on the right action to solve a problem through trial and error. Chimpanzees may notice that when you poke a stick in a termite nest, the termites emerge. Fifteen-month-olds may see that when you try the taped-over ring it fails, and doctors may observe that when you prescribe aspirin your patients' headaches go away. Then you can just repeat that action the next time.

But having a causal theory of the world makes it possible to consider alternative solutions to a problem, and their consequences, before you actually implement them, and it lets you make a much wider and more effective range of interventions. If you know that the hole allows the ring to descend on the post, or that the rake causes the toy to move with it, you can design a new strategy to deal with the taped-over ring or the distant toy. If you know that a cascade of electrical impulses on the trigeminal nerve leads the blood vessels to expand, which puts pressure on nerves, which leads to a headache, you can design drugs that influence just the electrical processes or just the blood pressure. When you take a drug like sumatriptan to relieve a migraine headache you are taking advantage of the causal knowledge about migraines that neurologists have discovered, and the possible remedies that it allowed them to design.

CHILDREN AND CAUSATION

Understanding what causes migraines and cancer, and using this knowledge to change the world, is, of course, the work of science. But are scientists the only people who can think about causation and use it to bring new worlds into being? Ordinary adults also seem to know a lot about the causal structure of the world and they irresistibly think about counterfactuals, even when all they do is lead to guilt and regret.

We saw that children are also extremely good at counterfactual thinking. If counterfactual thinking depends on causal understanding and is a deep, evolved part of human nature, then even very young children should also be able to think causally. In fact, it turns out that they do already know a great deal about the causal structure of the world—about how one thing makes another happen. In fact, this is one of the most important, and most revolutionary, recent discoveries of developmental psychology.

Just as psychologists used to think that children don't understand much about counterfactuals, they also used to think that young children don't understand much about causation. Children's thinking was supposed to be restricted to their immediate perceptual experience—they might know that one event happened after another but not that one event caused another. In particular, psychologists thought that children didn't understand the hidden causal relations that are the stuff of science—the way that something in a seed makes it grow, or germs make you ill, or magnets make iron filings move, or hidden desires make people act. Piaget, for example, claimed that children were "precausal" until they were well into the school-age years.

But over the past twenty years we have discovered that babies and young children do know a lot about how objects and people work, and they learn more as they grow older.

Piaget asked children about causal phenomena that they didn't know much about. He asked preschoolers interesting and hard causal questions like "Why does it get dark at night?" or "Why do the clouds move?" The children either simply got confused or produced answers that were deficient by adult standards though they sometimes had a logic of their own ("It gets dark so we can sleep" or "The clouds move because I want them to").

More recently psychologists decided to try asking children questions about things they know a lot about, like "Why did Johnny open the refrigerator when he was hungry?" or "How does a tricycle work?" Children as young as two gave perfectly good, and sometimes even elaborate, causal explanations. "He thought there was food in there and he wanted food so he opened the fridge so he could get the food." Very young children are consumed with insatiable curiosity about causes, as their unstoppable "why?" questions show.

The psychologist Henry Wellman spent a sabbatical year simply searching through CHILDES, a computer database of recordings of hundreds of children's everyday conversations. (Wellman, who once taught preschool, said that it was odd and touching to simultaneously be in the scholarly adult peace of the computer room at the Center for Advanced Studies in the Behavioral Sciences at Stanford and yet be surrounded once more by these invisible three-year-olds.) He found that two- and three-year-olds both produced and asked for dozens of causal explanations a day. They gave explanations for physical phenomena: "The teddy's arm fell off because you twisted it too far"; "Jenny had my chair because the other chair was brokened." They gave accounts of biological causes: "He needs more to eat because he is growing long arms"; "Mean hawks eat meat because meat is tasty for mean hawks." But most of all they liked psychological explanations: "I didn't spill it last night because I'm a good girl"; "I not gone go up there because I frightened of her." The explanations might not always have been the same ones a grown-up would give but they were perfectly good logical explanations all the same.

Other studies show that young children understand quite abstract and hidden causes. They understand that something in a seed makes it grow or that invisible germs make you ill. The Japanese psychologists Giyoo Hatano and Kayoko Inagaki explored children's everyday biology—their understanding of life and death. They found that when they're around five years old children around the world develop a vitalist causal theory of biology, much like the theory in traditional Japanese and Chinese medicine. These children seem to think that there is a single vital force, like the Chinese chi, that keeps us alive. They predict that if you don't eat enough, for example, this force will wane and you'll get sick. They think that death is the irreversible loss of this force, and predict that animals that die won't come back to life. (This new understanding of mortality is a mixed blessing. Younger children think that death is more like a move than an ending; Grandmom has simply temporarily taken up residence in the cemetery or in heaven, and might come back. Many children start to become much more anxious about death once they think of it as the irreversible loss of a vital force.) This theory allows them to make a whole network of predictions, counterfactuals, and explanations— like the child Henry Wellman studied who said that someone "needs more to eat because he is growing long arms."

Causation is what gives fantasy its logic. Think about the children in Paul Harris's studies who could work out precisely what the imaginary consequences would be if Teddy spilled the imaginary tea. A pretend game in which absolutely anything goes would just be a mess. Instead, pretend works by establishing imaginary premises ("I'm the mommy and you're the baby") and then working out the causal consequences of those premises quite strictly. Children can become quite passionate about whether the right causal rules are being followed: "You didn't get me with your ray gun 'cause I was behind the shield!" "You hafta drink your milk 'cause you're the baby!"

CAUSES AND POSSIBILITIES

Children develop causal theories of the world from a very early age. If causal knowledge and counterfactual thinking go together, then this might explain how young children have the parallel ability to generate counterfactuals and to explore possible worlds. If children understand the way things work, they should be able to imagine alternative possibilities about them. This might also explain the cases where children don't think counterfactually. Think back to the fifteen-month-old who futilely tries to jam the solid ring over the pole. It could be that she just doesn't understand yet how poles and holes fit together. Children might sometimes fail to think counterfactually because they don't have the right kind of causal knowledge, not because they're unable to imagine possibilities, just as I would have a hard time telling you what could have been done to prevent the space shuttle crash, or what should be done to prevent it in the future.

Henry Wellman showed that children talk about causes in their everyday conversations. Then he took the next step and asked children to say what was possible or impossible, based on their causal knowledge of the physical, biological, and psychological world. He found that children consistently used their knowledge to discriminate possibilities. They said, for example, that Johnny could simply decide to hold up his arm, but he couldn't possibly decide to simply jump in the air and stay there, or decide to grow taller, or decide to walk through a table.

One little boy we tested decided to demonstrate his counterfactual knowledge by actually acting out each of the possibilities after he had made the predictions. "You can't just jump in the air and stay there, look!" he said, jumping as high as he could. And then: "Watch! Table I will walk through you!" at which he dramatically and theatrically bumped against the table and said, "Ow, see, you can't do it."

Even the youngest children already have causal knowledge about the world and use that knowledge to make predictions about the future, to explain the past, and to imagine possible worlds that might or might not exist. But at a deeper level, what would children's minds have to be like in order to do this? One way Wellman, Hatano and Inagaki, and I tried to capture these ideas was by saying that children have everyday theories of the world—everyday ideas about psychology, biology, and physics. These theories are like scientific theories but they are largely unconscious rather than conscious, and they are coded in children's brains, instead of being written down on paper or presented at scientific conferences. But how could something as abstract as a theory be coded in children's brains?

MAPS AND BLUEPRINTS

Children's brains construct a kind of unconscious causal map, an accurate picture of the way the world works. These causal maps are like the more familiar maps we, and even computerized systems such as Mapquest, use to represent space. Many animals, from squirrels to rats to people, construct "cognitive maps" of their spatial world, internal pictures of where things are in space, much like the external pictures of printed maps. Once you represent spatial information in a map you can use that information much more flexibly and productively. We even know something about where and how those spatial maps are encoded in animal brains. They appear to be located in a region called the hippocampus—remove a rat's hippocampus and it will no longer be able to find its way around a maze.

One thing a map does is to let you make blueprints. A blueprint looks like a map, but instead of making the blueprint match the world, we change the world to match the blueprint. Once we know how to make spatial maps, we can also decide to make changes in the spatial layout of objects, including our own bodies, and predict the effects of those changes.

If you are in a strange city without a map, you may find yourself wandering around from the hotel until you hit on the train station or the restaurant, and you may repeat that route once you've found it. Once you have a map, though, you can discover that there were much shorter and more convenient routes you could have taken. The map lets you compare different routes to a place, and lets you discover the most efficient route, without having to actually take each one. You don't need a printed map to do this. Animals with good cognitive maps, like rats, can explore a maze, construct an internal map, and then immediately, without trial and error, find the shortest route from one location in the maze to another.

You might not think of using the map in this way as using the map as a blueprint. After all, the world the map represents stays the same. But you are, in fact, changing the location of one very important object on the map, namely the little red dot that means "you are here." When you imagine the different routes you could take you are imagining, creating really, different cognitive maps with that red dot in different locations. A map is a very efficient device for constructing different cognitive blueprints, pictures of what will happen as you move yourself around through space.

Moreover, with a map you can consider other, more complex, spatial possibilities. When you set out to design a new garden, for example, your first step is to make a map of the existing backyard (noting, for example, the slab of cracked concrete, the broken jungle gym, and the patch of weeds). But the second step is to construct a similar map of the ideal garden that will replace it (sketching in the fountain, the brick pathways, and the flowering trees). The great landscape garden designer Capability Brown once remarked, looking at a particularly sinuous stretch of the river Thames, "Clever!" Brown was thinking of the landscape as the outcome of a blueprint, as a human invention, rather than as a natural phenomenon accurately represented in a map. In a much simpler way, animals such as squirrels can use spatial maps to plan where to hide their nuts and then to recover the nuts later.

Once we have the new ideal map, the blueprint, we can set about acting on objects to realize it. We can move ourselves to a new location by the shortest route. Or we can move the jungle gym away to the dump and haul the fountain in to replace it. Maps also help us to consider all the spatial possibilities before we commit ourselves. We can consider whether it would be faster to take the side streets or stick to the boulevard. We can look at the assorted places that the fountain might be—the ways that it might interact with the brick path or the flowering tree—before we actually decide to go ahead and install it in a particular place.

CAUSAL MAPS

Human beings also construct a different kind of map—a map of the complex causal relations among events. The neurologist has a kind of map of migraines—outlining all the causal links between neural activity and pressure and pain. Or think about the children who could make all those predictions about the biological world. Rather than considering each of the causal relationships between life and death and growth and disease and food separately, children seem to have a single coherent vitalist picture of the world. They think that eating causes you to have more energy, while illness drains you of that energy—that growth lets you dial up your causal force while death robs you of it. They can make new predictions, often ones they've never heard about before. They'll say that as long as you keep eating you could just keep growing indefinitely, or that a grown-up who is taller must be older than one who is shorter (my own son insisted that, at five feet two inches, I couldn't really be friends with a young basketball-playing colleague because he was big and I was just little). Or they'll explain that you have to eat because it gives you power. This causal map of biology lets them draw all these consequences—and more.

While other animals clearly make spatial cognitive maps, it is not clear that they make causal maps in the same way. Other animals are able to understand specific kinds of causal relationships. For example, they understand that their own actions cause the events that immediately follow those actions—say, that poking the termite nest makes the termites come out—or they may understand a few particularly important causal links, such as the link between bad food and nausea. However, other animals don't seem to make the kind of maps that we see even in very young children. Other animals seem to rely more on the kind of trial-and-error learning that allows us to notice that aspirin makes our headaches go away, instead of the kind of theory making that lets us design a new drug such as sumatriptan to get rid of migraines.

In the nineties a group of philosophers of science at Carnegie Mellon University led by Clark Glymour started trying to give a mathematical account of how scientific theories might work. At the same time computer scientists at UCLA, led by Judea Pearl, were trying to write programs that would be able to make the same sort of predictions and recommendations that scientific experts make. The two groups hit upon the same set of ideas about causal maps. They worked out how to describe the maps mathematically and how to use them to accurately generate new predictions, interventions, and counterfactuals. The new mathematical descriptions, called "causal graphical models," have taken over artificial intelligence and have inspired new ideas about causation in philosophy.

You can make computer programs that use these causal maps, just the way that Mapquest uses spatial maps. Mapquest uses a single map to automatically produce millions of routes from one place to another. In much the same way the computer programs that use these causal maps can do the same kinds of sophisticated counterfactual reasoning that human scientists—and children—do. These programs can make medical diagnoses and suggest possible treatments, or make suggestions about what might help prevent climate change. NASA has explored using these ideas in the next generation of Mars robots.

The core idea of cognitive science is that our brains are a kind of computer, though far more powerful than any of the actual computers we know about. Psychologists try to find out exactly what kinds of programs our brains use, and how our brains implement those programs. Since children are so good at understanding causes, we thought that children's brains just might be constructing causal maps and using them in the same way as the computer programs. In fact, collaborating with the philosophers and computer scientists gave me the causal map idea in the first place. (For many years, in many bars, I argued with Glymour about whether my babies were smarter than his computers. The answer, of course, is that they're smarter in some ways but not others—but still, overall, after ten years of experiments, I've got him voting for the babies.)

DETECTING BLICKETS

How could we find out whether children really do make causal maps of the world around them, and use them to imagine new possibilities and to make the world different? How could we discover if they use the same kinds of programs as the expert computers? One thing we could do is actually to introduce three- and four-year-olds to new causal events and see if they could use that knowledge to make predictions, design new interventions, and consider new possibilities. That way we could know for sure that the children were drawing these conclusions based just on the causal information we gave them—the new map—and nothing else.

With the help of the guys in the shop and the graduate students in my lab, I invented a machine we call the "blicket detector." The machine is a square box that lights up and plays music when some blocks, but not others, are placed on top of it. We tell children, "Look, here's my blicket machine! Blickets make the machine go. Can you tell me which things are the blickets?" Children are fascinated by the machine and immediately begin to explore and experiment to find out more about how it works and which things are blickets—trying out blocks on the machine, pressing harder or softer, even scratching on the blocks to find out what might be inside them.

The truth, fortunately unsuspected by any of the children, is what we might call Wizard of Oz causality. There is a little man, or rather an undergraduate research assistant, behind a curtain pressing buttons to make the machine go. My youngest son, Andres, was a pilot subject—aka guinea pig—for the blicket detector experiments. After several months I finally explained to him how it really worked. He reacted pretty much like Neo in *The Matrix* when he wakes up and realizes that the world is just an elaborate deception. (At twenty, he has forgiven me, possibly because he thinks this experience is a precursor to saving the universe, or at least dating Carrie Moss.)

Once the children start to discover which blocks make the machine go, they can use that information to envision new possibilities and make new predictions, including counterfactual predictions. In one of the first tests we did we taught children that a particular block was a blicket that activated the machine, and then combined the blicket with a nonblicket and put both of them on the machine. The machine, of course, still lit up. One of the first four-year-olds we tested immediately came up with a counterfactual any philosopher would be proud of. "But s'pose," he said excitedly, "you didn't put on the blicket that time, s'pose you only put on that one (pointing to the nonblicket) then it wouldn't have gone."

If you ask children to make the machine go they will choose only the blickets. More tellingly, if you ask them to make the machine stop, they will say that you have to remove the blicket, even though they have never seen anyone stop the machine this way before. They can use the new causal information to draw the right kinds of conclusions, including counterfactual conclusions. They can imagine what will happen if you take the blicket off the machine or what might have happened if you had taken it off before.

New causal knowledge can lead to bigger changes, too. Figuring out which block makes the machine go or stop may not seem like a big deal. But my student Laura Schulz and I decided to do the same experiment in a different way. We showed the children a similar machine with a switch attached. The children didn't know how this new machine worked. Then we asked them whether the machine would go on if you flicked the switch, and whether it would go on if you just told it to go. At first, every single one of the children said that the switch could make the machine go, but simply talking to it couldn't. These children have learned that machines work differently than people do.

But then, if we actually demonstrate that talking to the machine causes it to light up, children change their minds. If you ask them to make the machine stop they very politely say, "Machine, please stop," instead of reaching for the switch. And if you ask the children to predict what will make a new machine go, they are much more willing to entertain the "talk to it" possibility than they were before, though they still think the switch is a better bet. Giving the children new causal knowledge changed the way they thought about possibilities, and changed the kinds of actions they would take. Children could imagine a listening machine that had seemed downright impossible before.

In the same way, for adult scientists, new causal knowledge

allows us to imagine possibilities that would have seemed unimaginable before. In science fiction films, where imagination should run riot, what strikes you most is that the directors' imaginations are so limited by their current knowledge. In *Blade Runner*, for example, Harrison Ford runs desperately to a pay phone—with a video screen. The screenwriters could imagine a pay phone with a TV, but not that pay phones would disappear altogether. Nothing is more dated than visions of the future, because to imagine the future's possibilities, we need to have the future's knowledge.

Often, people treat knowledge and imagination as if they were different, even as if they were necessarily opposed to each other, but the new work on causal maps suggests just the opposite. Understanding the causal structure of the world and generating counterfactuals go hand in hand. In fact, knowledge is actually what gives imagination its power, what makes creativity possible. It's because we know something about how events are connected in the world that we can imagine altering those connections and creating new ones. It's because we know about this world that we can create possible worlds.

This profoundly human blend of knowledge and imagination isn't just the province of adults. In fact, it underpins even the wildest childhood fantasies. The three-year-old pretending to be a fairy princess isn't just being adorable and creative. She's also demonstrating a uniquely human kind of intelligence. And with these new scientific ideas in hand we can think about many other kinds of imagination in new ways. In the next chapter I'll talk about the distinctive kind of imagination that creates imaginary people, and about the way this is related to the grown-up play of writers and actors.

2.

Imaginary Companions

HOW DOES FICTION TELL THE TRUTH?

❋

Plato disapproved of poetry. In fact, he went further: poets, and playwrights and actors and artists of all kinds, would be exiled from his ideal republic. He argued that poets by their very nature say a lot of stuff that isn't true. And worse, they persuade people to think that it is true—at least for the moment. Why let such liars loose in an ideal state, let alone pay them to create illusions? Poets aren't even very good liars—in some peculiar way they manage to deceive us even though we know perfectly well that what they say isn't true.

Now we can ask an evolutionary version of Plato's question. It's easy to see why the truth is important and helpful to organisms. Knowing what the world is like helps you figure out how to survive in that world. But why is fiction equally important? Why would it help an organism to tell lies, and to do it in a way that doesn't even effectively fool anyone? Why weren't poets eliminated by natural selection if not by the benign dictator of *The Republic*? Looking at children makes this evolutionary question particularly vivid. Children are the world's wildest and most enthusiastic creators of fiction. How come? What function does all this crazy pretense serve?

So far I've been talking about children's causal knowledge of the physical and biological world and about the kinds of counterfactuals—the kinds of imagination and possibility—that knowledge allows. We saw that children's causal knowledge is reflected in their pretend play—even babies pretend that a ball is an apple, or a block is a car, or a pencil is a comb, and they can work out the causal consequences of those counterfactuals (the apple can be eaten, the car moves, the comb smooths your hair). Knowing about how one event causes another lets you know what would happen as well as what actually did happen.

In this chapter I'll talk about a different kind of causal knowledge and a different kind of imagination that goes with it. Children also construct maps of the psychological world—theories of minds instead of theories of things, everyday psychology instead of physics. And those maps play an even more crucial role in children's lives. For a social species like ours, understanding what people can do, and acting to change what they do, is even more important than understanding and changing the physical world. Many anthropologists have suggested that the development of this "Machiavellian intelligence" was an engine of human cognitive evolution. Individual humans are pathetic creatures, literally unable to keep ourselves alive. Our survival depends on our ability to get other people to do what we want—to make alliances, construct coalitions, and form teams. Just as understanding how fire works can let us make a meal or ward off a tiger, understanding how desire works can let us make a friend or ward off an enemy.

You might expect that these psychological causal maps would also be reflected in children's pretend play. And, in fact, one of the most striking kinds of pretend play involves the invention of counterfactual people—imaginary companions. The creation of imaginary companions reflects a distinctively human kind of social and emotional intelligence. At first glance, weird phenomena such as imaginary companions seem hard to reconcile with the idea that children are also little scientists actively trying to understand how the world works. But, in fact, this sort of playful freedom is part of the evolutionary story of childhood. It's all part of the strategy of protected immaturity.

These psychological kinds of knowledge and imagination—knowing about how people work and imagining what they might do—also underpin adult fiction, the work of writers and poets, actors and directors. So understanding children's pretend play can help us understand why fiction is important to adults, too.

DUNZER AND CHARLIE RAVIOLI

One of the stories of my own childhood, a sort of Gopnik family "Turn of the Screw," was the gothic tale of Dunzer. According to my mother, when I was two I insisted that a peculiar little man named Dunzer lived in my crib. He was playful and friendly at first but "gradually became more and more hostile," as my mother put it with scary Jamesian vagueness. Eventually, I was so afraid of Dunzer that I refused to go to sleep. So my mother proposed that I exchange cribs with my brother, who was a year younger. But when they went to put the baby in my crib he screamed and clung to my mother and pointed in terror to precisely the spot where I had seen Dunzer.

Imaginary companions are a common and fascinating phenomenon of childhood and they've inspired a lot of psychological speculation. But, surprisingly, until recently no one had actually studied them systematically. The psychologist Marjorie Taylor decided to remedy this (she was inspired by her own daughter, who spent much of her childhood being Amber the Dog, and later became an actress in Hollywood). In her work we meet the likes of Nutsy and Nutsy, the raucous but charming brightly colored birds who live in a tree outside a little girl's window, and whose incessant talking sometimes amuses and sometimes irritates her; and Margarine, the little girl with floor-length golden braids who not only explains the exigencies of playgroup to the three-year-old who created her, but later helps the boy's little sister to make the transition to pre-school. A subtext of the Dunzer story, at least as my mother told it, was that my brother and I were uniquely imaginative (or possibly uniquely crazy). But Taylor showed that imaginary companions are surprisingly common.

Taylor asked randomly chosen three- and four-year-old children and their parents a set of specific questions about imaginary companions. Most of the children, 63 percent to be exact, described a vivid, often somewhat bizarre, imaginary creature. Taylor repeated the questions on several occasions and found that the individual children were quite consistent in their descriptions of their imaginary companions. Moreover, their descriptions matched the independent descriptions of their parents. This showed that the children really were describing their imaginary friends, not just making them up on the spur of the moment to please the interviewer.

Many of the imaginary companions had a poetic appeal: Baintor, who was invisible because he lived in the light; Station Pheta, who hunted sea anemones on the beach. Sometimes the companions were other children but sometimes they were dwarves or dinosaurs. Sometimes the children became the imaginary creatures themselves. As I was writing this, I glanced out the window at the garden of my building—the three-year-old in the next apartment was standing next to her mother, growling, with her hands tucked up, a hula hoop around her neck tied to a leash that her mother was holding. Her mother was saying to another three-year-old, "Don't worry, she's a very gentle tiger."

Rather depressingly, little boys seem to have a penchant for becoming supercreatures of enormous power, while little girls are more likely to invent small animals to pity and take care of. My own three sons showed both patterns: Galaxy Man, the scary superhero alter ego of my oldest son, and Dr. Termanson, the egg-headed, slightly comic, slightly sinister mad-scientist companion of my second, were later joined by the very small and needy Twins who lived in my youngest son's pocket.

Imaginary companions can be friendly or, like Dunzer, they can be hostile. They can even be unavailable. The little brother who was scared of Dunzer grew up to be a father himself as well as a writer for *The New Yorker*. His three-year-old daughter, grow-ing up in literary Manhattan, in turn created an imaginary com-panion. Olivia's imaginary friend was Charlie Ravioli and he was too busy to play with her. She would report sadly that she had bumped into Charlie at the coffee shop but he had to run, and she would leave messages on an imaginary answering machine: "Ravi-oli, this is Olivia, please get back to me."

Children from many cultures and backgrounds have imaginary companions and they seem surprisingly resistant to adult influence. Fundamentalist Christian mothers discourage imaginary compan-ions because they think they might be demons. Hindu mothers discourage them because they think the companions might be manifestations of past lives and that they may take over the life of the current soul. And although many American parents approve of preschoolers' imaginary companions, they discourage them later on because—well, because they're weird.

But the imaginary companions persist anyway. At least a few

children seem to keep their imaginary companions privately long after they have given them up publicly. Frida Kahlo painted her imaginary childhood friend in her self-portraits, and Kurt Cobain addressed his suicide note to his imaginary friend, Bodha (though admittedly these examples might seem to support the parental anxieties about weirdness). Like Dunzer, imaginary friends can also sometimes be passed from sibling to sibling. Usually, though, they eventually fade from the children's minds with hardly a trace. Dunzer lives on in family legend but neither my brother nor I can remember him.

NORMAL WEIRDNESS

In Taylor's studies there were a few relatively small statistical differences between the children who had imaginary companions and those who did not, but often these differences were not what we would expect. Older and only children were more likely to have imaginary companions than younger siblings, but outgoing children were also more likely to have imaginary companions than shy children. Children who watched a lot of television were less likely to have imaginary companions, but that was also true of children who read a lot of books—children who were immersed in someone else's imaginary world seemed less likely to create such a world themselves. Indeed, it seems almost a matter of chance whether a particular child ends up with an imaginary companion or not. Imaginary companions seem to be more characteristic of children in general than of especially gifted, or disturbed, or imaginative children.

As with pretend play in general, the vividness of imaginary companions, and especially the vividness of the emotions they generate, led psychologists in the past to conclude that they indicated children's shaky grasp of reality. Freudians have typically seen imaginary companions as indicators of some sort of therapeutic need—a sign of neuroticism that demands treatment. When my brother published an account of Olivia and Charlie Ravioli he was flooded with e-mail from thoroughly analyzed fellow New Yorkers diagnosing what was wrong with her. Imaginary companions play a similarly psychoanalytic role in popular culture, both in scary movies like *The Shining* and sentimental ones like *Harvey*.

But imaginary companions are not, in fact, an indication of either genius or madness. Children with imaginary companions are not, on the whole, markedly brighter or more creative or shyer or crazier than other children. Imaginary companions aren't the result of distress or trauma, and they aren't precursors of pathology. Some children do seem to use their companions to help sort out problems in their lives, but for most they seemed to be just plain fun.

Taylor found that even children with vivid and beloved imaginary companions knew perfectly well that those companions were really imaginary, just as children know the difference between reality and fiction, in general. Children had no difficulty discriminating between the imaginary friends and real people and they even spontaneously commented on the distinction. Taylor's method meant that children were confronted with an earnest adult interviewer asking for details about the name of Michael Rose's giant father or the length of Gawkin the Dinosaur's tail. The children often interrupted to remind the interviewer, with a certain note of concern for her sanity, that these characters, were, after all, just pretend—you know, not really *real*.

When children grow older, imaginary companions are usually replaced by a new kind of imaginary activity. "Paracosms" are imaginary societies rather than imaginary people. They are invented universes with distinctive languages, geography, and history. The

Brontës invented several paracosms when they were children, as did the teenage murderers who inspired the movie *Heavenly Creatures* (one of them, in real life, grew up to be the novelist Anne Perry).

Using her interview technique, Taylor found that many perfectly ordinary, unliterary, unmurderous ten-year-olds also created their own paracosms, just as most ordinary four-year-olds created imaginary companions. One child, for example, created a planet called Rho Ticris inhabited by gigantic hounds called dune dogs, the Blue (blue-skinned humanoids), and the Dire Grim, a sinister race with seven rows of teeth. Rho Ticris was an important part of his life from nine until twelve, when it faded away as the earlier imaginary companions do. And, of course, many of the favorite books and games of older children—from Harry Potter and the Narnia books to Dungeons and Dragons and Warcraft—also involve paracosms. Paracosms are probably less familiar than imaginary companions partly because they are less common and partly because they are more private and less likely to be communicated to adults.

MAKING A MAP OF THE MIND

Why do young children create imaginary companions? Earlier, we saw the close link between the ability to think counterfactually and causal knowledge. So we might expect a link between psychological counterfactuals and knowledge about other minds. Imaginary companions are a great example of psychological counterfactuals. When imaginary Teddy spills the tea the floor gets wet. In the same way, if there were a malicious little man at the end of my crib, or a busy New Yorker at the end of my answering machine, this is how he would behave. The imaginary companions reflect ways that people might be, and ways they might act. The heyday of imaginary companions is between about two and six years old. It turns out that this is also the period when children create an everyday psychology—a causal theory of the mind.

From two to six, children discover fundamental facts about how their own minds and the minds of others work. They formulate a causal map of the mind. They start to understand the causal connections between desires and beliefs, emotions and actions, just as they start to understand the connections between blickets and blicket detectors, or between food and growth or illness. One of the central tenets of this theory of mind is that people may have different beliefs, perceptions, emotions, and desires and that those differences may lead to different actions. People behave differently because they have different kinds of minds.

Even babies who can't talk yet already seem to understand something about the ways that people might differ, and they can make new and surprising causal predictions based on that understanding. For example, we showed fourteen-month-olds and eighteen-month-olds two bowls of food—broccoli and Goldfish crackers. All the babies, as you'd expect, loved the crackers and couldn't stand the broccoli. Then the experimenter tasted a bit of food from each bowl. She acted as if she were disgusted by the crackers and happy about the broccoli. She said, "Eew, yuck—crackers" and "Mmm, yum—broccoli," revealing that her tastes were the opposite of theirs. Then she put out her hand and said, "Can you give me some?"

The babies were a bit startled by the experimenter's perverse tastes—they waited awhile before they did anything. Nevertheless the fourteen-month-olds gave the experimenter the crackers. But although the eighteen-month-olds had never seen anyone crazy enough to reject Goldfish crackers, they made the right prediction.

They sweetly did what they thought would make the experimenter happy, however weird it might seem to them. Just as they immediately knew to use the rake to get the toy, even though they'd never done it before, they immediately knew to give the experimenter the broccoli instead of the crackers. Once you know how rakes and toys work you can do something new to make a distant toy move. Once you know how people's tastes work you can do something new to make them happy.

Slightly older children can understand the complex causal interactions among desire, perception, and emotion; they can predict all the possible actions that might stem from different psychological combinations. Henry Wellman told two-year-olds that his friend Anne was going to get a snack of either raw broccoli or Cheerios. Anne got the snack in a closed box. Then she peeked into the box and reacted (the children couldn't see what she saw). You can ask two- and three-year-old children a bunch of questions about this scenario, including questions about possible futures and possible pasts, and they will rattle off the right answers. If Anne saw the broccoli, she would be sadder than if she saw the Cheerios. If Anne looked in the box and then said, "Oh boy," she must have seen the Cheerios but if she said, "Oh no" she must have seen the broccoli. But if Anne wanted broccoli, then she'd have been happy if broccoli was in the box. And if she hadn't looked in the box at all, she wouldn't have been especially happy or especially sad.

Finally, even older children, around five or so, start to understand the relationship between our beliefs and the world around us. For example, suppose you show a child a candy box that turns out to be full of pencils. The children are very surprised when they see the pencils. But if you ask them what someone else will think is in the box three-year-olds confidently report that he will think there are pencils in there! You see the same thing in children's everyday explanations about why people do what they do. They start explaining actions in terms of thoughts and beliefs, especially false thoughts and beliefs, only when they are around four—they say things like "The people thought that the hunchback was mean, but he was really nice." By then, children understand the deeply important fact that our ideas about the world may turn out to be wrong. It's as if young children think there's a direct causal link between the world and our thoughts about the world. Older children begin to appreciate that the link is more tangled and indirect—there are many intermediate steps between seeing the box and knowing what's inside it, and some of those steps may go wrong.

Just as children construct a causal map of biology that relates growth and illness, life and death, they also construct a map that connects mental states to one another and to the world outside them. And with that map in hand they can explore all the possible combinations and permutations of human behavior, and imagine all the strange things that people might think, feel, and do. Oscar the Grouch on *Sesame Street* plays on this ability. Once young children know the general principle, that Oscar likes all the things that we don't, they can, delightedly, predict that Oscar will love trash, smelly food, and worms but hate puppies and chocolate—or that he'll be happy if you give him dirt but not if you give him flowers.

As we might also expect, those causal maps allow children to act to change the minds of others. If I know that Anne has a particular passion for broccoli I'll know that I can bribe her with broccoli to do what I want, or tease her by withholding broccoli, or make her like me by presenting her with a steaming green platter of the stuff, all techniques that will be worse than useless if she really only likes crackers. I'll know, too, that if I want her to get me some crackers from the cupboard I'd better make sure she knows they're in there; just asking won't help if she hasn't seen them. But if I want to keep her from getting the crackers I can lie and tell her that the cupboard is empty.

Children who can explain actions in terms of a theory of mind also seem to be more adept, for good or ill, at altering other people's minds. Children who better understand minds are more socially skillful than those who do not, but they are also better liars. They're more sympathetic but they're better at getting under your skin too. As any successful politician knows, understanding how people work can help you to make them happy—or to manipulate them for your own ends. Four-year-olds can be surprisingly crafty politicians, especially with parents as their constituents.

Lying is a particularly vivid example of the use of counterfactuals, and of the advantages of understanding how minds work. As Machiavelli himself could have told you, lying is one of the most effective forms of Machiavellian intelligence. Our human ability to deceive others, both our allies and our enemies, is a great advantage in managing our complex social lives. Very young children may lie, but they're not very good at it. My younger sister once shouted to my mother, "I didn't cross the street by myself!"—from the other side of the street. When they play hide and seek very small children will notoriously put their heads under a table with their behinds sticking very visibly into view.

You can see the same thing in experiments. In one study the experimenter showed children a closed box and then told them there was a toy inside, and not to peek at it. Then the experimenter left the room. For children curiosity is the greatest drive of all, and very few of them could resist the temptation. When the experimenter returned she asked if they had peeked in the box, and what was inside it. Even the three-year-olds denied that they had peeked inside the box. But then they immediately told the experimenter what was in there! Only at five or so could children deceive in an effective way.

More strikingly, understanding minds actually also lets us intervene in our own minds. It lets us change our own minds as well as the minds of others. At about the same time that children develop a causal map of the mind they also start to develop capacities for what psychologists call "executive control," the ability to control your own actions, thoughts, and feelings.

One of the most dramatic examples of executive control comes from striking, though rather mean, "delay of gratification" experiments. Back in the sixties Walter Mischel would sit a preschooler in front of two big chocolate-chip cookies (or marshmallows or toys). He explained that the child could choose: she could eat just one of the cookies now, or she could get both of the cookies if she waited until the experimenter returned in a few minutes. The few minutes seemed like an eternity to the children. The videotapes of them squirming in their seats, closing their eyes, and literally sitting on their hands are both comic and pathetic. Most of the younger ones just couldn't hack it—they gave in and took the single cookie. But children got much better at this kind of self-control between three and five.

One of the most striking things about these studies was not just that children got better but *how* they got better. You might think that children just developed more willpower, and there is some truth to that. But children also got better and better at doing things to their own minds to make them behave differently. The successful children put their hands over their eyes, or hummed, or sang. They did much better when they tried imagining that the marshmallows were merely big puffy clouds and not tempting treats. As adults we use similar strategies all the time to regulate our own actions. I put the chocolate up on a high shelf out of reach or promise myself that I'll get to go for a walk and buy flowers after the chapter is done, but not before.

These strategies for executive control are also especially powerful evolutionary mechanisms. Imagining the different ways that I could be and actually implementing them lets me control and change my actions in a way that is unprecedented in evolutionary history. Not only does understanding the world let me imagine alternative worlds and make them real, and imagine ways that other people could act and make them real. It actually lets me imagine other ways that I could act and realize them too.

These children learned some important things about how our minds work. For example, they learned that focusing on what you want makes your desires more irresistible, while thinking about something else makes your desires less intense. They were using their causal knowledge about how minds worked to make them work differently, just as they used their knowledge of other people to deceive them, or used their knowledge of the blicket detector to make the machine work.

IMAGINARY COMPANIONS AND
PSYCHOLOGICAL KNOWLEDGE

Marjorie Taylor discovered that children with imaginary companions tend to have a more advanced theory of mind than other children, even though they're no smarter overall. Children who had imaginary friends were better at predicting how other people would think, feel, or act than those who did not. Similarly, contrary to popular legend, sociable children were actually more likely to have imaginary companions than shy and lonely children.

There's no getting around the fact that, from the adult point of view, there's something spooky about imaginary friends. But in fact, as far as children go, they're not only commonplace, they're a sign of social competence. Having an imaginary friend isn't a replacement for real friends, and it's not a form of therapy. The children with imaginary companions really care about people and like to think about them even when they're not there.

The shift from imaginary companions to paracosms may also reflect shifts in children's causal knowledge of other people. Older children, who already understand how individual minds work, become more interested in what happens when minds interact in socially complex ways. These older children are no longer primarily interested in understanding individual people. Instead they are trying to understand the elaborate social networks that will be crucial for their adult lives. Middle-school classrooms are full of alliances, exclusions, and battles, leaders, henchmen, and outcasts, and children are often deeply absorbed in sorting them out. Paracosms are a way of exploring counterfactual societies, just as imaginary companions are a way of exploring counterfactual minds.

AUTISM, CAUSATION, AND IMAGINATION

Children with autism are a particularly striking example of the link between causal knowledge, imagination, and play. Autism is a complicated and mysterious syndrome. Children with many different kinds of underlying problems may all get labeled with the vague term "autism," but it's at least possible that some children with autism have special difficulty constructing causal maps, in general, and causal maps of the mind, in particular. And they often seem to have trouble imagining possibilities, too.

Children with autism often know a great deal about the physical world—they can become experts at railway timetables or they may know every kind of car model. They also often have exceptional capacities for perception and memory. A "savant" with autism, for example, may be able to tell you exactly how many matches spilled out of a box, even after they've been cleaned up. But there is at least some evidence that they don't spontaneously analyze the world in terms of deeper hidden causes. Temple Grandin, an author with autism, talks about "thinking in pictures," and this may be true for other people with autism. When we gave children with autism our "blicket detector" box they paid attention to the superficial appearance of the blocks—their color and shape—but didn't seem to care whether they made the machine go. And Lisa Capps found that children with autism didn't develop the same kinds of everyday biological ideas about growth and life and death that typically developing children do.

You can get along pretty well without knowing about biology. But without a causal theory of other people you'll have a great deal of trouble understanding them. In Mark Haddon's compelling portrait of a teenager with autism, *The Curious Incident of the Dog in the Night-Time*, the narrator, like other people with autism, has great difficulty understanding and interacting with others. The hero of Haddon's book is touchingly unable to see the obvious difficulties of his mother and father.

In Haddon's book there is also a point at which the hero's therapist gives him the candies/pencils problem I described earlier. He is baffled; the problem of figuring out someone else's beliefs seems insoluble. There is a great deal of systematic evidence that children with autism have trouble developing a theory of other people's minds.

People with autism also almost never have imaginary companions, or indeed, engage in pretend play at all. They often don't seem to even understand what pretend play is all about. The hero of the Haddon book feels that even when he's writing a story everything he says has to be strictly true. Without causal theories it's hard to consider counterfactuals. Children with autism have a great deal of difficulty constructing causal theories of other people's minds, and they also don't play with the possibilities of mental life.

There is a close relationship between understanding the variety of real minds and inventing a variety of imaginary ones. There is a close link between causal knowledge and counterfactual thinking. Children who have elaborate causal maps of the minds of others also produce elaborate imaginary counterfactual people and vice versa. Children with autism, who don't have these maps, also fail to imagine other people. Knowing about other people, and imagining them, seem to go hand-in-hand.

MAPS AND FICTIONS

Marjorie Taylor also discovered a link between the childlike ability to make up imaginary people and the adult ability to create fictional counterfactual worlds—the ability we see in novelists, dramatists, screenwriters, actors, and directors. The queen of the fairies with the sparkly cloak and the wild hair could be a three-year-old or she could be schizophrenic, but she could also be an actress playing Titania.

Imaginary companions bear many similarities to the characters of adult fiction. Many authors describe their fictional imaginings in much the same terms as children do, as if they were independent people who just happened to be nonexistent. In the preface to *The Ambassadors*, Henry James described an author's relation to his characters by saying, "They were always well in advance of him, he had, in fact, from a good way behind, to catch up with them, breathless and a little flurried, as best he could." And, of course, as adult readers we can be profoundly moved, or terrified, or consoled by fictional characters, even though we know they don't really exist.

Taylor looked at fifty people who identified themselves as fiction writers, ranging from an award-winning novelist to enthusiastic amateurs. She found that almost all of them reported experiencing their characters as autonomous agents, like Henry James or the children with imaginary companions. They felt their characters walk behind them on the street, or argued with them about their roles in the novel. Many of them reported that they often felt that they simply passively recorded what the characters did and said.

Moreover, almost half the writers said that they remembered an imaginary companion and reported the companion's features in some detail. In contrast, only a few ordinary high-schoolers reported that they could remember imaginary companions, though presumably many more actually had had them. For most adults they had silently faded away, like Dunzer. But fiction writers seemed to maintain an acquaintance with their old imaginary friends. Three-year-olds with imaginary companions aren't especially creative—perhaps because all three-year-olds are already as creative as they can be—but an adult who maintains her link with the imaginary life of childhood seems particularly likely to end up writing fiction.

You can use the idea of a map to think about fictions as well as facts. I explained earlier about how we can use the same kind of thinking to make both maps and blueprints. There is also a third kind of map, even more clearly distinct from the real spatial world. We can use a map to create a fictional space, one that does not, and will not, exist. One of the great charms of *The Lord of the Rings* is the detailed set of maps at the back of each book, with all their specific information about routes through the Misty Mountains and the exact distance between Osgiliath and Mordor. The map of Middle-earth uses exactly the same resources as the map of your local town, or the garden plan, but it allows you to imagine a fictional space rather than understand a real space or create a new one. In just the same way, we can use the apparatus of causal thinking to construct fictional counterfactuals as well as past and future counterfactuals.

The line between a fiction and a counterfactual is one of degree rather than kind. Fictions are counterfactuals that just happen to be further away from our real world than other possible worlds. A fiction is a counterfactual out there where the buses don't run. If past counterfactuals are the price we pay for future counterfactuals, then fictional counterfactuals are the free bonus we get. Because we can plan, hope, and be responsible for the future we can also wonder, daydream, and escape into the fictional.

WHY MINDS AND THINGS ARE DIFFERENT

The research shows that children's imaginary companions are linked to what they learn about other people. Children pretend so much because they are learning so much. And this early pretending seems to be continuous with adult fiction. This may help to explain an apparent conundrum. Why is it that, even for adults, the transparent lies of fiction seem mysteriously able to convey deep truths about the human condition? Why do plays and novels, poems and stories and myths, mean so much to us? Why is it that even a professional scientific psychologist like me feels that I've learned more about human personality and social life from Jane Austen than from the *Journal of Personality and Social Psychology*?

There are some important differences between causal maps of

the physical world and those of the psychological world. Just as maps of the physical world allow us to change that world, so do maps of the psychological world. But in the psychological case there is an even more intimate relation between causes and counterfactuals, maps and blueprints. To intervene in the physical world we need a lot of cooperation from the causal structure of that world. It may take years or even centuries to figure out the technology to build a bridge or dam a stream.

It seems to be much easier to intervene on minds, including our own minds. We can use our words, as they say in preschool. There is something almost supernatural about psychological causation—say a few words from across the room or even across the country and you can instantly make someone else sigh with love or boil with anger. Or think about the way that a single e-mail announcing a meeting can cause people from all over the world to move to exactly the same spot at the same time. Doing the same thing to rocks or trees would seem like magic.

In fact, just about everything in the psychological world is shaped by human intervention. We can, of course, change the physical world in quite radical ways and very "unnatural" physical worlds will result. Most of the physical structure of any modern city is the result of human intervention. But we can at least contrast this with physical worlds that have not been altered by human intervention (though we may soon have to go to Mars or the moon to do so).

In the psychological case there is no "natural" world, no unspoiled mental wilderness. Even hunter-gatherer cultures are shaped by the particular conventions, traditions, and intentions of their members. The Warlpiri Australian aborigines are just as different from the Baka pygmies of Africa as urban Americans are from urban Japanese. A wild animal or a wildflower is fully an animal or a flower. But a wild child, like the famous Wild Child of Aveyron, is a damaged and injured child.

The range of imaginative possibilities in the psychological world also seems wider than the range in the physical world, and the constraints seem to be less strong. The extraordinary variety of human cultures is testimony to that. Of course, there are some psychological universals. All humans have beliefs, desires, and emotions, are happy when their desires are fulfilled and unhappy when they are not, and so on. Not every psychological arrangement is possible, and evolutionary psychologists may be right to suggest that some arrangements are harder to sustain than others. It may be an evolutionary fact that we humans have a hard time maintaining monogamy or celibacy, but it is equally an evolutionary fact, and a more surprising and interesting one, that we humans can and do invent monogamy or celibacy, or democracy, or sexual equality or pacifism or any number of other brand-new psychological attitudes (not to mention the psychological states that constitute being a tea ceremony adept, a Deadhead, or a Cubs fan). The celibate or the Cubs fan actually takes on the desires and beliefs that come with that role, even if the desire not to have sex or the faith that the Cubs will win may seem highly irrational from an evolutionary point of view. To understand what the celibate or the Cubs fan does you have to understand those "unnatural" desires and beliefs.

As a result, it is often very difficult to tell whether children are learning about the causal structure of other people's minds or changing their own minds. An American child learns what American minds are like, and a Japanese child learns what Japanese minds are like, just as they learn what American and Japanese tables and chairs and landscapes are like. But, simultaneously, that learning seems to allow the child, indeed to invite her, to make her mind into an American or Japanese one. Does the child simply discover that the people around her value individuality more than cooperation? Or does that discovery make her become somebody who values individuality more than cooperation herself?

For all these reasons, in the psychological case it is hard to separate the maps and the blueprints. Many of the most central causal facts about other people, the facts about them we most need to know to predict and change what they will do, are the result of some past history of human intervention. What we do and think always reflects what other people have said and done to us, and even more significantly what we have said and done to ourselves.

But it is important to see that there is nothing mystical, or relativist, or antievolutionary about this. We, and those around us, may create our psychological worlds more than we discover them, and discover our physical worlds more than we create them, but the same distinctive human reasoning is involved in both cases. The causal maps in our minds allow us both to understand the existing physical and psychological worlds and to invent and realize new physical and psychological worlds. They simultaneously let us make predictions, imagine alternative possibilities, and create fictions.

SOUL ENGINEERS

In the physical case, our causal maps, our theories, seem to be primary, and the engineering applications of those maps, the blueprints, seem to follow after. And while there certainly are fictional physical counterfactuals—in science fiction, for example, we may imagine different ways that the physical world could work—they're less pervasive and compelling than psychological fictions.

In the psychological case the counterfactuals, the blueprints and fictions, seem especially important. A great work of fiction presents us with a blueprint of the many ways we and others could choose to be (or not to be), and a kind of outline of the causal consequences of those choices. It tells us about the ways that people might be. Lady Murasaki tells us something new about the possible ways to love, as Proust tells us about snobbery, or Homer tells us about heroism. The writer Joseph Škvorecký, quoting Josef Stalin, of all people, said that novelists were the engineers of human souls—and this may quite literally be true.

Children work out the imaginary consequences if Teddy spills the imaginary tea, or if you try to have lunch with Charlie Ravioli, or get into the crib with Dunzer. Writers work out the imaginary consequences of Genji's imaginary charisma or Marcel's imaginary social climbing or Achilles' imaginary pride.

The child who works through the tragicomic story of Teddy's tea tells us that he understands teddies and teapots. The charm of the story of Charlie Ravioli is that three-year-old Olivia had already figured out the peculiar causal structure of busy New York literary life. She knew that if you bump into somebody in the street, the right thing to say is "Let's have lunch sometime" and even that leaving messages on a busy person's answering machine is unlikely to be effective. Though she was only three, she'd taken all her individual experiences of New York life and turned them into a single coherent theory of New York. By telling the story of Charlie Ravioli, Olivia conveyed just how much she knew about how that particular New York psychology worked. Her laid-back California cousins could work out what that life must be like, just by listening, even though they had no firsthand experience of yellow cabs and corner coffee shops.

The stories of Genji, Marcel, and Achilles convey more sophisticated adult psychological knowledge—a kind of knowledge that we might not have had until we read the book. Just as we could work out what twenty-first-century literary New York must be like from Olivia's story, we can work out what eleventh-century Japanese life, or nineteenth-century French life, or ancient Greek life was like from theirs. More, we can discover aspects of our own lives that are also implicit in those stories.

W. H. Auden, reviewing *The Lord of the Rings* when it first came out, pointed to the apparent conflict between the superficial unreality, not to say silliness, of much of the book—those awful Orcs and twee elves—and its simultaneous deep appeal. Auden said that all lives viewed from the outside, as we might view a physical sequence of events, were like a certain kind of grim realist fiction—one boring, somewhat depressing thing after another. But, he went on, all lives viewed from the inside are a matter of choices, selecting a path among many counterfactual possibilities, making one's way through many possible worlds. Even in the most commonplace life, trivial goals become imbued with the overwhelming importance and significance that is necessary to initiate action, while ordinary frustrations become mountains and chasms. From the inside, from the psychological perspective, any human life takes on the structure of a possibly hopeless but crucially important quest against overwhelmingly daunting obstacles. Fictional counterfactuals, even wildly fictional ones like *The Lord of the Rings*, help provide maps and guides for that sort of journey.

THE WORK OF PLAY

Even the youngest children ubiquitously create fictions in much the same way that adult writers and readers do. The curious thing about children's pretense, though, is that children actively seek out the wild fictive counterfactuals that are cognitive lagniappe for adults.

From the adult perspective, the fictional worlds are a luxury. It's the future predictions that are the real deal, the stern and earnest stuff of adult life. For young children, however, the imaginary worlds seem just as important and appealing as the real ones. It's not, as scientists used to think, that children can't tell the difference between the real world and the imaginary world. (Recall that the children in Harris's and Taylor's experiments knew very well that the pretend monster or the imaginary companion wasn't real.) It's just that they don't see any particular reason for preferring to live in the real one.

When we see our children immersed in their pretend worlds we say, "Oh, she's playing." This is very revealing. In adult life we distinguish between useful activities, such as cooking dinner or building bridges, and activities such as reading novels and going to the movies, that are just, as we say, "fun" or "entertainment"—in other words, play. Since young children are protected from the pressures of everyday life, since they are, to be blunt, completely useless, everything they do looks like play. They aren't out building bridges and plowing fields and they don't make dinner or bring home a paycheck. And yet their obsessive and unstoppable pretend play—that parade of fictional counterfactuals—reflects the most sophisticated, important, and characteristic human abilities.

This apparently useless behavior may be very functional from a broader evolutionary perspective. Think about the evolutionary picture I outlined in the first chapter. There is a kind of division of labor between our young selves and our older selves. Our young selves get to freely explore both this world, and all the possible counterfactual worlds, without worrying about which of those worlds will actually turn out to be inhabitable. We adults are the ones who have to figure out whether we want to move into one of those possible worlds, and how to drag all our furniture in there too.

While children may be useless, they are useless on purpose. Because, as children, we don't have to restrict our imaginings to the immediately useful, we can freely construct causal maps and exercise our ability to create counterfactuals. We can compute a wide range of possibilities, not just the two or three that are most likely to pay off. We can consider different ways the world might be, not just the ways the world actually is. As adults our causal maps of the physical and psychological worlds, and our ability to consider other ways the world might be, will let us conquer the stern and earnest universe of future possibilities.

This division of labor may lead to other differences between adults and children. I mentioned earlier that one of the clearest differences between babies and young children on one hand, and older children and adults on the other, is what psychologists call the development of inhibition—the ability to keep yourself from acting impulsively. Inhibition lets us avoid doing what we feel like immediately, in the service of our larger goals. The commonplace that babies and young children are uninhibited compared with adults is literally true, and we even have some ideas about the brain changes in the prefrontal cortex that lead to those changes in inhibition.

Usually psychologists act as if this childish uninhibitedness is a defect. And, of course, if your agenda is to figure out how to get along well in the everyday world—how to actually do things effectively—it is a defect. But if your agenda is simply to explore both the actual world and all the possible worlds, this apparent defect may be a great asset. Pretend play is notably uninhibited; young children just can't help themselves from following up any random imaginative thought. And young children, unlike adults, don't seem to prefer the close counterfactuals of planning to the distant counterfactuals of fiction. They don't choose to explore only the possibilities that might be useful—they explore all the possibilities.

The evolutionary outcome of this uninhibited exploration is that children can learn more than adults can. But children aren't wild pretenders because they are consciously trying to learn about the world or other people. They are wild pretenders because they are children and that's what children do. It's only from the broader evolutionary perspective that their uninhibited useless pretense turns out to be among the most deeply functional human activities.

Adult fiction sits between the wildly uninhibited counterfactuals of childhood and the sternly practical ones of adulthood. One way of thinking about adult fiction writers is that they combine the cognitive freedom of childhood with the discipline of adulthood. Adult dramatists, unlike most adults and like children, are exploring the possibilities of human experience for their own sake. But unlike children, and like their fellow adults, they do this on purpose and with the dedication and discipline that all adult endeavors require.

The idea that art and literature reflect our capacity for play is not new, of course, but thinking about the cognitive role of children's play gives this old idea a new force. The wild, harebrained, uninhibited three-year-old may be quite unable to do something as simple as get her snowsuit on (there are so many distractions: she has to play with the imaginary tiger and make sure her imaginary friend is dressed too). But she is, in fact, exercising some of the most sophisticated and philosophically profound capacities of human nature—though admittedly that may be cold comfort to the parent who has to make it to work on time.

3.

Escaping Plato's Cave

HOW CHILDREN, SCIENTISTS, AND COMPUTERS

DISCOVER THE TRUTH

✳

Socrates is talking to Glaucon:

Behold! human beings living in a underground den, which has a mouth open towards the light and reaching all along the den; here they have been from their childhood, and have their legs and necks chained so that they cannot move, and can only see before them, being prevented by the chains from turning round their heads. Above and behind them a fire is blazing at a distance, and between the fire and the prisoners there is a raised way; and you will see, if you look, a low wall built along the way, like the screen which marionette players have in front of them, over which they show the puppets.

I see.

And do you see, I said, men passing along the wall carrying all sorts of vessels, and statues and figures of animals made of wood and stone and various materials, which appear over the wall? Some of them are talking, others silent.

You have shown me a strange image, and they are strange prisoners.

Like ourselves, I replied; and they see only their own shadows, or the shadows of one another, which the fire throws on the opposite wall of the cave?

True, he said; how could they see anything but the shadows if they were never allowed to move their heads?

And of the objects which are being carried in like manner they would only see the shadows?

Yes, he said.

And if they were able to converse with one another, would they not suppose that they were naming what was actually before them?

Very true.

And suppose further that the prison had an echo which came from the other side, would they not be sure to fancy when one of the passers-by spoke that the voice which they heard came from the passing shadow?

No question, he replied.

To them, I said, the truth would be literally nothing but the shadows of the images.

—*from Plato's* Republic

Socrates' point, of course, is that we are these prisoners. This famous, ancient picture, the chained prisoners in the smoky cave, is still a compellingly creepy statement of one of the oldest philosophical problems. *The Matrix* used much the same image with the same impact, though with more elaborate special effects. All that reaches us from the world are a few rays of light hitting our retinas, and a few air molecules vibrating at our eardrums—images and echoes. So how can we really know anything about the outside world? Where do our theories of the world come from and how do we get them right?

Developmental psychologists have known for a long time that babies and children are prodigious learners. Some of us even have suggested that children use the same powerful learning techniques that scientists use. However, we didn't know very much in detail about how this learning was possible—either for scientists or children. In fact, I thought that this was a problem that would not be solved in my lifetime—but I was wrong. In the last few years we've made amazing progress in understanding how at least some kinds of learning are possible and how scientists and babies can accurately discover the truth about the world around them.

In the last two chapters we saw that even very young children know about the causal structure of the world. They make causal maps. This knowledge gives them remarkable abilities to imagine alternative worlds and to change this one. And these causal maps develop: five-year-olds know more than three-year-olds, who know more than one-year-olds. Children's causal maps get better—they represent the world more and more accurately, and this allows the children to imagine more powerfully and to act more effectively. Children are correctly learning how the world works. So babies must be born with powerful causal learning mechanisms.

But even if we know that these causal learning mechanisms must be in place, can we say anything more about what they're like and how they could allow us to grasp the truth? Causal learning is a notorious example of the gap between experience and truth. The great philosopher David Hume originally articulated the difficulty: "where we have observed a single event followed by another, we are not entitled to form a general rule or foretell what will happen in like cases, it being justly esteemed an unpardonable temerity . . . And there is nothing in a number of instances different from every single instance."

All we see are contingencies between events—one event follows another. How do we ever know that one event actually caused the other? And the problem gets worse. In real life, causal relations rarely involve just two events. Instead, dozens of different events are related in complicated ways. And in real life, it's actually rare for one event to *always* follow another. Usually, the cause just makes the effect more likely, not absolutely certain. Smoking causes lung cancer, but not always, and whether a particular smoker actually gets cancer depends on a complex web of other factors.

Like any good philosophical problem, the problem of causal learning is still far from completely solved, but there's been a lot of progress. The same philosophers of science and computer scientists who worked out the mathematics of causal maps also worked out techniques for learning those maps. They developed a mathematical account of how an ideal scientist could learn about causes. And they've started to turn that abstract mathematics into real computer programs, programs that can actually learn about the world.

These programs depend on the logic and mathematics of probability. When we think about logic, we usually think in terms of cut-and-dried certainties, absolute answers. But in science, and in ordinary life, we don't get those kinds of answers. The accumulated evidence may make some possibilities more or less likely, but it rarely gives us certainties.

However, to say that there is no absolute answer doesn't mean that there is no answer at all. In fact, we can be quite certain about uncertainties, and quite precise about imprecise knowledge—we can formulate a kind of probabilistic logic. Much of the recent work takes off from ideas about probability that were first formulated by the philosopher, mathematician, and theologian Reverend Thomas Bayes back in the eighteenth century. Bayes's published work, with titles such as *Divine Benevolence; or, An Attempt to Prove That the Principal End of the Divine Providence and Government Is the Happiness of His Creatures*, is long forgotten, but the unpublished essay on probability that was found in his papers after he died has become the foundation for much of twenty-first-century computer science and artificial intelligence. (In a search for Bayes on the net, the *Encyclopedia of Philosophy* article was followed by a commercial site that advertised Bayesian methods for fixing cars and winning government contracts.)

Rev. Bayes's big idea was that learning is about the probabilities of possibilities. For Bayes nothing is ever certain; instead we just think that some possibilities are more likely than others. As we get more evidence about how the world works we systematically update the likelihood of all those possibilities. A little evidence can nudge one hypothesis just a bit past another one. If the evidence is strong enough even the most unlikely possibility can turn out to be true. Learning is a long, slow process with many false starts and revolutions; things we once thought were hardly possible at all turn out to be true (or at least the best account at the moment). Bayesianism gives you precise mathematical ways to get closer and closer to the truth, even if you don't ever entirely reach it.

Combining Bayesian learning ideas with the causal maps I described in the last chapter has turned out to give computer scientists an extraordinarily powerful way of constructing learning machines. In fact, causal graphical models are often called "Bayes nets." Suppose I have two different possible theories about the world—two possible causal maps. How can I decide which one is actually right?

Recall that the maps let you make predictions. With a map I can say that some outcomes are likelier to happen than others. If I think that smoking causes cancer I can predict that preventing smoking will lower the probability of cancer. If it doesn't cause cancer—if the causal map is different—then preventing smoking won't have this effect. Then I can do an experiment or clinical trial or even just a big epidemiological study and find out what actually happens.

If the map predicted that evidence, then the probability that that is the right map will go up. The new evidence will make one map more likely than another: if the probability of cancer goes down when people stop smoking, the probability that smoking causes cancer goes up. Causal maps give you a way to make predictions about what the world will be like. By comparing those predictions with what actually happens, you can figure out systematically how likely it is that any particular causal map is actually true.

The famous Turing test proposes that you sit at a computer terminal and try to figure out whether you are interacting with a computer or another person. Turing, who invented the modern computer, said that if you can't tell the difference, you will have to grant that the computer has a mind. Servers like Hotmail now do real Turing tests, like asking a user to recognize a blurry word, to make sure they don't give e-mail addresses to spammers' computers. But to be truly convincing a Turing test would have to be more stringent. In his original paper Turing also argued for a "child computer" test. The computer should be able to do the same things as a human adult, but it should also be able to learn how to do those things like a human child.

Computers are far from passing that Turing test, but they're getting a lot better. The new Bayesian ideas let us build computers that can actually learn about the world. Computer scientists working for NASA have begun to design programs that can let a robot learn about the mineral composition of rocks on Mars, without having to consult Earthbound experts. Biostatisticians are designing programs that can take masses of genetic data and learn about the complex causal sequence of events that turns a genome into an organism. NASA scientists are even designing programs that can take satellite data and figure out how the temperature of the ocean off Latin America causes monsoons in India.

These programs work by mimicking the procedures of science. How do scientists solve the problem of causal learning? They use three techniques. They can do statistical analyses of evidence, they can learn from their own experiments, and they can learn from the experiments of others. If I'm a doctor and I want to know if smoking causes cancer, I can analyze the epidemiological data about cancer rates in smokers, I can design a randomized controlled experiment—say, getting half a group of patients to stop smoking, and letting the other half continue—and I can read the journals and find out what experiments everyone else has done. Ideally, I'd do all three. At first glance, these ways of learning about the world seem very complex and abstract. And, in fact, when ordinary adults have to consciously analyze statistics, or design experiments, or evaluate the experiments of others, they usually have a miserable time. Anyone who has taught, or taken, an introductory statistics course can testify to that.

Often, though, people can do things intuitively that they can't do consciously. When we drive, we are unconsciously making very complicated computations about the speed of the car, the effects of the steering wheel, and the nature of the road. When we understand sentences we are unconsciously making very complicated computations about sounds and syntax. It turns out that even the youngest children can use statistics and experiments to learn about the world, in much the way that the sophisticated scientists and NASA computers can.

OBSERVATION: BABY STATISTICS

In statistics we calculate the probabilities of various combinations of events and then use that information to draw causal conclusions. For instance, we can count up the number of smokers and nonsmokers who do or don't get lung cancer. Then we can calculate how likely it is that people who smoke will get cancer and compare that to the likelihood that people who don't smoke will get cancer. Then we factor out other measures such as age and income to show that the link between cancer and smoking isn't due to other causes. With enough information like this we can eventually conclude that smoking causes cancer.

In 1996, in a groundbreaking paper in *Science*, Jenny Saffran showed that even babies as young as eight months old were sensitive to statistical patterns. This paper launched a flood of exciting research about babies' statistical learning abilities.

How could we possibly show that babies can do statistics? Saffran looked at how they learn words. Suppose, for example, you hear the words "pretty baby." When we hear someone say words, as opposed to reading them on the printed page, there aren't actually any pauses, the words just follow one another continuously. (This becomes vivid when you try listening to a foreign language.) So "pretty baby" actually sounds like "prettybaby." How do you know that "pretty" and "baby" are words and "tyba" is not?

If you have listened to English for eight months (especially if you have a typically fond and sappy mom) you will often have heard "pre" followed by "ty" (not only in "pretty baby" but in "pretty boy" and "pretty darling"), and "ba" followed by "by" (not only in "pretty baby" but in "darling baby" and "angel baby"). But you will have heard "ty" followed by "ba" much less often. You might use that probabilistic information ("ty" often follows "pre" but "ba" rarely follows "ty") to figure out that "pre" and "ty" go together but "ty" and "ba" don't.

To see if babies do this, Saffran used a technique for trying to understand infant minds, habituation, in a very clever experiment. Habituation depends on the idea that babies prefer to look at or listen to new things instead of old ones. If you play babies the same kind of sound over and over again, for example, they get bored and turn away from the sound. Play them something new and they become attentive and start listening and turning to the sound again.

You can use this technique to see whether babies are sensitive to statistics. For example, you can play them long strings of nonsense syllables without pauses in various combinations. In one string "ga" is always preceded by "ba," but "da" can follow many different syllables, including "ba." So if you hear "ba" you will definitely hear "ga" next, but there is only a one-third chance that you will hear "da." Then you can play the baby different nonsense "words" in isolation, like, for instance, "bada" or "baga." Remember that babies prefer to listen to things that are new rather than things that are familiar. Will they recognize that "bada" is more unusual than "baga" and prefer to listen to that combination of sounds? They do, as the babies can unconsciously use the pattern of probabilities to figure out which syllables are likely to occur together.

Is this ability to detect probability patterns limited only to language? People such as Steven Pinker or Noam Chomsky would argue that there are very specialized parts of the brain designed just for dealing with language. But eight-month-olds can also detect patterns of probability when you do the same experiment with musical tones (if you hear E followed by D, then C is likely to follow D, the beginning of music appreciation) or with visual scenes (like figuring out that when you see a door you'll also often see a window nearby).

In a particularly dramatic recent study, Fei Xu at the University of British Columbia showed that even nine-month-olds understand some important statistical ideas. She showed babies a transparent box full of mixed-up red and white Ping-Pong balls. Sometimes the balls were mostly white with a few red ones mixed in, sometimes they were mostly red with a few white ones. Then she covered the sides of the box to hide the balls. The experimenter took five balls out of the now opaque box in succession, either four red and one white one or vice versa. If you think about it, it should be surprising, though of course possible, that you just happen to pull mostly red balls out of a mostly white box. It could happen but it's not very likely, and certainly much less likely than pulling out mostly white balls.

Very young babies seemed to reason about probabilities in the same way. They looked longer at the experimenter when she pulled out mostly red balls from a mostly white box than when she pulled out mostly white balls from a mostly white box, or mostly red balls from a mostly red box. Like Reverend Bayes, these nine-month-olds could consider the probabilities of possibilities.

So even nine-month-olds detect the patterns of probability that are the basic data of statistics. Will they use those patterns to draw conclusions about what causes what, in the way that scientists do? At least by the time they are two and a half, and probably earlier, children can also use probabilities to make genuinely causal inferences.

To test this we went back to the blicket detector machine I described in the last chapter. We showed the children complicated patterns of contingency between the blocks and the detector. The children were like scientists looking at a big data table about smoking levels and cancer rates. Instead of asking what causes cancer or how to stop it, we asked similar questions about our machine. We asked the children which blocks made the machine go, and we also asked them to get it to stop.

For example, we showed children the two patterns of blocks in the figure below. In both cases, the white block makes the detector go three times and the black block makes it go two out of three times. If children were just looking at how often the blocks made the detector go they should behave the same way in both experiments. But the pattern of probabilities is different: black makes the detector go only if white is there too. You have to "factor out"

Screening-off Procedure

ONE-CAUSE CONDITION

Object A activates the detector by itself.

Object B does not activate the detector by itself.

Both objects activate the detector (demonstrated twice).

Children are asked if each one is a blicket.

TWO-CAUSE CONDITION

Object A activates the detector by itself (demonstrated three times).

Object B does not activate the detector by itself (demonstrated once).

Object B activates the detector by itself (demonstrated twice).

Children are asked if each one is a blicket.

Figure 1. The "Is It a Blicket?" experiment.
Source: Gopnik, Sobel, Schulz, and Glymour, 2001

the white block, the way we factor out age or income when we explore the link between smoking and cancer.

Three- and four-year-olds, and even two-year-olds, get it right. They say that the white block is a blicket but the black one is not in the first "one-cause" case, but that they both are blickets in the second "two-cause" condition. They make the sort of statistical inferences a scientist would make in order to find out the truth about the machine.

What is more, children can use their new knowledge about blickets to make changes, though admittedly rather small ones, in the world around them. For example, we can show children the sequence of events in the next picture. The black block goes on and nothing happens. Then we take it off and put the white block on by itself. The detector lights up and plays music. Now we add the black block to the top of the detector and the box still lights up and plays music. So both blocks are on top of the box and the box is playing. Then we ask the children to make the machine stop. Children have never actually seen anything make the machine stop, but nevertheless they make the right decision: Taking the white block off will work and taking the black block off won't. In a small way, the children in these experiments have learned how to change the world. In the "two-cause" condition, on the other hand, children figure out that they must take off both blocks.

We can even show that these young children are unconsciously calculating probabilities. We showed the children one block that made the detector go two out of six times and another that made it go two out of four times. Four-year-olds, who can't yet do simple addition, said that the second block had more of an effect on the detector than the first one. And in other experiments we showed that they used even more sophisticated Bayesian reasoning to calculate the probability of causes and effects.

Procedure used in Gopnik et al. (2001), Experiment 3

ONE-CAUSE CONDITION

Object B is placed on the detector and nothing happens.

Object B is removed.

Object A is placed on the detector by itself and the detector activates.

Object B is added to the detector with Object A. The detector continues to activate. Children are asked to make it stop.

TWO-CAUSE CONDITION

Object B is placed on the detector and the detector activates.

Object B is removed. The detector stops activating.

Object A is placed on the detector by itself and the detector activates.

Object B is added to the detector with Object A. The detector continues to activate. Children are asked to make it stop.

Figure 2. The "Make It Stop" experiment.
Source: Gopnik, Sobel, Schulz, and Glymour, 2001

EXPERIMENTATION: MAKING THINGS HAPPEN

In addition to making observations, scientists also learn about the causal structure of the world by performing experiments. In an experiment, the scientist intentionally acts on the world, she intervenes, just as she does when she uses her knowledge of the world to change it. But in an experiment the goal isn't to make something happen, it's to figure out *how* things happen. The scientist deliberately brings about a new event. She adds sulfuric acid to the sodium, or puts penicillin in the Petri dish of bacteria, and then observes what happens to the rest of the world, what other events follow. She can use this information to draw conclusions about the causal links between sodium and sulfuric acid or penicillin and bacteria out in the real world, even when she isn't intervening. Armed with these conclusions she can then go on to effectively change the world in a big way. She can cure tuberculosis and cholera by prescribing penicillin, for example.

When we just observe two events co-occur, it could always be because there's some hidden common cause we don't know about—maybe everyday stress makes people have high blood pressure and it also makes them get heart diseases. But now suppose we take a group of people and randomly give half of them a drug that lowers their blood pressure. If they get less heart disease, it must be because of the drug. Mathematically speaking, we can use Bayes-net models to show that these inferences about causation are justified by particular patterns of experimental results. Mathematicians can also show why experimentation is a particularly powerful way of learning about causes, providing much more accurate results than observation alone. And this work shows that you don't have to do the kinds of formal experiments that scientists perform to learn about causes. Other kinds of interventions that look more like children's play can also help us learn.

Can babies do experiments? Even very young babies pay special attention to the consequences of their actions. For example, we can attach a mobile to a three-month-old baby's leg with a ribbon, so that the baby's kicking makes the mobile move, and the baby will kick like mad. Is this a kind of experiment or is it just that the baby likes to see things move? To test this, you can show the same baby a mobile that does exactly the same things but isn't connected to the baby's own body. Babies prefer to look at the mobile that they can influence themselves, and they smile and coo at it more too. This suggests that it isn't just that they like the effect—they really are trying to make the effect happen and to see the consequences. They are happy because the experiment succeeds.

Moreover, babies will systematically explore the contingencies between various limb movements and the movements of the mobile—they'll try kicking with one leg and then another and then try waving an arm, watching the mobile's responses all the time. And if you take them out of the crib and then put them back in again they'll immediately wave the correct leg to make the mobile move. These explorations really do seem to be experiments. They are actions designed to find out about how the world works, rather than just actions designed to bring about particular events.

These very early experiments seem designed to find out about the direct causal links between what a baby does and what happens next. But by the time they are a year old babies will systematically vary the actions they perform on objects. Piaget described this kind of experimental play long ago. Rather than just doing the same thing over and over, say banging the block on the table, babies will first bang the block harder and then softer or first bang it and then shake it, carefully observing what happens all the while. And they don't just watch the immediate consequences of their actions; they watch the further consequences "downstream." Give an eighteen-month-old a set of blocks and you can see her trying different combinations, placements, and angles, seeing which ones eventually lead to stable towers and which end in an equally satisfying crash.

By the time children are four they do more complex experiments. Consider another demonic machine Laura Schulz and I designed—the gear toy. Like the blicket detector, the gear toy presents children with a new causal problem. It's a square box with two gears on top and a switch on the side. When you flip the switch the gears turn simultaneously. By itself that doesn't tell you how the toy works. But if you take off gear A and flip the switch, gear B turns by itself; if you take off gear B and flip the switch, gear A doesn't turn. With both these experiments together, you can conclude that the switch is making gear B move and that gear B is making gear A move.

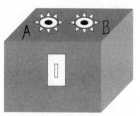

Figure 3. The gear toy.

If you feel a little shaky about following this, don't worry, you're in good company. When we did similar experiments with UC Berkeley undergraduates they got flummoxed when they tried to think it through. They did much better when we told them to just follow their instincts.

(My deception of my poor son Andres over the blicket detector came back to bite me with the gear toy. As psychologists, and thus mechanical incompetents, we asked the guys in the machine shop to make the toy for us. Several months later the machine broke and we asked them to replace the wires between the switches and the gears. They explained that actually there was no causal relationship between the gears and the switch at all. They had designed it so that each component had an independent microchip that made it act the right way—their version of the little man behind the curtain. This time I was the one who felt like Neo in *The Matrix*.)

We told four-year-olds to figure out how the toy worked and we left them alone and filmed them with a hidden camera. The children, just as you'd expect, played with the machine. They spun the gears around, listened to the inside of the box, even sniffed the machine. But they also kept flicking the switch, taking off gears and putting them on again. In the course of merely playing around, most of the children solved the problem.

Laura Schulz then provided even more striking evidence that young children use play experimentally to figure out causal problems. She showed four-year-olds a box with two levers. In one version the experimenter said, "Here's your lever and my lever. Let's find out what these levers do," and pushed on her own lever simultaneously with the child. A duck popped out of the box. This meant that the children didn't know which lever caused the duck to appear—it could have been either one. The other version was exactly the same except that this time the child and the experimenter pushed the levers separately and the duck appeared only when one of the levers was pressed—it was obvious that that lever made the duck appear. Then Schulz simply left the children with the box. They played with the box much more in the first version than in the more obvious second one, pressing and manipulating the levers until they figured out just how the box worked.

In another experiment Christine Legare took our blicket detector and added in a small twist. One group of preschool children saw that blocks made the box go. But another group saw that three blocks worked, but then saw that one block didn't work. Christine asked the children, "Why did that happen?" and then she let them play with the box. Children gave a bunch of interesting explanations: "You put it in the wrong place!" or "The battery's dead!" or "It just looks like a blicket, it isn't one really." The children who saw the puzzling event played with the box much longer than the children who saw the regular box. And they played in a way that reflected their explanations—the kids who said the last block wasn't really a blicket carefully made a pile of the good blickets and segregated them from the defective one.

This won't surprise anyone who has spent much time with babies or young children. We take it for granted that young children are perpetually "getting into things." In fact, a major job for caregivers is to keep this instinct for getting into such things as plugs and electric fans from causing harm. As a do-it-yourself exercise in developmental psychology, find any child between one and two, and simply watch her play with her toys for half an hour. Then count up the number of experiments you see—any child will put the most productive scientist to shame.

But when you think about it more closely this is a very odd thing for children to do. They don't get into things in order to satisfy their immediate needs; their immediate needs are taken care of by adults. Why do young children expend so much energy and time, even putting their own safety at risk? It makes perfect sense, though, if you think of toddlers as causal learning machines. Experimentation is one of the best ways of discovering new causes and their effects and understanding the causes you've already observed. The Mars rovers, perhaps the most dramatic recent discovery machines, get into everything too.

Although preschool teachers and parents have long felt intuitively that play contributes to learning, these experiments actually show scientifically that this is true. Just as imaginative play helps children explore possibilities, exploratory play lets them learn about the world. You can only hope that this will slow down the Dickensian administrators who seem to want to take play out of the early curriculum.

The drive to experiment seems to be innate, but experimentation provides us with a way of learning things that are not innate. What are built in are techniques for discovering all the things that aren't built in. Experimentation, in children or in scientists, provides us with a continuous series of shocks, little unexpected confrontations with nature. It's the key to solving Plato's problem. When we actively experiment on the world, we are really and truly interacting with a real world outside ourselves, and we can't tell beforehand what lessons that real world will teach.

DEMONSTRATION: WATCHING MOM'S EXPERIMENTS

Finally, there is a causal learning technique that lies somewhere between statistical analysis and active experimentation. It may be the most important kind of learning for us humans. Scientists learn from other people's experiments as well as their own. In fact, much scientific practice, from reading journals to going to talks, to holding lab meetings, helps you learn from other people. We scientists make the assumption that the interventions of others are like our own interventions and that we can learn the same things from both sources. By now each issue of a journal such as *Science* reflects the accumulated experiments of tens of thousands of scientists.

Learning from the actions of others was a basic mechanism of human culture long before organized science. By watching what others do and learning from it, we can go beyond the brief scope of an individual life. We can benefit from the accumulated learning of all the generations before us.

Experimental interventions are a particularly powerful way of learning about the causal structure of the world, much more powerful than mere observation alone, but there is a tension between the two kinds of learning. We can draw much stronger conclusions from experimentation than from observation, but it is much easier to observe than it is to experiment. Experimenting means acting and acting takes energy and resources and determination. However, if you assumed that other people's actions were similar to yours, you could vastly extend the scope of your experience with little expenditure of effort yourself. You could let other people do your experiments for you.

If those other people already knew more than you did, you could get special benefits from watching their interventions. Like the lab demonstrations in a science class, the interventions of "experts" can teach you what causes what.

Babies are particularly well designed to learn from other people in this way. They already know that other people intervene in the world the same way that they do. Seven-month-olds, for example, appreciate that actions are directed toward particular goals. To show this, Amanda Woodward used the habituation technique. You can show the babies two toys, say, a ball and a teddy bear on a table (see figure 4). A hand reaches in and grasps the teddy bear. Now you switch the locations of the two toys, so that the teddy bear is where the ball was and vice versa. What will the baby predict will happen next? Will the person they're watching move to the other side of the table to get the teddy bear? Or will she just go to the same side of the table as before? Seven-month-olds seem to predict that she'll reach for the teddy bear—they look longer when she goes to the ball instead. Even more strikingly, they don't make this prediction if a stick, rather than

a. Habituation   b. New Goal   c. Old Goal

Figure 4. The Woodward "Understanding Goals" experiment.
Source: Courtesy of Amanda Woodward

a hand, touches one object or the other. So seven-month-olds know that Mom's hands, like their own hands, try to make things happen.

Other kinds of experiments also show that a baby can link her own actions and the actions of others. For example, very young babies can imitate the actions of others—they will reproduce the actions they see someone else perform. Andy Meltzoff is the king of imitation research. Back in the seventies he showed that literally from the time they are born babies imitate the gestures and actions of other people. Nine-month-old babies can use this kind of imitation to learn about causes. These babies don't just imitate actions, they recognize and reproduce the results of those actions. For example, a one-year-old walks into the lab and sees the experimenter tap his head on a box, which makes it light up. A week later she returns to the lab and sees the box on the table. She'll immediately use her own head to get the box to light up.

By the time they are eighteen months old babies can imitate in an even more sophisticated way. Gyorgy Gergeley showed babies an experimenter touching her head to the box, but now she had a blanket wrapped around her so that her hands weren't available. If the other person's hands are free the babies will tap their own heads on the machine. But if she's wrapped up in the blanket and she taps the machine with her head, the babies will instead use their own hands. They seem to have figured out that you would use your hands if you could, but since you can't you're using your head instead.

Or suppose you show the baby someone trying to take apart a two-part toy dumbbell, as Meltzoff did. The baby sees the other person try and try again, but never manage actually to succeed. When they get the toy the babies immediately pull apart the toy themselves. As all parents wryly recognize, children don't just learn by imitating your successes. They learn by avoiding your mistakes, and understanding your limitations, too.

These babies go beyond simply imitating the other person. Instead they recognize the complex causal relationships among human goals, actions, and outcomes.

By the time they're four, children can use information about your interventions to make very complicated new causal inferences. For example, take the "gear toy" experiment I described before. The children experimented on the toy until they saw the right pattern of evidence to figure out how the toy worked. But instead of trying out all the different possibilities themselves, they could just watch what another person did to make the toy go. It turns out that children will also solve this problem if they simply see an adult demonstrate the right experiments on the toy, as well as when they perform the experiments themselves.

This suggests that other people, especially caregivers, can serve as implicit causal tutors for children—long before children have any formal education. When adults demonstrate actions, and encourage babies and children to imitate them, they also encourage causal learning. They demonstrate the particular tricks and tools of their individual culture, but they also point to the causal relations that those tricks and tools exploit.

In fact, for most of human history, this kind of demonstration was the most significant educational technique. In preindustrial societies it still is. Barbara Rogoff studied Mayan mothers and children in Guatemala. She found that the Mayan children developed a remarkable degree of skill with complex and dangerous tools at a very early age. Young children are constantly with the adults as the adults practice these skills—the village square is both the workplace and the childcare center—and adults make sure that even the youngest babies carefully watch what they do.

This kind of demonstration also provides a powerful mechanism for change and innovation. A single new discovery by a clever, or lucky, experimenter can spread through an entire community and on to the next generation, until it seems second nature to the generation that learned it as small children. Each culture can develop its own special expertise this way. Barbara Rogoff told me that, on a trip to the city, the Mayan mothers marveled at the way Barbara's own children effortlessly coped with the complexities of a bathroom, manipulating all those complicated levers and taps with hardly a second thought. The Mayan mothers had the same astonished reaction that Barbara did when she saw the Mayan children skillfully manage machetes and cooking fires.

You can learn a causal map by watching the consequences of particular actions—by seeing how a number of experiments turned out. But once you've learned the map you can do much more than just reproduce the actions you've seen. Causal maps also let you consider new possibilities and make new plans. The children who watched us manipulate the gear toy could figure out new ways to make it go or stop. Watching an expert demonstrate how to use a machete doesn't just let you perform the same moves that the expert does. It also lets you understand how machetes work, and so lets you think of new ways to use the machete to solve new problems.

UNDERSTANDING MINDS

So far, I've talked about how babies learn about physical causes—gears and switches, blickets and blicket detectors. But for human beings psychological causes are just as important—maybe more so. We saw earlier that just as babies and children learn a great deal about physical causes they also learn a great deal about psychological causes. Even the youngest babies already seem to understand some basic facts about emotion and action. But as they grow older they gradually develop an understanding of desire, perception, and belief, personality traits, moods, and prejudices, all the way up to the detailed and subtle psychology we can appreciate in Lady Murasaki or Proust. But though we've shown *that* children learn about other minds, we haven't yet explained *how* they learn.

Children learn about physical and psychological causes in similar ways. At first it might seem that there's not much connection between the statistical analyses that let us discover that smoking causes lung cancer, or even that the blickets make the detector go, and everyday psychology. But, in fact, statistical patterns may actually help us to identify which things have minds in the first place.

Think about the ways we interact with people and with things. When we manipulate things, typically it's all or nothing. When I pick up a ball it follows my every move. When I put it down it doesn't do a thing. The same with light switches and remote controls. But with people it's all much more complex and delicate. Sometimes when you smile at Mom she smiles back, but sometimes she's distracted or busy. And if you do smile at Mom and she smiles back that will make you more likely to smile, which will make her more likely to smile, and so on. Sometimes we interact with a physical object that has the same pattern of complex responses as a person. My computer, for instance, mostly does what I tell it to do, but sometimes it's practically perverse, refusing to perform no matter what I do, or worse, behaving itself one minute and then seizing up the next. In those cases we often feel as if the computer has a mind of its own.

Even one-year-olds are sensitive to these contingency patterns, and use them to differentiate people and things. The psychologist Susan Johnson endowed a very clearly nonhuman thing, a sort of brown robotic blob, with the ability to react contingently to a baby. When the baby made a noise, the blob chirped, and when the baby moved, the blob lit up, and so forth. A second identical blob made the same chirps and lit up the same way but did so in a way that was entirely unrelated to what the baby did. The events were the same, but the statistical relations between the events were different—the chirps were correlated with the babies' actions in one case but not the other.

Then each blob turned so that one end of it faced away from the baby and toward an object. The babies turned to follow the "gaze" of the reactive blob but not the unreactive blob. They seemed to think that the reactive blob could see. And the babies babbled and gestured more at the blob that interacted with them than at the blob that didn't.

They also treated the reactive blob as if it had goals. They seemed to think that it wanted things. Remember that babies understood that someone was trying to pull apart a toy dumbbell even when they didn't manage to succeed. They didn't react the same way to a machine. But when Johnson gave the machine interactive abilities, when it chirped and lit up in response, then the babies did act as if the machine was trying to pull apart the toy. In short, they treated a reactive object, even a very peculiar reactive object, as if it had a mind, and as if the pattern of its chirps and lights and movements were indications of what it saw and wanted to do.

We can also do psychological versions of exactly the same experiments we did with the blicket detector. By the time they're four years old children will use statistical patterns to make inferences about individual minds. This time, instead of showing children blocks and machines, we showed them a toy bunny in a basket. The bunny, we told them, is scared of some animals but not others, and we wanted them to figure out the bunny's fears. Then children saw various patterns of contingency relating the bunny and other toy animals. A zebra showed up in the basket by itself and the bunny shook with fright. But when an elephant appeared by himself, the bunny welcomed him in. Then the elephant and the zebra both appeared in the bunny's basket and the bunny shook with fright again. Could the children "factor out" the effects of the elephant, and conclude that the bunny was really scared only of the zebra?

Four-year-olds drew the right conclusions about what made the bunny scared—they analyzed the data and figured out the right answer. They could also intervene in the world to change it based on this knowledge—they would remove the zebra from the basket to ensure the bunny's peace of mind (and indeed the sympathetic preschoolers were quite anxious to do so—they practically rushed in to evict the scary animal from the basket even before we asked them to).

Children can draw conclusions about personality traits in the same way. My student Elizabeth Seiver and I showed four-year-olds different patterns of contingency among people, situations, and actions. Anna and Josie were little dolls that could play on a miniature trampoline and bicycle. We showed half the children that Anna happily went on the trampoline and leaped on the bicycle three out of four times but Josie could bring herself to get on the trampoline and bicycle only one out of four times. We showed the other half of the children that Anna and Josie both happily bounced on the trampoline three out of four times but dared approach the bicycle only one out of four times. Again the events were the same but the statistical patterns were different.

Then we asked the children to explain why Anna and Josie acted the way they did. The first group said it was because Anna was brave and Josie was timid, and they predicted that Anna would continue to be brave in new situations—she'd go off the diving board, too. The second group said the dolls acted that way because the trampoline was safe and the bicycle was dangerous. Watching the pattern of playground behavior can lead children to some deep conclusions about what other people are like.

Often these inferences are right, of course, but even very young children, like adults, may make profound decisions about someone's character with just a little data. You may be quick to decide that a colleague is a really good guy when he smiles at you a few times (and then be startled to discover what he's really like). Sometimes this can even be a matter of life and death. People in general concluded that the abusive Abu Ghraib guards had deep-seated evil personality traits, even though psychological research suggests that many, even most people, might act similarly in those situations.

Children learn from the patterns they see, but they also perform psychological experiments to explore the inner as well as the outer world. For example, Ed Tronick got nine-month-olds to watch their mothers suddenly adopt a perfectly still pose—a kind of impassive, iron face. As you might expect, the babies were perturbed by this, and often even started crying. But they would also produce a large number of unusual and expressive gestures, as if they were trying somehow to test what was wrong. In another study, instead of having a baby imitate an adult, the adult imitated the baby, mimicking everything that the baby did. Faced with this extremely peculiar behavior, one-year-olds performed a different kind of experiment. They produced odd exaggerated gestures as if they were testing whether the experimenter really would imitate those actions too. They would wiggle a hand in some particularly strange way to see if the adult would do the same. The babies were as intrigued by the mimicry as they were by the stone face and, in each case, they tried to get a reaction from the adult that would help them figure out what was going on.

Perhaps most potent of all, children can learn about the mind by observing the interactions and interventions of people around them. Watching how the people around you influence and manipulate others is a particularly powerful source of information about psychological causes. Younger siblings, for example, rather surprisingly seem to learn about minds more quickly than older siblings, though they typically do worse on IQ and verbal tests. Younger siblings develop exceptional emotional and social intelligence, while older ones develop more conventional schoolroom intelligence. Younger siblings are more likely to be peacemakers and charmers, while older siblings are the serious achievers. Watching an older brother or sister interact with Mom and Dad may be a very important way of learning how minds work. Younger siblings have especially rich opportunities to see Machiavellian intelligence in action. When he was two, my middle son would stare from his high chair with utter fascination at his three-year-old brother—noting every argument lost and won, every negotiation, every little bit of three-year-old diplomacy and strategy.

Language plays an especially potent role in learning about the mind. In fact, there are consistent and strong correlations between children's language abilities and their understanding of the minds of others. After all, a major way that we come to understand what is going on in other people's heads is by hearing what they say. We can figure out how objects work by looking at them and we can even figure out what people want by looking at what they do. But to figure out what people think, you have to hear what they say.

Perhaps the most dramatic example of the power of language comes from deaf children. Deaf children of deaf parents, who learn sign as a native language and are surrounded by other signers, have no trouble understanding minds. However, most deaf children have hearing parents. Even when those parents learn sign, as most do nowadays, they use it rather haltingly as a second language, the way I would speak Spanish if I suddenly tried to learn it now. As a result deaf children of hearing parents often don't understand what the people around them are saying. This means they miss much of the psychological interaction that is going on around them. They also have a particularly hard time understanding minds. Remember that five-year-olds, unlike three-year-olds, usually understand that beliefs can be false—they say that Nick will think there are candies in the candy box, even though really it's full of pencils. But deaf children of hearing parents who don't use sign may not solve this problem until they are eight or nine.

Even more dramatically, studying deaf children lets us see what happens when a language is actually created. In Nicaragua, as in many poor and small countries, deaf children were traditionally isolated from one another—they didn't have a common language and no one taught them sign language. In the seventies, for the first time, Nicaragua opened a school for the deaf, where all the children could meet one another and communicate. The children actually started to invent a new sign language. By the time the next generation of children arrived they could learn this new language instead of trying to cobble it together themselves. It was a natural experiment on the benefits of language.

Jennie Pyers went to study these children. She discovered that the first generation of children—the ones who had to invent the language—had a terrible time understanding how other people's minds worked, like other deaf children of hearing parents. You could see this in laboratory tests but you could also see it in their everyday lives. Even adults couldn't solve the simple problem about the pencils in the candy box. If you asked them to describe a video of a man absentmindedly taking a teddy bear from a hat rack and putting it on his head instead of a hat, they never mentioned that maybe he had made a mistake. The other deaf people at the school commented on how hapless their older friends were at keeping secrets or manipulating other people. The second generation of children, who had all learned a common language, had no trouble understanding how minds worked. Even though they were younger than the previous generation they had no trouble solving the candies-and-pencils problem. They immediately said that the man in the video must have thought the bear was his hat.

In fact, psychology is an arena where the premodern ways of teaching are still the most effective ones, even in contemporary life. We don't teach psychology in elementary schools, because we don't need to. Every distracted or commanding teacher, every successful bully or heroic defier of bullying, every charming flirt or captivating class clown, is a rich psychology tutorial of their own.

While a new tool or technique, a wheel or a lever, may be impressive, the psychological wheels and levers are really the things that move the world. Mastering physical causality can give us the means to explore space or destroy the world. But psychological causality, the words spoken by some humans to others, actually makes the rockets go up or the bombs come down.

Our ability to represent the causal structure of the world and the mind and to imagine and create possible new worlds and minds is one powerful engine of human change. But our ability to revise and transform those representations, to observe and experiment, and to learn from those observations and experiments gives us an even more powerful engine of change. A single accurate causal map already allows us to change the world in myriad ways. But the ability to create new and ever more accurate causal maps, both of the world and ourselves, lets us do even more.

This ability to learn about the causal structure of the world may lie at the heart of what makes us distinctively human. The two most prominent theories of the evolution of human intelligence both emphasize causal knowledge. One school emphasizes the importance of understanding physical causes—the sort of understanding that allowed us to use complex tools. Another emphasizes the ability to understand psychological causes—the sort of understanding that allowed us to maintain complex social networks and to develop culture.

Our ability to learn about causes may underlie both these valuable and distinctively human abilities. We should, of course, be wary of saying that there are things that only humans can do. Many animals are better at using tools and understanding the actions of other animals than we once thought. And we should avoid the hubris of thinking that these capacities are somehow "higher" or "more evolved" than others. We have been around for only about one-hundredth as long as the dinosaurs, and our capacities for tool use and complex social networks may yet lead to our extinction.

However, even if other animals have some of these capacities, we are, at the very least, much better at these kinds of learning than any other animal, and we devote far more of our time and energy to their pursuit. And we do this most of all when we are very small children.

Thinking about Plato's problem—how we learn—can help us understand many otherwise puzzling facts about children, such as their obsessive, tireless experimental play and their ceaseless observation and imitation of adults. Why does my one-year-old get into everything? Why does my two-year-old always press my buttons? Where on earth did my three-year-old get *that* from? Children act this way just because they are designed to rapidly and accurately learn the causal structure of the physical and psychological worlds around them.

At the same time, the discovery that even the youngest children are so deeply engaged in causal learning, and are so good at it too, suggests a new way of thinking about the ancient philosophical questions. Plato and other philosophers asked, "How can we know so much about the world?" The scientific answer is that methods of experimentation and statistical analysis seem to be programmed into our brains even when we are tiny babies. Very young children unconsciously use these techniques to change their causal maps of the world. Those programs allow babies, and so the rest of us, to find the truth.

4.
What Is It Like to Be a Baby?

CONSCIOUSNESS AND ATTENTION

✳

The great developmental psychologist John Flavell once told me that he would trade all his degrees and honors for the chance to spend just five minutes inside the head of a young child—to genuinely experience the world as a two-year-old once more. I think this is the secret wish of almost all developmental psychologists however scientifically we may talk about neural plasticity and fundamental learning mechanisms. And it occurs to every parent, too. What is it like to be a baby? How do babies experience the world? What does knowing about consciousness tell us about babies and young children? What can babies and young children tell us about the nature of consciousness?

At least since the scientific revolution began, consciousness has been one of the thorniest problems in philosophy. All of us know that we have specific vivid experiences—the special tint of a blue-grey sky, the distinctive taste of ripe strawberries, the particular pitch of a pigeon's coo. Philosophers invent technical terms to capture this special quality of our experience like "subjectivity" or "qualia." But perhaps the best philosophical expression of the problem comes from Thomas Nagel. In a famous essay Nagel asked, "What is it like to be a bat?" The problem of consciousness is about what it is like to be me.

Before we knew much about the brain it was possible to see consciousness as a mysterious feature of a special kind of substance—whether you call it mind or soul. But a hundred years or more of scientific study of the brain has convinced almost all philosophers that everything we experience must be connected to, or caused by, or based in the brain (the very profusion of prepositions is revealing). Still, though, the problem of how that is possible is not much nearer a solution than it was one hundred years ago. How can the electrical activity of a few pounds of grey goo produce the blue of the sky and the song of the dove?

For most problems, including most philosophical problems, we can at least get a hint of what the possible solutions might be. The problem is to decide which solution is the right one. But consciousness is one of those really tough, frustrating problems where we don't have a clue about what the solutions should even look like. The one thing that seems clear is that the possibilities on offer are all pretty hopeless.

Usually in cognitive science we explain how the mind works by thinking about the actions we produce or the computations we perform. We explain the fact that we can produce new sentences by saying that we know linguistic rules. If we had different rules we would produce different types of sentences. However, consciousness doesn't seem to be just the result of having a brain that produces certain behaviors or performs particular computations. At least it seems as if we might have just the same rules and produce just the same kinds of sentences, and yet experience language completely differently. It even seems possible that robots could produce those behaviors or perform those computations without any awareness at all. Consciousness also seems to be more than just the result of having particular kinds of neural connections, or a particular evolutionary history. We can at least imagine zombies who were like us in every respect but had no awareness.

Another possibility, dualism, the idea that there is some separate spooky substance responsible for consciousness, just doesn't fit with everything else we know about science—even when it's dolled up in talk about quantum mechanics. This hasn't stopped philosophers from arguing for all these options and more, but I think at heart even the most fervent advocates feel unsatisfied with the answers.

There are two rays of hope in this otherwise dismal picture. First, we've been here before. For centuries, the problem of life loomed as large and seemed as intractable as the problem of consciousness does now. How could all the special properties of living things come from a collection of atoms and molecules that aren't alive at all? The answer turned out to be that the question was wrong—instead of a single explanation of "life" we have lots of little explanations about how particular configurations of molecules could lead to particular properties of living things.

This example may be particularly relevant because of the other ray of hope. While we don't know how "Capital C" Consciousness is related to the brain, we know an increasing amount about how particular features of consciousness are related to particular psychological and neural states. We actually know quite a lot, for example, about why green seems to be composed of yellow and blue, why the moon appears larger when it's near the horizon, why the rest of the world disappears when we are absorbed in work, and so on.

Much of what we've learned about consciousness is counter-intuitive. For example, consider "blindsight." Certain patients with brain damage have no conscious visual experience at all; they swear up and down that they are blind in part of their visual field. But if you insist that they just make a wild guess—"You don't understand," they protest, "I can't *see*"—they can figure out where objects are and even what shape they are. They will reach accurately for a ball they can't see. Recently, scientists showed that you could get just the same effect in ordinary people by temporarily inactivating their visual cortex.

Even in everyday life sight is more complicated than it seems. It turns out that we don't actually get any visual input at a central spot near the back of the eye; it's called the blind spot. If a light shines at that particular spot on your retina you won't see anything. But, of course, we don't experience that hole at all. We "fill in" so that it seems we have a smooth, unbroken visual field. Surely we should know what we see, but does the person with blindsight really see the ball? Do we see the blind spot?

Looking at the way babies and young children experience the world can provide us with equally counterintuitive insights about consciousness. Just as the experience of blindsight patients may ultimately give us cues about consciousness, so we can hope that understanding children's experience will ultimately help us understand how consciousness can exist at all.

How can we tell what it's like to be a baby? Babies and young children can't tell us about their experiences. None of us accurately remembers our infancy, and even our memories of early childhood are very hazy and unreliable. Nevertheless, it's possible to at least make an educated guess about what infant experience is like. We can use our knowledge about the psychological and neurological bases of adult experience, and our additional knowledge about the psychological and neurological differences between adults and children.

As adults, we become vividly aware of objects when we pay attention to them. When we pay attention to objects our brains produce neurotransmitters that make certain neurons work better and change more easily. Babies pay attention in systematically different ways than adults, and their brains work differently too. These differences suggest that baby consciousness may be systematically different from that of adults.

This leads to a counterintuitive but fascinating conclusion. Many philosophers have suggested that babies are somehow less conscious than adults are, if they are conscious at all. After all, babies don't have the ability to talk or to explicitly reason their way through a problem or to make complex plans, abilities that are related to consciousness for adults. The philosopher Peter Singer has even notoriously argued on this basis that disabled infants have no more intrinsic right to live than nonhuman animals do—for Singer we have as much justification to kill babies as to kill other animals for meat. Whatever you think of Singer's ethical claim, or about animal consciousness, I think his factual claim is just wrong. The data lead to just the opposite conclusion—babies are, at least by some measures, *more* conscious than we are.

EXTERNAL ATTENTION

Attention and consciousness seem to be closely related. When I attend to something carefully I become vividly conscious of it. Many psychologists use the metaphor of a spotlight to describe these effects of attention—when we attend to something it's as if we shine a beam of light on it that makes all its details brighter and more vivid.

Sometimes we pay attention because an external object catches our eye—a big truck suddenly looms in front of us. Psychologists call this exogenous attention. But we can also voluntarily shift our attention, and our consciousness, from one object to another— endogenous attention. We can say to ourselves, "This is a danger- ous corner. Pay attention!" and the traffic suddenly comes into clear and vivid focus.

New or unexpected events are especially likely to catch our attention. Some kinds of events, like loud noises, may just be in- trinsically startling. But we also pay attention to more subtly unex- pected events. When you live near a railway and become used to the trains you may wake up startled when a train doesn't go by at the usual time. When we experience something new, or startling, or salient, our brains produce characteristic electrical patterns— brain waves—that are associated with attention. As we try to make sense of the new event our bodies change as well as our minds— our heart rate slows in a distinctive way—and we enter an espe- cially vivid state of consciousness.

You can do an experiment that is the equivalent of the train that doesn't go by. You play a certain pattern of sounds repeatedly, and then fail to play a sound at the accustomed time. Although nothing has actually happened, your brain responds as if it had heard a startling new sound. Paradoxically, we may actually be- come more aware of the deafening silence than we were of the sound. (In a good suspense movie the moments of expectation when nothing actually happens are often far more vivid than all the explosions and shoot-outs.)

Just as an unexpected silence can be deafening, an expected noise can become silent. After a while, as we take in all the infor- mation we can, we become used to the sound, "habituated" like the babies in the looking and listening experiments I described earlier. We get bored, and both our attention and our vivid con- sciousness trail off. When we become completely habituated to an event our consciousness of it may disappear almost entirely. We may literally no longer hear the train that goes by each day at noon. When we first move into a new house we are aware of every detail of each new room, but after a few months the place can become practically invisible.

Similarly, when we first master a new skill, such as riding a bike or using a new computer program, we are painfully conscious of every step. But by the time we become expert we can literally be completely unconscious of what we are doing. We know so much about the house or bicycle riding or the computer program, and what we know is so well learned, that we no longer need to pay attention. We no longer need to take in any additional information or learn anything new about the event or skill—we just do it. In adult life it sometimes feels as if hours and even days can go by when we are on autopilot this way—perfectly functional, walking, talking, teaching, meeting-attending zombies.

INTERNAL ATTENTION

For adults, attention can also be endogenous, directed voluntarily at particular objects, like that spotlight. In this case, attending to one thing can actually make us much less conscious of the other things around us, even salient or new or unexpected things. When I'm walking down the street absorbed in a problem I'm notoriously likely to bump into the lamppost that would otherwise be perfectly apparent—a living cliché of the absentminded professor, as my children often point out.

There are some startling experimental demonstrations of this effect. Some psychologists call it "inattentional blindness." In one dramatic experiment, designed by Dan Simons, you look at a video of several people throwing a ball. The instruction is to count the number of times the ball goes from hand to hand. The players weave in and out so this takes some effort; it's like trying to follow the pea in the old shell game. Then the experimenter asks if you noticed anything strange. "Nothing," you say. Now he plays the video again, but this time he says you don't have to follow the ball. And you see that someone in a gorilla suit walked slowly right through the middle of the scene! You were looking right at the gorilla but literally didn't see it, because your attention was so focused on the ball. (I saw this video again recently at a meeting of the Association for the Scientific Study of Consciousness. The presenter first said, "All of you know this clip." And indeed all of us did except George Johnson, a science journalist for *The New York Times*, who was sitting beside me. George stared completely blank-faced, counting the balls, utterly oblivious as the gorilla walked through the scene and everyone laughed. At the end he turned to me, puzzled, and said, "What was the point of that? Why did they laugh?")

It turns out that there are neurological bases for these effects. When we attend to something our brain releases a particular kind of chemical, called a cholinergic transmitter. This chemical affects how well neurons function—it makes them conduct information better. The nicotine in cigarettes mimics these transmitters and literally makes you more attentive, just as opium mimics the natural transmitters that kill pain. When we pay attention our brains release these transmitters quite selectively, just to the particular parts of the brain that are processing information about the event we attend to. At the same time our brains also release inhibitory transmitters and activate inhibitory neurons that have just the opposite effect on other parts of the brain. (Coffee also makes us alert but it seems to do so by inhibiting some of these inhibitors— coffee opens up our attention and cigarettes let it narrow in on a particular target. It's no wonder they're the preferred drugs of journalists, who have to take in all the information about a breaking story and then summarize it in 250 words by a deadline.) What your brain actually does depends on the balance between the inhibitory effects and the excitatory ones. So paying attention literally boosts some parts of your brain and shuts down others.

Attention not only makes some parts of your brain work better, but it also makes those parts of your brain more plastic—that is, those parts of your brain change more easily than other parts of your brain. The evidence for this comes from studies of monkeys by Michael Merzenich and his colleagues. Neuroscientists can actually record the activity of a monkey's brain cells and see that different cells respond to different kinds of events. Some cells respond to particular kinds of sounds, for example, and others respond to touch.

The experimenters got the monkeys to pay attention to one type of event instead of another. A monkey hears a stream of sounds, say, and feels a sequence of touches. If he moves his hand when he hears a particular sound he gets some juice, but touch isn't rewarded. The monkey pays more attention to the sounds as a result, just as in a crowded room you might focus your attention on overhearing a potentially rewarding conversation and ignore the irrelevant ones.

When they checked the monkeys' brains they discovered that the sound cells had been rewired by these experiences—they responded differently—but the tactile cells were the same. In fact, more of the monkeys' brain cells responded to sound after they had been trained, but the number of touch-responding cells stayed the same. When they reversed the experiment so that touch was more rewarding, they got the reverse effect. These changes seem to be at least partly mediated by the cholinergic transmitters. If the monkeys were given a chemical that blocked those transmitters, the changes were less likely. This plasticity effect also seems to fit our intuition that when we attend to things carefully we can learn more about them than when we do not. When we learn we literally change our minds and brains in the light of new information.

Voluntary endogenous attention—as when I tell myself to pay attention to the traffic—is a way to persuade our brains to learn. It makes us treat something as if it were novel or unexpected, even when it isn't. As an adult I can simply decide that I need to get extra information in the service of some larger goal, like the monkey who pays attention to the sounds that will get him the juice. For example, I can force myself to follow the often mind-numbingly boring scientific papers on the neuropsychology of attention because I think the information will help me to be accurate when I'm writing my book. Given that goal, it's as important for me to attend to the papers as it is for me to take in information about some intrinsically attention-grabbing unexpected event—like the first scene of a Hitchcock movie. Or I can force myself to attend to the perfectly ordinary traffic at the busy corner because I know abstractly that something dangerous may happen.

So while we don't have a Big Explanation of Consciousness, we do have a story about how a particular kind of vivid, narrowly focused awareness is related to the mind and the brain. When we have this kind of consciousness our minds take in information about some parts of the world and shut out distracting information from others. And we can use the attended information to learn something new. Certain things also happen in our brains—they release cholinergic and inhibitory transmitters appropriately. In turn those transmitters both make the relevant parts of the brain function more efficiently and allow them to be reshaped more easily.

There is also a related story about a particular kind of unconsciousness. Many psychological and brain processes are simply never conscious at all. But in other cases, we actually make potentially conscious events become less conscious. When events or activities become familiar, well understood, and highly practiced they also become, as we say, automatic—less conscious than they were before. Similarly, when we focus our attention on one event we become less conscious of other unattended events. Inhibitory brain processes seem to be involved in both these kinds of unconsciousness.

BABY ATTENTION

What does all this have to do with babies? We don't know exactly what babies' conscious experience is like but we do know something about their capacity for attention and about their brains (or at least we know about the brains of baby monkeys and rats). Babies and young children are both similar to and different from adults in significant and revealing ways.

In the bad old days, psychologists thought that babies could attend only in an entirely automatic and reflexive way, without even using their higher brain centers at all. This was part of what I think of as the myth of the brain-deficient baby, the idea that newborn babies were crying carrots, vegetables with a few reflexes.

In fact, when babies attend to something they seem to take in information about it and to be conscious of it in the same way as adults. When they see even a subtly unexpected event they show the same brain waves that adults do. They look steadily and intently at the event, their eyes scan the important features of the event, and their heart rate decreases in the same way. Every sign is that they are vividly conscious of the event in the same way that we adults are. If the event is interesting enough they can pay attention for a surprisingly long time. But after a while, like adults, they gradually become bored and look away.

This fact is at the heart of the habituation technique I described earlier. Presenting something that is even subtly unexpected immediately rivets babies' attention and they will reliably look at unexpected events for longer than expected ones. Babies seem to have an infinitely voracious appetite for the unexpected. This is fortunate for psychologists, since we can rely on this attention to the new to tell us how babies organize the world. But it is also striking in its own right. And, of course, the younger you are, the more novelty and unexpectedness you will experience, both in the external and internal worlds. Both the objects around you and your own internal feelings will start out being unexpected.

But there are also differences between attention in babies and in grown-ups. We saw that for adults, attention can be governed either by external events or internal decisions—it can be exogenous or endogenous. But for babies, attention is much more exogenous than endogenous. They can, at times, show some control of attention. However, this is much less true earlier than later in development. For babies, attention is much more likely to be captured by interesting external events than directed by internal plans and goals. Babies would give up following the ball rather than miss the gorilla in the room. Endogenous attention seems to develop quite slowly all the way through the preschool years.

You can see this in everyday life. If you want a two-year-old to give up a toy, giving them a new toy that catches their attention is much more effective than trying to persuade them, even bribe them, to voluntarily turn away from the old one. In fact, babies sometimes become captivated by interesting things that they really don't like, like an unusually bright light or loud noise. They cry and fuss but seem unable to look away, like adults watching a horror movie.

It's interesting that the habituation technique actually becomes more difficult to use as babies grow older. For older children, attention gradually becomes more controlled by their internal agenda rather than by the intrinsic interest of external events. So it becomes more difficult to use their attention as a reliable indicator of what they see. And for adults, of course, if we decide to attend to the ball even the wildly unexpected gorilla won't distract us.

A second difference between babies or young children and adults involves inhibition. Babies and young children don't seem to inhibit distractions as well as we do—their attention is less focused. An event at the periphery of their vision can easily turn them away from their original focus.

This can be both a curse and a blessing. Babies and young children are not as good as older kids and adults at concentrating on just one thing. But they may be better at picking up incidental information. Suppose, for example, I give children a memory task. They look through a pack of cards, two at a time. They are told that they will have to remember what's on the left-hand card but not the other card, so they should just pay attention to that card. Then at the end you test children on their memory for both cards. Older children are much better at remembering about the left-hand card than the other one—like adults they inhibit the unattended information, and they are also better at remembering the attended card than the younger children. But for younger children the two types of learning are much more similar. In fact, the younger children actually do better at remembering the unattended card than the older children do.

You can also see this informally when you play a card-matching memory game such as concentration. This is the sort of game where cards are placed facedown on a table. At each turn a player picks a card from a deck and then gets to turn over one of the cards on the table. If they match he gets to keep both cards. The secret of concentration is to notice which cards are where, even when it's not your turn and when those cards don't seem relevant to your immediate success. Young children are surprisingly good at this, better than grown-ups sometimes. And we have all had the startling experience of hearing a child come out with some phrase or idea from an adult conversation—even though it looked as if the child wasn't paying any attention.

So rather than determining what to look at in the world, babies seem to let the world determine what they look at. And rather than deciding where to focus attention and where to inhibit distractions, babies seem to be conscious of much more of the world at once. They aren't just picking up information about the specific objects that are useful to them—they are picking up information about all the objects around them, especially when that information is new. And, of course, much more of the information is new for babies than it is for us.

This capacity for very general attention makes babies such terrific learners. We saw in the last chapter that babies can and do learn causal maps from even subtle new statistical patterns. This means that babies must be soaking up information about every interesting event they see, whether or not it is obviously useful or important. This lets babies and children construct new maps, and change their old ones, much more quickly and easily than adults do.

Neuroscience studies also seem to mirror this picture. Infant brains have abundant cholinergic transmitters but the inhibitory transmitters only develop later. Interestingly, babies require relatively higher concentrations of anesthetics to put them out—which may be because anesthetics act on these neurotransmitters. One way to define consciousness is that it's that thing that anesthetics get rid of, so this also suggests that babies have more of this mysterious stuff than we do. Babies' brains are also much more generally malleable, more plastic, than adult brains. For example, when children suffer from brain injuries they recover much more quickly and thoroughly than adults. Other parts of the brain take over from the injured parts. Adult brains are much less flexible. Like the proverbial old dog, old brains have a harder time learning new tricks.

When Merzenich did the same monkey experiments I just described with baby monkeys he got very different results. Young monkeys' brains don't differentiate the auditory and tactile events in the way that the adult brains do, just as human babies seem to have more trouble focusing on just one thing. On the other hand, you can also do a rather different experiment by simply giving animals lots of stimulation without making them pay particular attention to one aspect of it or another. For example, you can simply bathe animals in sounds that have some systematic pattern. When Merzenich and his colleagues did this the young animals' cells changed; they responded to sounds differently, even when there was no payoff. Older animals don't show this sort of general plasticity.

Moreover, we know that different parts of the brain are involved in different kinds of attention. The parietal cortex, in the middle of the brain, seems to govern the ability to orient to new or unexpected events in the world; the occipital cortex, in the back of the brain, seems to be involved in sustained attention to the visual world—the parietal cortex alerts us to something new and the occipital cortex makes sense of it. Both these parts of the brain are active quite early in infancy.

The usual inhibitory suspects—namely parts of the frontal lobes of the brain—are more involved both in internally driven attention and in the ability to inhibit distractions. These parts of the brain are potentially active from very early in infancy. But the connections between the frontal regions and other parts of the brain gradually become stronger and stronger as babies and children grow older. These connections are still being formed even in adolescence. The connections underlie our increasing ability to inhibit distractions and control our attention.

A fascinating series of studies by Rafael Malach and his colleagues makes the difference between these kinds of attention and these parts of the brain particularly vivid. Malach and his colleagues put people in a Functional Magnetic Resonance Imaging (fMRI) machine. These machines track how much blood goes to different parts of your brain as you solve some problem or do some task, and that in turn tracks how that task activates different parts of your brain. You can use it to make those pictures of brains "lighting up" that you see all the time in *Scientific American*. Most of the time the poor guinea pigs in these machines either get some tedious task to do, like clicking a button when a red *x* appears, or else they just lie there. In both of these cases frontal areas of the brain are active—more active when the subjects perform an intentional planned action, but still buzzing along even when they just lie in the machine daydreaming.

But Malach's lucky subjects got to watch an absorbing movie instead, *The Good, the Bad and the Ugly*, with Clint Eastwood. Rather amazingly, the brain patterns of nearly everybody tracked the events in the movie in the same way—Sergio Leone really knew how to get into your head. Even more striking, the frontal parts of the brain, the parts that plan and think and keep track of the self, were actually inhibited as people watched the movie. The back parts of the brain, the parts that are active in young babies, lit up instead. The subjects were plainly conscious but they weren't self-conscious. They weren't making plans or considering or judging or weighing the movie, they were just totally into it. For a baby, watching a Mickey Mouse mobile may be like being utterly, blissfully, selflessly captivated by a good movie.

Often, psychologists assume that the changes in children's attention are the result of maturational changes in these parts of the brain. Brain changes could be like the changes in children's height as they grow older—they don't learn to get taller; it just happens. In the same way, the brain could just change as a result of some unfolding genetic program, and changes in children's minds would follow. But you could also draw the opposite conclusion; as children learn new things, and as more of their experience and skill become familiar and habituated, their brains change accordingly.

In fact, there are two complementary kinds of brain processes that depend on experience in this way. Brains make more and more connections between different neurons, but they prune the less-used connections and retain only the most-efficient ones. Both these processes take place simultaneously throughout development. Both are shaped by external events. But the balance changes—earlier in life we make more connections, and as we grow older we begin to prune more connections. These processes may reflect complementary psychological processes, and even reflect the quality of our experience. Early in life we are sensitive to more possibilities, while later in life we just focus on the possibilities that are most likely to be important and relevant to us.

So the psychological picture of attention and the neurological one complement each other. This picture of attention development also makes a lot of sense in terms of the evolutionary division of labor between babies and grown-ups. If you want to act on the world effectively it makes sense to limit your attention to just a few events. You want to focus on learning about just the aspects of the world that are relevant to your goals and plans—like the monkeys who focus only on the sounds that will lead to juice. As adults we can decide beforehand what information will be useful to us and what will just be a distraction. Our brains enhance the first kind of information and suppress the second. Similarly, to act effectively you want most of your brain to be quite stable and robust and unchangeable—you alter only the bits you need to alter, and if it ain't broke leave the rest of it alone.

The evolutionary imperative for babies is to learn as much as they can as quickly as possible. Their job is just to make accurate maps of the world around them. They learn and infer, make causal maps and draw counterfactual conclusions, and they don't need to worry if what they learn is relevant to some particular plan or goal. Parents do that sort of worrying for them. They're better off paying attention to everything, particularly new, fascinating, information-rich events, rather than just paying attention to events that are immediately useful or relevant. The gorilla may be more informative in the long run than the ball. Watching the Clint Eastwood movie may tell us more than clicking the button when a red x appears.

YOUNG CHILDREN AND ATTENTION

We can't ask babies what their consciousness is like directly, but we can try to figure it out by looking at abilities such as endogenous attention that are associated with characteristic kinds of consciousness. We can use this indirect method with young children, too. We could also just ask them what their experience is like. This blindingly obvious idea didn't seem to occur to anyone until the mid-nineties. John Flavell—who I quoted at the start of this chapter—is one of the few developmental psychologists in the National Academy of Sciences, and one of the greatest developmentalists of all time. As he himself would be the first to say, the honors should really go to "the Flavells"—his wife, Ellie, has played an integral part in the work. At a meeting I went to in 1993 John got up and quietly said, "Ellie and I were wondering: What do children think about consciousness? So we went to the preschool and asked them." Sometimes it takes a genius to see the blindingly obvious. He went on to describe some startling and philosophically intriguing results. The Flavells found that practically everything we think is self-evident about consciousness isn't self-evident at all to preschoolers.

Preschoolers have very different ideas about attention than adults do. They don't seem to understand about attentional focus. For instance, we can show them Ellie staring at an interesting photograph of the kids in the preschool in a very plain frame. Ellie points to various kids in the picture, describing what they were like. Then we ask the children if Ellie was thinking about the kids in the picture and they all say yes. But we can also ask if she was thinking about the frame of the picture and they say yes, she was thinking about that, too. They don't think she was thinking about everything—they say she wasn't thinking about the chair in the next room. But they do believe that she will be thinking about everything she sees—they don't understand about inattentional blindness. This could just be because they are confused about consciousness, of course. But it could also be because their own consciousness is actually not like Ellie's. It could be because they themselves experience consciousness in a less-focused way. So even when we directly ask children about their conscious experience, we find clues that their consciousness may be very different from our own.

WHAT IS IT LIKE TO BE A BABY?

What can all this tell us about what it is like to be a baby? It's plausible that babies are actually aware of much more, much more intensely, than we are. The attentional spotlight in adults seems more like an attentional lantern for babies. Instead of experiencing a single aspect of their world and shutting down everything else they seem to be vividly experiencing everything at once. Their brains are soaked in cholinergic transmitters, with few inhibitory transmitters to allay their effects. And their brains, as well as minds, are dramatically plastic, profoundly open to new possibilities.

Babies also seem less subject to certain kinds of unconsciousness than we are. Less of their experience is familiar, expert, and automatic, and so they have fewer habituated unconscious behaviors. While they inhibit distractions less well, more of the field of consciousness will be available to them. This also suggests that they are more conscious than we are.

In adults, vivid awareness accompanies attention, and attention is linked to brain plasticity. In adults, attention literally allows us to change our minds and brains. If we made the backwards inference that brain plasticity implies attention, which implies vivid awareness, it would seem that babies are more conscious than we are.

Still, this is all rather indirect. We can certainly say that babies are less habituated, less focused, and more plastic than we are. More of the world is new to them and they are learning more about it. But what does it feel like to be this way? To resolve this question it might help to look at what adult awareness is like when adults have to do the same things that babies do. What is *our* consciousness like when we put our minds and our brains in a position that is similar to the position of babies? Do we lose awareness or gain it?

TRAVEL AND MEDITATION

First, think about the adult experience of travel—particularly, say, when an American travels to an exotic place like India or China. An adult in a strange place is like a baby in many ways. There is a great deal of new information available at once. And the traveler is not in a good position to make "top-down" decisions beforehand about exactly what kinds of information are going to be relevant. Like the baby, the traveler's attention is likely to be caught by external objects and events, rather than determined by her own intentions and decisions.

This is especially true if the traveler makes her journey for its own sake rather than in pursuit of some particular goal such as a conference or a business deal or even a tourist destination. In fact, paradoxically, travel is an adult activity whose goal is largely not to have a goal. At its best, travel is not about seeing the Taj Mahal or the Great Wall but about trying to absorb the full texture of an unfamiliar culture. And travelers often point out that the serendipitous, unexpected events are the most informative and vivid—a good traveler leaves herself open to chance.

This kind of traveler, like a baby, is devoted to making new discoveries about the world without being quite sure what those discoveries will be. When we travel we notice the small things that we take for granted in our own country: the way that everyday Japanese life is ferociously aesthetic, or the knowing way that people look at each other in a French café, even the subtle intonations of an unknown language. This may lead us, in turn, to re-shape our causal maps of our own culture and country—our own desires and actions—and this new knowledge lets us imagine new ways that we could live ourselves, with Japanese baths or Italian passion or French wit. The cliché says that travel broadens the mind, but this may be literally true. When we travel we return to the wide-ranging curiosity of childhood, and we discover new things about ourselves as well as others.

When we travel, at least when we travel in this way, our attention and awareness are enhanced, not shut down. Life seems more vivid, even painfully so at times. In fact, the few days of a trip seem packed with experience—overflowing with consciousness. We remember more from that handful of intense days in Beijing or Paris than we do from weeks of routine, unconscious everyday life at home. On the other hand, planning and action suffer—we're so distracted by all the new information that an everyday task like shopping for food or finding the post office becomes effortful and exhausting, and we're likely to leave a trail of forgotten jackets and misplaced phone chargers behind.

Or consider certain types of meditation. Meditative practices involve manipulating attention in novel ways. In some of these traditions, the idea is to focus and sustain vivid attention on a single object—a mandala or a koan or a crucifix. But in other types of meditation the idea is to distribute attention as much as possible. Certain types of "open awareness" meditative practices are about *not* focusing on a single object. They are recipes for defeating inattentional blindness, and escaping attentional inhibition.

In these practices you begin by heightening your overall level of attentiveness and arousal. You sit in an upright and unsupported posture—you don't lie down or sit in chairs, because you don't want to just get drowsy. Meditators also imbibe notoriously large quantities of caffeine. Indeed, tea was originally cultivated by monks in China who had discovered how helpful a little neurotransmitter modification was for maintaining attention. It is still a mainstay in every Zen monastery, and evidently many modern Japanese monks are devoted to thick, awful, instant Nescafé.

At the same time, you rob this awareness of its usual objects by sitting still in front of a blank wall. Normally in these cases your attention would go inward—adults pay as much attention to their internal experience as to the external world—but meditators also work to prevent this from happening. They consciously try to avoid planning or thinking. They do things like mentally count breaths, which disrupts the captivating flow of inner speech. (It's hard to make a logical argument or a plan and count your breaths at the same time.)

The experience that results, at least for brief moments, is very striking. Suddenly, as your attention to specific external events and internal plans diminishes you become vividly aware of everything around you at once. The texture of the floor, the delicate movement of light on the walls, the sound of the birds and passing cars, even your aching knees, all seem to be illuminated simultaneously, with little distinction between the trivial and the important, or the internal and the external.

Travel and meditation lead to the same kind of experience by opposite means. When you travel you expose yourself to so much new and unexpected external information that you overwhelm the usual mechanisms of attentional selection and inhibition. Everything around you is more interesting than the things that you would normally attend to (like getting to a particular meeting). When you meditate, you starve the usual mechanisms of attention. You give them almost nothing to work with and you consciously try to avoid focus, inhibition, and planning. The result is similar: just as a lot of new information can overwhelm the inhibitory mechanisms, so shutting down the inhibitory mechanisms can make even everyday information seem new.

Meditation and travel seem to end up causing what philosophers call the same phenomenology—the same type of subjective experience. In fact, a lovely thing about meditation is that you can visit Beijing without leaving your room. It's like the lantern consciousness of childhood as opposed to the spotlight consciousness of ordinary adult attention. You are vividly aware of everything without being focused on any one thing in particular. There is a kind of exaltation and a peculiar kind of happiness that goes with these experiences too.

Lantern consciousness—that vivid panoramic illumination of the everyday—is often one part of some kinds of religious or aesthetic experience. Lantern consciousness also seems to accompany other kinds of activities, such as falling in love, hunting, or even mania. But there are also many other kinds of religious and aesthetic experience, other kinds of exaltation and ecstasy, that have different qualities.

For example, I'd argue that this expansive lantern consciousness is almost the opposite of the distinctive adult happiness that comes with what psychologists call "flow." "Flow" is the experience we have when our attention is completely focused on a single object or activity, and we lose ourselves in that activity. It is the sort of experience that comes from executing plans beautifully and efficiently—the experience of dancing or shooting a basket or writing really well. In flow we enjoy a peculiarly pleasurable kind of unconsciousness. When we're completely absorbed in a task we lose sight of the outside world and even lose consciousness of each particular action we must take. The plan just seems to execute itself. Lantern consciousness also seems unlike the kinds of religious experience that result from sustained concentration on a single object, or the kinds of mystical experience in which the external world seems to disappear altogether.

Lantern consciousness leads to a very different kind of happiness. There is a similar feeling that we have lost our sense of self, but we lose our selves by becoming part of the world. Lantern consciousness is invoked by writers like Virginia Woolf and Emily Dickinson and artists like Henri Cartier-Bresson. It is William Blake's world in a grain of sand, William Wordsworth's splendour in the grass.

This kind of phenomenology has historically often been associated with childhood. The Zen master Shunryu Suzuki called it "beginner's mind," the mind as it is uncontaminated by expertise. The Romantic poets such as Wordsworth, who made something of a specialty of invoking this sort of experience, explicitly identified it with childhood. They thought childhood was especially valuable because children experienced the world with this sort of infinite wonder.

Developmental psychology and neuroscience suggest that this intuitive identification is accurate. I think lantern consciousness is what it is like to be a baby. Babies, like Buddhas, are travelers in a little room. They are immersed in the almost unbearably bright and exciting novelty of walls, shadows, voices. William James, the greatest writer of all psychologists, has a typically striking image that might help invoke the experience. He himself applied it not to babies but to the brilliant but scatterbrained among adults. In some people, he says, the field of consciousness is like a narrowly focused beam with darkness all round it. For others, and I would argue for babies, "we may suppose the margin to be brighter, and to be filled with something like meteoric showers of images, which strike into it at random, displacing the focal ideas."

Not all kinds of heightened or mystical experience are characteristic of childhood—many, like flow, may appear only in adulthood. And infants and children are clearly not in this state all the time. In fact, it may be just because they are in this state more than we are that babies spend much of the rest of their time either asleep or miserably fussy. Think about how frazzled you can get on a trip. The traveler, like the baby, may also show a tendency to wake up crying at three o'clock in the morning.

And for adults this kind of abandonment of control and discipline is, of course, the result of a highly controlled and disciplined and very adult training. Experienced meditators can decide not to decide, choose not to choose, plan to give up planning. Travelers have to save and spend and organize to get to India or China in the first place. Babies and young children are in this state whether they want to be or not.

Developmental psychology and neuroscience can help tell us what it is like to be a baby, and travel, meditation, and Romantic poetry can even give us an empathetic first-person taste of infant experience. Babies can also tell us about consciousness itself. Just as blindsight patients tell us that action and consciousness may be dissociated, babies tell us that different kinds of psychological abilities may be dissociated, and may lead to different kinds of consciousness. The kind of consciousness that accompanies learning may be quite different from the kind that accompanies planning. Almost all the experimental studies of adult consciousness involve focused attention and a particular narrowly defined task. But babies suggest that this is only one tiny piece of what awareness is all about.

Perhaps, in fact, there is a broader lesson philosophers could learn from babies. Philosophers and psychologists have tended to look for one single key to the problem of consciousness—whether that's a particular oscillation rate of neurons, or a particular brain region, or a particular ability such as language or high-level planning or self-reflection. Thinking about babies suggests that the answer is likely to be more varied and dynamic. Instead of thinking about one Big Explanation for Consciousness we should be looking for little explanations for all the many different kinds of consciousnesses—endogenous focus and exogenous openness, self-conscious planning and unself-conscious absorption, spotlight and lantern. Changes in consciousness as we grow older, or wiser, or develop new ways of learning about the world can be especially revealing. Rather than focusing in on just one aspect of consciousness that will prove to be the explanatory key, we should perhaps be more open to the whole manifold, variegated universe of experience.

5.

Who Am I?

❋

Consciousness isn't just our awareness of the outside world. It is a distinctive internal experience. Our consciousness is as dominated by our memories and plans, by our obsessions and fantasies, as it is by our experience of the world outside us. We time travel—moving back and forth from vivid visions of the past to glowing (or glowering) anticipations of the future. And we hear a constant "inner speech" monologue—that voice that natters on inside our heads. Often, more waking moments seem spent in these internal reflections than in registering the world outside.

This babbling stream of consciousness is closely related to our sense of personal identity. My experiences happen to *me*. The great philosopher René Descartes thought that this internal experience, in fact, is the only thing I know for sure: I think therefore I am. But who is this "I"? She is the inner observer with the front-row seat watching my life unfold. She is the constant self who unites my memories of the past and my anticipations of the future. She is the person my life has happened to, the person who plans the rest of that life, and the person who is the beneficiary of those plans. She is my inner eye, my autobiographer, and my CEO.

Can we say anything about this internal consciousness in babies and young children? Do they have a stream of consciousness or an inner observer like ours? Do they have that sense of a constant unified self? Again, without actually being a baby it's hard to be sure. But just as in the last chapter, we can use information from other kinds of studies to say something about what very young children's internal consciousness might be like. We can look at the psychological functions that are associated with internal consciousness in adults and see how they change and develop in childhood.

CONSCIOUSNESS AND MEMORY

Just as attention is closely linked to our external consciousness, memory is closely linked to our internal consciousness. Psychologists distinguish different types of memory. Any influence of our past experience on our current behavior is memory of a sort. Even very simple organisms like sea slugs have that kind of memory. When an experimenter touches a sea slug's siphon gently it withdraws its gills a little. But suppose that gentle touch is repeatedly followed by a sharp blow to the sea slug's tail. Now as soon as the sea slug feels the gentle touch it withdraws much more strongly. It seems that the slug remembers that the gentle touch will lead to the sharp blow—the way that Pavlov's dogs remembered that a tone would lead to a shock.

Memory can also refer to the knowledge someone has accumulated over a lifetime. I say that I remember that Paris is the capital of France, for instance, or that cat is spelled "c-a-t," but I don't remember exactly when I found this out or when I first knew it—I don't have a *memory* of Paris being the capital of France—I just know that it's true.

But there is a special kind of conscious experience that makes my memories mine and allows me to make a continuous story of my life. Psychologists call it episodic or autobiographical memory. This is the kind of intense, bright, specific, conscious memory that I have of my first Picasso painting, at the Guggenheim Museum in New York when I was four, or my first kiss, at the Philadelphia Museum of Art when I was fourteen.

These different kinds of memory involve different parts of the brain. People with certain kinds of brain damage can learn new information but can't create new episodic memories. The most famous of these patients, known by his initials as H.M., had surgery for epilepsy when he was a young man. The operation destroyed his hippocampus. H.M. could learn new skills, like using a computer, and he could even sometimes learn new facts. But his autobiographical memory, and so his personal identity, effectively ended in 1953. Each time he met his doctor, H.M. reintroduced himself—he had no memory of meeting him before. And he was surprised every time he looked in the mirror and tried to reconcile his aging face with his sense that he was a man of twenty-seven.

Though plainly H.M. was conscious, his consciousness was profoundly different from the consciousness of the rest of us. It's dizzying even to imagine what it would be like if your conscious span extended back only a few moments—if your earlier experience no longer belonged to you. In the movie *Memento*, the protagonist has just this sort of "anterograde amnesia." The weirdness of the film effectively captured how dislocating and strange this experience would be. At every moment the hero has no idea what happened the moment before—he walks into the same bar where he just had a conversation and everyone in it is entirely new to him. He makes a plan to go to a motel and then finds that he's in the motel with no idea how he got there.

Where do our episodic memories come from? It may appear as if autobiographical memory is just a kind of internal-consciousness DVD drive that records your life and then lets you play it back again, but it's not that simple. For example, when I remember my first kiss, I remember it as if I were looking at the two figures in the rain on the garden bench outside the museum. Of course, I wasn't actually looking in from the outside, I was looking out from the inside. A real DVD of my experience would show the edge of my nose and a looming face.

Even the most vivid "flashbulb" autobiographical memories, the kind that we experience after a terrible event such as the *Challenger* spaceship explosion or 9/11, may turn out to be wrong. Psychologists recorded people's experiences of the *Challenger* disaster shortly after it happened. They got people to answer questions like "Where were you?" or "Did you see it on TV or hear it on the radio?" Then three years later they asked the same questions again. The memories of the dramatic explosion were just as vivid and people were very confident that they were accurate, but many got the answers wrong—they didn't actually remember the events as well as they thought they did. Even these exceptionally vivid memories weren't just a transcription of the original experience.

We can even create detailed autobiographical memories that are completely false—memories of experiences that never occurred at all. These may be dramatic memories of alien abduction or satanic abuse, or even of committing a crime, but they can also be quite ordinary memories like getting lost in the mall when you were a child.

Elizabeth Loftus and her colleagues have done startling experiments about creating false memories in perfectly ordinary people.

They began by suggesting that some event, like getting lost in the mall, had actually happened ("Your mom says you once got lost in the mall"). Then they asked people to try hard to bring the memory to mind, and suggested some of the details ("Remember, you hid by the fountain?"). By the end of the process, the people they tested were absolutely positive that they could remember that they had gotten lost in the mall. They had vivid episodic memories of the event, even though it had never actually happened.

Episodic memories are different from other kinds of memory because they have so much sensory detail. I can recapture the exact feel of the rain and the precise texture of that first kiss, but I just know that Paris is the capital of France. You can lead people to have equally detailed and specific mental images by telling them to imagine just how an event might have felt and looked and tasted. When you do this, whether in a memory researcher's lab or in a therapy session or in a police interrogation, you can actually create autobiographical memories. These false memories are so seductive because they "feel" just like real memories—our conscious experience of them is indistinguishable from the real thing.

Even people who say they remember being abducted by aliens aren't crazy and aren't lying. They genuinely do experience the memories they describe. The best explanation of the alien-abduction phenomenon is that it starts with a particular kind of sleep disturbance. The disturbance makes you feel paralyzed and also makes you feel that some unknown person is in the room. Most people who have these experiences just stop there, but a few interpret them in terms of the stories about aliens they have heard before. They elaborate them into a more detailed memory of weird lights and probes, just as the subjects in Loftus's experiments elaborated her suggestions into a memory. These memories feel very different from the "Paris is the capital of France" kinds of memories.

CHILDREN AND MEMORY

How do babies and young children fit into this picture? Do they have fully elaborated episodic memories like us or truncated memories like H.M.? As with external consciousness, the answer turns out to be more complicated than either of these alternatives. Even very young babies have episodic memories, but they are different from our memories. Over the first five years of a child's life they gradually develop into something that looks much more like adult autobiographical memory. These memory changes suggest that children's internal consciousness is changing in parallel too.

Psychologists used to think that babies didn't have episodic memories at all—more of the brain-deficient crying-carrot myth—but, in fact, infants have specific memories of particular events. Think about the imitation experiments, for example. The babies saw the experimenter touch the box with his forehead to make it light up once. A month later when they saw the box again, they leaned down and touched the box with their own forehead. They plainly remembered this specific unusual event.

Once they can talk, one- and two-year-olds can report specific events that occurred to them in the past. My eighteen-month-old son Alexei had raptly watched the stars and moon with his grandmother when she visited. When she returned a month later, in broad daylight, he immediately shouted "Moon" and tugged on her arm to take him outside.

But children start to weave those memories into a continuous narrative—a narrative in which they are the hero, or at least the protagonist—only when they are older. Robyn Fivush recorded an everyday event such as a mom and her child going to the zoo. A few days later she asked the children to recount what had happened. Two-year-olds could say something quite specific about the event, like "The elephant went poo." But surprisingly almost everything they said turned out be a direct echo of things that their moms had said during the visit. If Mom didn't explicitly mention the elephant at the time, her child didn't remember it. I feel that my episodic memories are *mine*, not, for example, my brother's. But for these very young children it was almost as if their memories belonged to Mom as much as they did to the child. Five-year-olds, in contrast, could produce complicated and original narratives about what had happened to them.

You can see this difference between younger and older children in more experimental settings, too. Three-year-olds don't seem to have the same sort of memory as older children. When someone asks, "Where were you on the night of the twenty-seventh?" I seem to unroll my episodic record of the past few days to find the right memory. And in everyday recollection my mind travels back to memories that unfold in all their detail. Psychologists call this free recall. But you can also see if someone remembers something by giving them a cue: "When you were in the bar on the night of the twenty-seventh, did you see a man with a black fedora and a violin case?"

These cued memories are also episodic, but they're prompted from the outside rather than generated from the inside. It's not that the interrogator is just telling you the answer, the way that the moms told the two-year-olds to remember the elephants or the experimenters told the undergraduates to "remember" getting lost in the mall. The information you remember is really in there, but you couldn't have retrieved it without the cue. It's like the difference between exogenous and endogenous attention. Your memory is controlled from the outside instead of the inside.

In an experiment I might give you a list of words and either ask you to remember as many of them as you can or tell you one word and get you to remember the next one. For all of us, cued memory is easier than free recall, but the difference is much greater for preschoolers. They have terrific specific memories when they are cued but have a very hard time with free recall.

You can see this in everyday life. You go through the preschool pick-up ritual and ask, inevitably, "What did you do today, honey?" The equally inevitable reply is "Nothing" or "I played." This is in spite of the fact that the child went on an exciting trip and rode the rocket in the science museum, or fell dramatically off the jungle gym, or played snakes and ladders for the first time. Good preschools often include a little list of what has happened during the day for parents to consult. When you ask about each event, the same child who stubbornly said "Nothing" will be full of exciting details. It isn't that the child is being balky, it's just that she can't seem to access her memories freely in the way an adult or even a six-year-old would.

KNOWING HOW YOU KNOW

One of the other characteristics of conscious autobiographical memory is that you not only know about events, you know how you know about them—you know, or at least believe, that your knowledge comes from some quite specific experiences in the past. I don't know how I know that Paris is the capital of France, but I do know that I know about the bench and the rain at the Philadelphia Museum of Art because I was actually there. Some philosophers have suggested that this is one of the hallmarks of conscious experience. It seems contradictory for me to say that I consciously remember the kiss, but I don't believe I experienced it. False memories can feel like true ones because we become equally, though mistakenly, certain that we know their source.

People with brain damage who lose their autobiographical memory also can't remember the sources of their knowledge. They might be able to learn how to program a computer, for example, but they couldn't tell you anything about how they learned to program—it is as if the new knowledge just appeared out of the blue. Even people with milder forms of brain damage who can create some new memories often have special trouble with sources.

Very young children also have special difficulty remembering where their beliefs come from. For instance, in my lab we showed children a little cabinet with nine different objects inside different drawers: an egg, a pencil, and so on. Sometimes we actually pulled out the drawer and showed the children the object. Sometimes we simply said, "There's a pencil in this drawer," without opening it, and sometimes we said, "Let's see if you can figure out what's in this drawer—look, here's a clue, it goes in this egg carton." Then we closed all the drawers, pointed to each one, and immediately asked two questions: "What's in here?" and "How do you know? Did you see it or did I tell you about it, or did you figure it out from a clue?"

All the children could remember what was in each drawer, but the three-year-olds had a great deal of difficulty remembering how they knew—they often said they had seen the egg in the drawer when they had been told about it or vice versa. The five-year-olds, on the other hand, could tell you both about what they knew and about the particular experiences that led to that knowledge.

This "source amnesia" also leads children to be particularly suggestible—so much so that there are real legal issues about whether children's testimony should be admissible in court. Simply saying something to a child like "He touched you, didn't he?" can lead him to believe that the event actually happened.

When my son Alexei was in kindergarten he came home with a series of disturbing stories about the vice-principal; he yelled at kids, beat them up, and punished them harshly. I was worried, of course. But then it turned out that the vice-principal was also supposed to live in an underground cave and eat live bats for dinner. The reports came from a playground urban legend and not Alexei's direct experience (though the legend may have captured a facet of the vice-principal's personality).

The old wisdom was that children were suggestible because they couldn't discriminate truth and lies or fact and fantasy, but we've seen that this isn't true. Children know the difference between truth and fiction and are genuinely trying to tell the truth. Suggestibility has more to do with the sources of information— children don't discriminate where they got information from, and so playground gossip or an inference from a leading question may be confused with real memories.

One of my undergraduate students at Berkeley, Jessica Giles, had been very involved in the children's legal system. We did an experiment to see whether children's suggestibility was linked to their understanding of sources. We showed children a movie and asked them questions about it. Some of them were source questions: "How do you know that the boy had yellow boots? Did you see them on the screen or did the boy tell you about them?" Some were the sort of leading questions that measure suggestibility. We might say, "The boy had red boots, didn't he?" even though the boots were yellow. We discovered that the children who could remember how they knew something were much more likely to resist the leading questions. And if we asked the children about sources first, and then asked the leading questions, they were much less suggestible. Making the source of the information vivid allowed even four-year-olds to resist the leading questions.

Three-year-olds have a hard time remembering the source of their beliefs, but they also have a hard time remembering their earlier mental states. We can see this in the "false belief" experiment I described before. Children see a closed candy box, which turns out to be full of pencils. The children are understandably both surprised and disappointed by this discovery. But then we asked what they thought was in the box when they first saw it. Although they had discovered the truth with great surprise only moments before, they still said that they had always known the box was full of pencils. They had entirely forgotten their earlier false belief.

We wondered if children forgot past desires as well as past beliefs. First, we asked children if they wanted crackers, and when they said yes we gave them crackers till they were positively stuffed, and refused to eat any more. Then we asked if they had wanted crackers when they first sat down, before they actually ate them. Half the three-year-olds said that they had never wanted the crackers at all. These children had no difficulty at all remembering past physical events, but they had a hard time remembering how they had felt about those events.

Trying to imagine what it is like to be a child in these experiments is as dislocating as trying to imagine what it is like to be H.M. You look at the tightly closed drawer and clearly hear me say there's an egg inside it, you are shocked to discover that there are pencils in the box, you are ravenous for the crackers. But literally minutes later you blithely, confidently, and sincerely remember that you saw the egg, believed that the box was full of pencils all along, and never wanted the crackers. It would seem that nothing could be more self-evident than our immediately past conscious experiences. And yet three-year-olds, who can remember specific events like moon watching for months, can't seem to recapture the experiences they had minutes before.

We adults may make these sorts of mistakes after a long time.

We may come to think that we always saw through communism, or that we actually attended the rally we only saw on TV, or that we couldn't possibly ever have liked Donovan. But children make these mistakes after just minutes have passed. They must be living in a very different world than we are.

CONSTRUCTING MYSELF

Autobiographical memory plays an important role in personal identity. I'm not continuous with my earlier and later selves because we share some particular characteristics—I am, after all, more like other fifty-year-old women developmental psychologists than I am like the three-year-old I was or the eighty-year-old that (with luck) I will be. And it isn't even because I maintain the same physical body over time—after all, my current body is (sadly) completely different from the body I had thirty years ago. The secret is memory. I can remember what I felt and thought and did earlier, even the now-strange thoughts and feelings of the six-year-old me (who believed that everyone in China lived in houses made of paper, and who was irrationally afraid of venturing into dark basements), or the even stranger thoughts and feelings of the sixteen-year-old me (who believed that everyone in China welcomed the Cultural Revolution, and who was irrationally unafraid of venturing into dark alleys).

Those memories are *mine*, and they are mine in a very distinctive and significant way. I may know about the equally strange thoughts and feelings that my brother once had, but I don't remember them and they aren't *my* past thoughts and feelings. In *Star Trek*, the most philosophically profound program ever to appear on television, there is a story that makes this point particularly clearly. Jadwiga Dax is a creature who consists of two parts, a regular body (Jadwiga) and a separate symbiont (Dax) that is transferred from one body to another as each body dies. Jadwiga takes on the accumulated knowledge of all the past lives of the symbiont, his skills at diplomacy and gambling, for example. But what actually makes Jadwiga and Dax a single person is that she also takes on the memories of all of Dax's previous lives, and experiences them in the same way that she experiences her own memories.

The philosopher John Campbell argues that the conscious experience of autobiographical memory depends on the causal relationship between our past selves and our current and future selves. As adults we think of our lives as a single unfolding causal story that links our past, present, and future experience. What we will do, feel, and believe in the future depends on what we do, feel, and believe now, which depends on what we did, felt, and believed in the past. This single timeline seems self-evident to us adults, but we could organize our experiences quite differently. People with dissociative or multiple-personality disorders, for example, have separate timelines for separate selves, so that what I do as Jekyll will influence Jekyll's future actions, but not my actions as Hyde.

Very young children already have some sense of self. For example, when they get to be around eighteen months old, children start to recognize themselves in the mirror. You can show this by surreptitiously putting a sticker on the baby's forehead and then putting her in front of a mirror. One-year-olds act as if there is another baby in the mirror and they point to the image of the sticker in the mirror. Two-year-olds, in contrast, immediately touch their own foreheads to see if the sticker is there.

But they don't seem to understand how this self is related to past and future selves—they don't have a single timeline. Teresa McCormack showed children two different series of pictures on two successive days. Then she asked the children which pictures they had seen, and whether they had seen them today or yesterday. The three-year-olds were very good at recognizing that they had seen the pictures but very bad at saying when they had seen them. By six years old children could do this about as well as adults.

Danny Povinelli did an even more dramatic experiment. Nowadays nearly all parents go around making videos of their preschoolers and playing them back, and even three-year-olds understand the basics of how videos work. In the experiment a grown-up played with a child and in the course of playing surreptitiously put a sticker on the child's forehead, just as in the experiment with the eighteen-month-old and the mirror. Immediately afterward he played a videotape of what had just happened back to the child. Five-year-olds were amazed to see the sticker in the videotape and immediately touched their foreheads to see if it was still there—they integrated the past self in the video and their current selves—but the three-year-olds were unfazed. They could recognize their present selves in a mirror, but they couldn't integrate the present and the past. Although they remarked that there was a sticker on their head in the video, they didn't seem to put that information about their past self together with their current self. They didn't seem to realize that having a sticker put on them five minutes ago meant that right now the sticker was still sitting on their forehead.

Tellingly, the three-year-olds also referred to the child on tape by using their own names, while the fours said that the child on the tape was "me." At three Johnny would say, "Look, Johnny has a sticker on his head," and make no attempt to touch his own head. At four he would say, "Look, I have a sticker on my head," and immediately reach to take it off. The younger children knew that the kid on the tape was them at an earlier time, but they didn't see the connection between the earlier Johnny and the person they were now.

All this has led many psychologists to argue that babies and young preschoolers don't have autobiographical memory in the same way that older children do or that we do. Memory researchers often treat episodic memory and autobiographical memory as two terms for the same thing—and, in fact, this seems to be true for adults. But you could say that babies and young children have episodic memory but not autobiographical memory. Although they are very good at remembering specific events in the past, they don't put these events into a single coherent timeline, don't remember how they know about the events, and don't remember their past attitudes toward events. They also don't privilege events that they have directly experienced over events they have learned about in other ways. And they don't have a single "inner autobiographer," a self who links their past and present mental states. They don't experience the "me" who used to think that there were pencils in the box, or who wanted the crackers before receiving the snack, or who had the sticker put on his head.

CHILDREN AND THE FUTURE

At the same time that four-year-olds begin to understand that their minds may have changed in the past, they also begin to understand that their minds may change in the future. In one experiment, Cristina Atance showed children pictures of different landscapes: a desert with a hot sun, or a snowy mountaintop. She said, "Suppose you were going to go for a trip here tomorrow. What should you take?" Children could choose between different objects: sunglasses or a seashell, a warm jacket or an ice cube.

Then she asked, "Why did you choose that?" Four- and five-year-olds chose the right option to protect against the perils of their imagined future (sunglasses for the desert, a warm jacket for the snow). They also explicitly explained those choices in terms of their anticipated future states: "In case my eyes hurt" or "I'm gonna get cold." But three-year-olds were much less likely to do this. They were as likely to think that you should take a seashell to the desert as sunglasses.

There is other evidence that babies and young children don't project themselves into the future in the same way that we do. At just about the same time that children are developing autobiographical memory they are also developing "executive control" abilities. Executive control is our ability to suppress what we want to do now because of what we will want in the future. We already saw that between three and five, children become able to act to change their own minds. They can sing or whistle or close their eyes to keep from trying to get that terribly tempting cookie.

We saw earlier that even young babies can make plans for the future. They can imagine an alternative way the world might be and act to make that alternative into reality. But executive control demands more than just making plans. I don't just have to imagine alternative ways the world might be, I have to imagine alternative ways that I might be. Usually when I make plans I do something to get what I want right now. Executive control becomes important when there is a conflict between what I want now and what I will want in the future. It requires me to understand the causal link between the way I feel now and the way I will feel later. Right now I don't need sunglasses and would love that one cookie. Afterward, when I get to the desert, or lose the two cookies, I'll feel differently. Executive control requires me to care as much about my future self as my current self.

For adults, executive control, like autobiographical memory, is closely associated with consciousness. We can act and plan and negotiate a complicated route through traffic unconsciously, mindlessly, as we say. But suppose we want to alter a plan in midstream, or to inhibit what we want to do now in favor of what we have to do in the future? That requires the conscious sense of a "me" who does the acting. Think of all those times when "you"—that is, your current self—are mindlessly but skillfully making your way back home, negotiating obstacles, turning corners, when the executive "you" suddenly springs into consciousness and realizes that today you have to go in entirely the opposite direction.

Or think of how deeply, even painfully, willpower and self-control seem to require consciousness. The executive you has to be constantly awake and alert, keeping watch over the poor, impulsive, habitual, mindless you—ready to pounce just to keep her from eating that one extra croissant or hitting the send button on that indignant e-mail.

In our everyday experience, the inner observer of consciousness, and the inner autobiographer of episodic memory, seem to be closely related to the inner executive—they seem, in fact, to be the same person: me. We feel that we have executive control because we have an überself who negotiates between our current, past, and future selves, and ultimately hands down the orders. Woody Allen vividly captures this everyday picture in *Everything You Always Wanted to Know about Sex*. Tony Randall sits in a big chair at the control center inside the hapless seducer's brain, desperately trying to coordinate the visual input on the big TV screen and the hydraulic machinery that controls his actions—"Damn, who flashed that scared expression!" As the philosopher Jerry Fodor puts it: Somebody has to be in charge so, by God, it better be me.

From a scientific point of view, of course, this can't be right. The inner executive, like the inner biographer who witnesses my memories, is what philosophers call a "homunculus"—a little man inside your head. But we can't explain what a person experiences or decides by assuming there is another littler person inside their head experiencing and deciding. Explanations like these don't explain anything—there is no überself, no inner Tony Randall in the brain, no mission control where everything gets decided.

Still, it certainly does feel that way. From a purely phenomenological point of view there does seem to be a close connection between autobiographical memory and executive control and the observing, remembering, and deciding "me"—the resident homunculus of internal consciousness. Scientific psychology tells us that we can't explain inner consciousness by saying that there really is a mysterious self that we look at with our inner eye, any more than we can explain external consciousness by saying that there really is a spotlight that sweeps over the outside world. Instead there must be a more indirect link between our capacity for autobiographical memory and executive control and the shape of our inner consciousness. Somehow, the fact that we have autobiographical memory and executive control leads us to have the experience of the inner eye and the constant self. Since autobiographical memory and executive control are so different for young children, it's likely that their internal consciousness and their sense of self are different too.

THE STREAM OF CONSCIOUSNESS

We could simply ask children what their internal consciousness is like. This is just what the Flavells did. Just as children's ideas about external awareness are very different from ours, their ideas about internal consciousness are equally peculiar. We assume that we have a stream of consciousness, that thoughts, feelings, and memories flow inexorably and constantly through our minds. But even five-year-olds don't agree. Suppose the children see Ellie, who is sitting still in a chair and staring at the wall. You ask, "Is Ellie thinking? Is anything happening in her mind right now? Is she having thoughts or feelings or ideas?" Five-year-olds deny it—if she isn't doing anything or looking at anything her mind must be a blank.

Even more surprisingly, children think the same thing about their own minds. If you ask them whether they can keep their minds totally blank for hours they confidently say yes. They continue to say this even in circumstances when it's clear to us that they must have been thinking. For example, suppose you get four-year-olds to listen to a bell ring every thirty seconds. Then the bell doesn't ring. The children are startled. But if you ask them what they were just thinking they say, "Nothing." Even more amazingly, if you explicitly ask them if they were thinking about the bell during the silence they still say "No." Older children, like adults, report that they were thinking about the bell, wondering why it hadn't rung, or waiting for it to ring again. The young children believe that you yourself think only when there is something right there to think about, just as Ellie thinks only when she is actually looking at something. One four-year-old summarized it this way: "Every time you think for a little while, something goes on and something goes off. Sometimes something goes on for a couple of minutes and then for a few minutes there is nothing going on." This is very different from the adult picture of a constant stream of consciousness.

Moreover, these young children deny experiencing visual imagery or inner speech, although they understand perfectly what a picture or a sentence is like. Suppose you say to children, "I want you to answer a question in your head, but don't say the answer out loud. Where would you find a toothbrush in your house?" Most of us do this by picturing the different rooms of the house, and then discovering the toothbrush in the bathroom. Then you ask the children if they were imagining the bathroom. Four-year-olds say no, they weren't thinking about the bathroom, although they get the answer right if you then ask them to say it out loud.

They also say you can't talk to yourself in your head. The Flavells asked them to think about how their teacher's name sounded. They denied that there was any voice in their head doing the naming, and if you explicitly asked them they were as likely to say that there was a picture in their head as a voice.

Preschoolers do seem to understand other aspects of thinking perfectly well. They know that if you decide something or pretend something or solve a problem you think about what you are doing. If Ellie is staring at a magic coin trick they say she is thinking about how the trick works. If you ask her whether she'd like Chinese or Indian food for dinner, and she says "Hmm" and sits contemplatively, they say she is thinking about where to go for dinner. They get the idea of thinking about something; they even understand that you can think about something without doing anything. But they don't understand that your thoughts can be internally generated. They don't understand that thoughts can simply follow the logic of your internal experience instead of being triggered from the outside.

LIVING IN THE MOMENT

What does all this tell us about what it is like to be a baby? Babies—unlike, say, H.M., the amnesic patient—can consciously remember specific past events, differentiate them from current events, and retain those memories for months. They can also plan, imagining ways that the world might be and turning those possible worlds into reality.

However, babies and young children don't yet have autobiographical memory and executive control. They don't experience their lives as a single timeline stretching back into the past and forward into the future. They don't send themselves backward and forward along this timeline as adults do, recapturing for a moment that past self who was the miserable loser or the happy lover, or anticipating the despairs and joys of the future. And they don't feel immersed in a constant stream of changing thoughts and feelings.

In fact, for babies and young children there doesn't seem to be the same kind of "me" making these projections into the past and future. They don't keep track of their past mental states. While they remember that something happened, they don't seem to remember what they thought or felt about it. And although they can plan for the immediate future, they also don't seem to anticipate their future states. They don't project what they will think and feel later on.

Even very young babies have some sense of self. They can recognize themselves in a mirror and distinguish themselves from other people. The three-year-olds, after all, know that that is Johnny in the video and not some other kid. But they don't seem to have the experience of the inner observer, the autobiographer, the executive in the way that adults do.

So what is it like to be this way? I think that young children's consciousness includes all the elements of adult consciousness. There are images of past events, visions of intended goals, counterfactuals like the bizarre fantasies of pretend play, even abstract thoughts. Children can recognize the difference between these types of mental events, between present perceptions and past memories, current fantasies and future goals. But for three-year-olds these events aren't organized into a single timeline, with memories in the past and intentions in the future (and fictions and fantasies off to one side). And children may not have the experience of a single inner executive. Instead, the memories, images, and thoughts pop in and out of consciousness as they are cued by present events, or by other memories, images, and thoughts.

If for adults external consciousness is like a spotlight, internal consciousness is like a path. It is my own particular path, the track that I make as I move through the world. I can look back at it and see where I've been and look forward to peer, however dimly, toward my destination. The path pulls us forward and gives our lives their peculiar momentum. This path can, of course, easily become a rut, a narrow track that we endlessly and obsessively traverse.

Just as attention in children is more like a lantern, their inner consciousness may be more like wandering than voyaging—a journey of exploration rather than conquest. They paddle in the pond of consciousness instead of coursing down that rushing stream. Safe in the protected compass of immaturity, they can go anywhere they want. Pooing elephants over here! Weird machines that you touch with your head right this way! Now a quick detour to the rocket ship at the science center, a zigzag to touch base with Charlie Ravioli, and a beeline for the vision of the really wonderful tower I'll make with these blocks.

INTERNAL CONSCIOUSNESS, FREE ASSOCIATION, HYPNAGOGIC THOUGHT, AND INSIGHT MEDITATION

I suggested in the last chapter that we could get an empathetic glimpse of babies' external consciousness through travel or open awareness meditation. Although focused attention is the canonical example of adult external consciousness, there are many other kinds of awareness even in adults. In the same way, although the focused inner monologue of plans and memories is the canonical example of our inner experience, there are other adult experiences that may be more like the experience of young children. We may be able to get a glimpse of babies' inner consciousness through adult experiences like the "free association" of psychoanalysis, or the kind of "hypnagogic" thought we experience as we fall asleep. Before we lose consciousness altogether a stream of images, thoughts, and feelings flows through our minds. (As an incorrigible insomniac I've sometimes had the experience of briefly pulling out of the hypnagogic state and thinking, "Wait a minute, that last thought made absolutely no sense, thank God, I must be falling asleep"—the last gasp of that persistent inner observer holding on to consciousness when she really wants to release it.) Some types of "insight" meditation intentionally cultivate a similar state. Meditators try simply to observe the shifting contents of their minds without trying to control them.

In all these experiences we either deliberately or accidentally give up control of our thoughts—we intentionally turn off autobiographical memory and executive control, or we simply lose them as we doze off. But, unlike travel or open awareness meditation, in these experiences we turn inward rather than outward. In all these cases, our consciousness becomes surprisingly fragmented and labile, shifting from image to memory to thought without much apparent rhyme or reason. But it also becomes surprisingly rich; we may be startled to see how rare and strange the contents of our minds can be. The image of a convoluted purple flower morphs into a childhood memory of hiding under the table, which transforms into a sudden sensation of formless anxiety. Just as turning off the attentional spotlight can make us realize the variety and richness of our external perceptions, turning off executive control can make us realize the surprising variety of our internal experience. We can let our minds wander, as we say, and see where they go.

However valuable and interesting they may be, however, these experiences are very different from the experiences that are characteristic of everyday adult internal consciousness, and that reflect some of our most important adult abilities. In these states of consciousness the mind doesn't formulate coherent multiparagraph logical arguments or make step-by-step plans for all the contingencies of the child-care building project, or lovingly replay last weekend moment by moment from Friday to Sunday. You can't or at least don't do any of these things when you are engaged in free association or hypnagogic thought or insight meditation. Children don't seem to do this sort of focused long-range planning or systematic recollection either.

Moreover, the sense of a single conscious "I" seems to become at least attenuated in these childlike states. The inner observer fades away. Indeed, one of the insights of the insight-meditation tradition is supposed to be precisely that there is no "I." Whether or not this is true for adults, it does seem plausible that it is true for babies and very young children.

WHY DOES CONSCIOUSNESS CHANGE?

By the time they are six or so children seem to have developed the basics of autobiographical memory, executive control, and the inner observer. They have a roughly adult understanding of consciousness, too. What causes these changes in inner consciousness?

The development of language almost certainly plays a role. Autobiographical memory and executive control are developing in tandem with the ability to use language, which provides us with a medium for telling ourselves, as well as others, what happened and what to do. Recall the children who went to the zoo and remembered only what their mothers had told them about the animals and their adventures. It is also striking that for adults this inner linguistic monologue—the constant babble of inner speech—is one of the most important and characteristic features of internal consciousness. But Flavell's findings suggest that for children inner speech is much less prominent.

Language certainly plays a role in our adult consciousness. That inner voice nags and urges and instructs and persuades us. There is another possibly apocryphal story about the philosopher Jerry Fodor (he's the Yogi Berra of philosophy). Someone asked what his stream of consciousness was like as he wrote philosophy. His reply was that it mostly said, "Come on, Jerry, you can do it, Jerry, keep going, Jerry." We all seem to have those inner voices. But for children that voice at least seems less hectoring. After all, they have the real voice of their parents to direct them and restrict them and generally keep them on target and out of trouble.

These differences in the internal consciousness of adults and children, like the differences in their external consciousness, reflect the general division of labor between children and grown-ups. Children's characteristic consciousness is shaped by their characteristic agenda—learn as much about the world as you can as quickly as you can. Take source amnesia, suggestibility, and the purging of past false beliefs. Suppose you just want to update your beliefs as quickly and efficiently as possible. It makes sense to simply discard your past false beliefs, and not to retain information about where those beliefs came from.

This is especially true if, like babies, you are constantly updating and changing many of your beliefs at once. Babies and young children learn so much so quickly that their entire stock of knowledge turns over every few months—they go through whole paradigm shifts between their third and fourth birthday. We saw in chapter 3 that children are constantly learning and creating brand-new causal maps of the world. In developmental psychology we talk breezily about the big differences between nine-month-olds' and twelve-month-olds' conceptions of objects, or three-year-olds' and four-year-olds' understanding of minds. But what this means is that in just a few months, these children have completely changed their minds about what the world is like. Imagine that your worldview in September was totally different from what it was in June, and then completely changed again by Christmas. Or imagine that your most basic beliefs would be entirely transformed between 2009 and 2010, and then again by 2012. Really flexible and innovative adults might change their minds this way two or three times in a lifetime.

As we grow older our beliefs will become more and more well confirmed—we'll have gathered more and more evidence supporting them. So, quite properly, we'll be more reluctant to change them. If your agenda is not to change your beliefs, but to hold on to as many of them as possible, only changing a few of them very deliberately when you are sure you need to, you might act quite differently. Then it makes more sense to keep track of the history and sources of your beliefs. You want to change your beliefs only when you are sure the new information is robust and reliable—and more robust and reliable than the existing beliefs.

Other aspects of baby consciousness may also reflect these differences. Anecdotally, at least, there is a relation between adult states such as free association and hypnagogic consciousness, and innovation and creativity. Patients feel that they have made break-throughs in self-understanding as they lie on the couch, and scientists report that they get great ideas in the middle of the night. And, of course, insight meditation is precisely supposed to provide insights. Even for adults, uncritical "brainstorming," a process that feels much like free association or hypnagogic thought, is a good way to encourage new ideas. Babies are all about innovation and creativity. These experiences may be the phenomenological markers of an underlying thought process that puts together ideas and information in new ways, just as vivid attention seems to be a phenomenological marker of learning and plasticity.

On the other hand, autobiographical memory and executive control both reflect our characteristically adult ability to conceive and execute long-term plans. By seeing my experience as a single coherent whole, connected in the past, present, and future, I can do things like put up with a graduate-student salary in the hope of a professorship later on, or struggle through the first pages of a book that will only be published five years later. In our evolutionary past, these abilities let us plant seeds now to establish a future harvest, or invest now in making a tool that we will only use later.

The executive-control one-cookie/two-cookie experiments were first done back in the sixties. Years later they turned out to be a remarkably good predictor of teenage success at school. Children who were more able to defer gratification when they were five years old became teenagers who were more likely to be rated as competent and mature, and their SAT scores were consistently higher than those of children who couldn't tolerate the delay.

Some psychologists have even suggested that teenagers who literally don't feel that they have a future are most likely to behave self-destructively. Michael Chandler looked at teenagers in aboriginal communities in Canada. These teenagers are notoriously at risk for suicide, as well as less drastically self-destructive actions.

Chandler found that adolescents at risk for suicide had a less co-herent sense of themselves. They were less likely to connect their current, past, and especially future selves than children who were less at risk.

A MAP OF MYSELF: CONSTRUCTING CONSCIOUSNESS

So far I've argued that developmental cognitive science can tell us something about what it is like to be a baby or a young child. It's quite different from what it is like to be an adult. But can these differences tell us something more about consciousness itself?

Thinking about children illuminates a central debate in philosophy. Is our conscious experience irrefutable, the bedrock of our knowledge and our lives? Or is consciousness itself a construction, even a kind of illusion?

Until about a hundred years ago philosophers thought our conscious experiences caused us to act in the way we do. If we examined our own minds, we would see the ideas, emotions, and decisions that made us act. That was Descartes's method, and he argued that conscious experience was the one thing we knew for certain. It was also the method of the earliest scientific psychologists, like Wilhelm Wundt and William James. And this kind of introspective meditation is crucial to Asian philosophy and psychology.

But introspection leads to troubling contradictions. When we look at our own minds are we also changing how our minds work? For example, do we actually experience the inner self, that extended observer, biographer, and executive, or not? David Hume famously argued that we do not: the self is an illusion, it disappears whenever we try to look for it. The Buddhist tradition makes a similar claim. Is this because there is no fundamentally experienced self or because the experienced self disappears when you try to look at it? Does introspection reveal your true experience, or does it change that experience into something else?

As psychological science has developed we have found more and more cases where introspection is misleading. In fact, sometimes our conscious experience is directly contradicted by our actions or other psychological evidence. In inattentional blindness, for example, we feel sure that we are consciously seeing the entire scene, and yet it turns out that we are missing the gorilla. In blindsight, patients feel that they can't see something that they can accurately reach for. In autobiographical memory, we feel sure we remember events that we never actually experienced, ranging from the details of our initial reaction to 9/11 to alien abductions. In experiences of executive control, we often feel sure we are making a rational choice when, in fact, we are in the grip of some irrational unconscious bias. And in all of these cases we experience a homunculus, the inner observer, biographer, and decider that we know just can't exist.

These contradictions have led some philosophers, notably Daniel Dennett, to argue that consciousness doesn't really exist at all. That's a pretty extreme view. But Dennett holds down one end of a continuum. This continuum runs from "anticonsciousness" philosophers such as Dennett or Paul and Patricia Churchland to "proconsciousness" philosophers such as John Searle and David Chalmers. The first camp emphasizes the changeable and contradictory nature of conscious experience. The second camp emphasizes the special first-person certainty of consciousness. For philosophers like Chalmers the gap between consciousness and the brain suggests that consciousness is immaterial, not that it is illusory. Chalmers thinks that the conscious mind and the brain are fundamentally different kinds of things, though he wouldn't identify the mind with a mystical soul.

Looking at children doesn't explain away consciousness but it does weigh in on Dennett's side of the argument. Thinking about children makes consciousness seem even more confusing and contradictory. Are children accurately reporting conscious experiences that are different from ours? Or have they just got mistaken ideas about what their consciousness is like? Do children really not remember that they thought there were candies in the box? Or are they just mistaken about their past experience? Can we be conscious at all if we don't have an inner self? What does it mean to have a conscious experience without knowing that it is *my* conscious experience? And if children can be mistaken about their own conscious experience, surely we adults can also be mistaken?

Many aspects of consciousness that we take for granted, like the idea that we know what we thought a few seconds ago, or that our consciousness is a single unbroken stream, or that we have a unified self, fall apart when we look at children. Looking at children tells us that consciousness is not a single unitary phenomenon with special features. Our vivid awareness of the external world may be different from our sense of an executive "I," which may be different from the capacity to fantasize or to recapture past events. Children are conscious but their consciousness seems very different from ours.

Looking at children also makes us appreciate the gap between conscious experience and psychological explanation. We saw in earlier chapters that children are unconsciously the most rational beings on earth, brilliantly drawing accurate conclusions from data, performing complex statistical analyses, and doing clever experiments. But these brilliantly rational learning abilities are accompanied by a kind of consciousness that looks and feels irrational.

Piaget and Freud also speculated, as I have, that children's consciousness might be like free association or hypnagogic thought. Talk a while with a three-year-old and it's hard to avoid that conclusion. But they took the further step of concluding that this was what children's actual thinking was like—irrational, incoherent, and solipsistic. And that clearly isn't true. That may be what a three-year-old mind feels like but it isn't what a three-year-old mind really is like. The gap between the way the mind functions and the shape of conscious experience is even greater for children than for adults.

Looking at how consciousness changes also emphasizes the complex and indirect interactions among what we think, what we know, and what we experience. Children's consciousness changes because they learn more about the world and about how their own minds work. When they begin to understand that other people's desires or beliefs may change, for example, they start to experience those changes themselves. Looking at children suggests that there is a constant interweaving between largely unconscious processes of learning and the detailed texture of our conscious experience. When we change the way we think, we also change the way thinking feels to us. When what we know changes, our experience changes too. Consciousness isn't a transparent and lucid Cartesian stream. Instead it's a turbulent, muddy mess. Philosophers may have to resign themselves to just playing in the mud for a while yet. At least children can tell us it might be fun.

6.

Heraclitus' River and the Romanian Orphans

HOW DOES OUR EARLY LIFE SHAPE OUR LATER LIFE?

✳

Heraclitus, one of the very first recorded philosophers, questioned whether we stay the same throughout life. Recall his famous aphorism that a man never steps in the same river twice because neither the river nor the man are the same. The nature of our personal identity, whether and how we remain the same person over time, is a classic philosophical question. Philosophy is often as much about stories as arguments, and the problem of identity has led to some wonderful stories.

One story is the tale of Ulysses and the sirens. Ulysses knows that the siren song will lure him to his death but, consumed by his characteristic curiosity, he wants to hear it anyway. So he has his sailors tie him to the mast of his ship, and gets them to fill their ears with wax so that they won't be influenced by the sirens themselves and won't hear anything he says. He commands them to keep sailing forward. Sure enough, as soon as he hears the song, he curses his earlier precautions and commands his men to untie him; but the men, deaf to his commands, obliviously sail on. The question is, what does Ulysses want? Does he want to be untied or not? It seems almost as if the earlier Ulysses and the Ulysses who hears the sirens are two different people.

The philosopher Derek Parfit tells an even more troubling version of this story. "In several years, a young Russian will inherit vast estates. Because he has socialist ideals he intends, now, to give the land to the peasants. But he knows that in time his ideals may fade. To guard against this possibility, he first signs a legal document, which will automatically give away the land, and which can be revoked only with his wife's consent. He then says to his wife, 'Promise me that if I ever change my mind, and ask you to revoke this document, you will not consent.' He adds, 'I regard my ideals as essential to me. If I lose those ideals I want you to think that I cease to exist. I want you to regard your husband then, not as me, the man who asks you for this promise, but only as his corrupted later self. Promise me that you would not do what he asks.'" Sure enough, later, when he inherits the land he insists that his wife revoke the document as a relic of his youthful folly. What should she do?

And here is another even more disturbing tale from Parfit. Scientists have finally discovered a way to offer you immortality. They raise a set of clones, perfect young physical bodies. When you get old, they duplicate all of your neural circuitry in the brain of one of those clones, they make the brain identical to yours in every respect, matching all your memories and thoughts and feelings. Then they kill you. Would you accept this offer?

These philosophical stories all vividly raise the question of what makes me *me*. In what sense do I remain the same throughout my life? What are the relationships among all the phases of my existence, the young rebel, the old conservative, Ulysses before and after the temptation of the sirens?

In the last chapter, we saw that even very young children, four or five years old, already have a single autobiographical story that links their past and their future. They know that the "I" who wore the sticker in the past is the same as the "I" watching the video now, and the "I" who might need sunglasses in the desert in the future. This identity doesn't just emerge automatically, though. Instead, children actively create that "I"—that sense that they are the unique protagonist of their own autobiography. In fact, in the deferred-gratification experiments children are starting to be able to act like Ulysses, with cookies as the sirens. They can frustrate their current selves in the interest of their future selves.

These cases involve short time spans—putting together the "I" right now with the "I" of a few minutes ago or a few minutes to come. When we look at the long scale of an entire life, the questions become even more acute. It's hard enough for children to work out the relationship between the present self and the self of a few minutes ago. It's even harder to unify my present self and the self of forty years ago. And yet we live our lives as if there is a single story that makes the child father to the man—that unites childhood and adulthood. In fact, that story feels like an essential part of our personal identity. Knowing how we were will tell us how we are now.

How do our early childhood experiences influence our lives later on? These questions, more than any others, dominate public and private discussions of childhood. What did my parents do right (or more often wrong) to make me the person I am today? What can I do to ensure that my child turns out well?

Our everyday intuitions about these questions veer wildly. We all feel that what happened to us when we were children shapes who we are now. This is one reason that Freudian ideas continue to be so popular, in spite of the fact that many of them have been discredited scientifically. This intuition may also be responsible for the popularity of self-help and parenting books, and it even underlies the enthusiasm for grim and depressing childhood memoirs.

On the other hand, we also feel that later events can override the influence of childhood. A happy marriage or a fortunate vocation or even a good friend can rescue us from early misery. More powerfully, we believe that we can actively shape our lives in a way that allows us to escape from childhood determinism. The memoirs of childhood unhappiness are more likely to have an uplifting ending, a celebration of the possibility of "recovery," than they are to have an equally unhappy conclusion. (There is, of course, a striking dearth of memoirs that describe how, in spite of a wonderful childhood and warm and loving parents, the author of his own free will made himself into a rotten grown-up.)

Philosophers, preoccupied with the troubles of Ulysses and the Russian nobleman, haven't paid as much attention to these questions about childhood. This is too bad because a little philosophical clarity would be helpful. There are a number of ways to think about early childhood and its impact on later life and they often get confused. We might think that certain childhood events simply cause us to have certain adult characteristics. Alternatively, we might think that our experiences as children cause us to have certain kinds of beliefs about the world and other people, and those beliefs shape our adult thought and action.

As we'll see, there is some evidence for both these views but the scientific picture is complicated. The complications emerge precisely because of our human capacities for change. Our ability to change our environment makes the relation between childhood and adulthood especially intricate and complex.

There is also a more subtle but important way that early childhood influences our adult lives. Because of autobiographical memory and our sense of self, my childhood simply is, for good or ill, part of what I am as an adult. It isn't that my childhood causes me to be an adult of a particular kind—it's that what I am as an adult includes my childhood.

LIFE CYCLES

Are there particular childhood events—especially things that parents do or don't do—that directly influence our later lives? When I give talks to parents, at least three-quarters of the questions I get are along these lines: If I let my child watch TV will she have attention problems? If I read to her in the womb will she be smarter? If I play Mozart will he do better in math class? Or (more generally) if I do x (work/don't work, let him sleep in my bed/don't let him sleep in my bed, let him cry/don't let him cry) will he end up as a hopeless neurotic? This is often half, but only half, ironically phrased as "What will he tell his shrink about me?"

These questions are irresistible—I've been asking myself the same questions about my children for thirty years. But there is surprisingly little scientific evidence for this simple view of the effects of early experience on later life. Take a particularly striking and sad example: the children who were abandoned in Romanian orphanages during the tyrannical regime of Nicolae Ceauşescu. Although these children weren't physically abused, they suffered terrible social and emotional deprivation. No one played with them or held them or talked to them or loved them. Babies lay alone in their cribs for hours, indeed days and weeks, at a time.

After the regime fell and the horror of the orphanages was discovered, many of these children, by then three or four years old, were adopted and taken into British middle-class homes. They looked completely different from other children. They were physically much smaller, they appeared to be severely retarded, they barely talked, and their social behavior was bizarre.

And yet by the time the children were six they had largely caught up. Their average IQ was only a little lower than a similar group of more fortunate children. They loved their adoptive parents in the same way that other children love their parents. In fact, most of the Romanian orphans were completely indistinguishable from other children.

Some of the children, though, continued to suffer. Although these children had recovered compared with their pitiful beginnings, they still seemed to lag behind other children both cognitively and socially. The longer the children had been in the orphanages, the more likely they were to have problems later, and the more severe the problems were likely to be. This suggests that the early experiences really were responsible for the later problems. So the story of the Romanian orphans is a story both of resilience, for all those children who recovered completely, and of risk, for those children who didn't.

The Romanian orphans are a dramatic case in two ways: they were dramatically deprived as babies, and their circumstances changed equally dramatically when they were adopted. But this combination of risk and resilience is the moral of studies of more typical development as well. Being abused as a child makes you more likely to abuse your own children, but the overwhelming majority of abused children don't become abusive parents. Somehow they escape from the circumstances of their early lives.

THE PARADOX OF INHERITANCE

You might think this means that, in fact, childhood experience has no influence at all on later life, and that most of what we are is shaped by our genes. But this doesn't seem to be true either. Instead, we see so much variation in development because our genetic inheritance and our experience interact. By itself, this is a banal observation. It's more interesting to see how complex and multifaceted those interactions can be.

Psychologists often talk about "heritability." People growing up in the same environment can vary in how smart or how sane or how miserable they are—in what psychologists call their "traits." Then you can ask if there is a mathematical relationship between these similarities and differences in traits and genetic similarities and differences. If you're smarter, or crazier, or sadder than other kids, were your parents likely to be smarter or crazier or sadder than other parents? How much of the difference between people on some individual trait is predictable from the differences in their genes?

Twin studies are a particularly good way to do this. We know that identical twins share all the same genes while fraternal twins don't, but both fraternal and identical twins share the same environment. If identical twins are more similar on some trait than fraternal twins, that indicates that the trait is "heritable." For example, if one identical twin is alcoholic, there's a good chance that the other twin will also suffer from alcoholism. If the twin is fraternal, there is less of a chance, though the fraternal twin is still more likely to be alcoholic than a random unrelated person.

Another technique is to look at adopted children. Are adopted children more similar on some trait to their birth parents, who share the same genes, or to their adoptive parents, who share the same environment? Again, children with alcoholic birth parents, who are adopted by people who aren't alcoholics, are more likely to suffer from alcoholism themselves than other similar people without that genetic background. You can also just measure these traits in a group of parents and then in their children. People with alcoholism are more likely to have alcoholic parents than people with other kinds of problems. So alcoholism is heritable.

Using these techniques, some psychologists propose a precise number that indicates the heritability of some trait. Based on the kinds of studies I just described, psychologists may say that in a standard white, middle-class group of people, the sort of people included in these studies, alcoholism has a heritability of .40. Similarly, you can measure the heritability of IQ in a standard white, middle-class group of people. The correlation between variation in IQ scores and variation in genes in that sort of group is estimated to be between .40 and .70. Even a heritability of .40 is pretty substantial.

People often assume that very heritable traits must be due to genes while less heritable traits are due to environment. These kinds of studies underlie the headlines about "genes for" everything from criminality to creativity. But heritability measures variation within a certain environment, and human beings create their own environments, particularly their own social environments—many of the environments they create are unlike any that have gone before. We've seen that our (genetically determined) capacities for counterfactual thought and causal intervention mean that we can act on our environment to make it a different environment. This is the rule rather than the exception in human life. The trouble is that the very same genes may have very different effects in that new environment than they did in the old one. This makes it conceptually difficult to sort out the effects of genes and the effects of the environment.

Take a very simple and striking case. When babies are born in hospitals they're immediately tested for a rare genetic disorder called phenylketonuria, or PKU. Children with PKU are unable to metabolize certain chemicals in food. If they have a normal diet they become severely retarded, but if they get a special diet that avoids these chemicals they are fine. So the mental retardation of PKU is absolutely 100 percent due to genes and it is also absolutely 100 percent due to environment. It was completely heritable when the chemicals were always present and it is not heritable at all now that they can be removed.

Human beings have used their innate cognitive abilities to discover the causal link between PKU and retardation and have intervened to change the environment of children with the defective genes. For other animals, without these abilities, the effects of PKU would indeed be entirely due to genetics. But for us they are not.

You can also see these paradoxes of heritability in more ordinary cases. For example, Eric Turkheimer at the University of Virginia discovered a database of very poor twins. All the earlier twin studies involved middle-class children. It turns out that IQ is far more heritable for rich children than for poor children. In fact, for poor children the effect of genes on IQ almost disappears—there is little correlation between how smart parents are and how smart their children are, and identical twins' IQ is no more similar than that of fraternal twins. So it seems that poor children's IQ is less affected by their genes than rich children's IQ. But how can that be? Surely poverty can't change your DNA?

The answer is that small variations in a poor child's environment—going to a better or worse school, for example—make a big difference to their IQ. Those differences swamp any genetic differences. Rich children are generally already going to good schools, so the differences between them are more likely to reflect genetic variation. Notoriously, Charles Murray and Richard Herrnstein in their book *The Bell Curve* suggested that the heritability of IQ meant that programs such as Head Start were futile. But, in fact, the new heritability results lead to just the opposite conclusion: changing a poor child's environment can have enormous effects.

Historical studies also show how new environments can change the effects of genes. Absolute IQ scores have skyrocketed at a startling pace in the past century, although our genes have remained the same. One compelling explanation is that a hundred years ago we embarked on an unprecedented gene-environment experiment. We started putting developing brains in a brand-new environment: school. Before then only a few people experienced schooling. It turned out that in this new environment those brains performed in a way they never had before, and once everybody started going to school there was one of those characteristically human interactions between nature and nurture. Bright people (or at least people who do well at school) become brighter as a result of going to school, and they therefore want still more schooling, and the more schooling is available the brighter people can become.

This environmental experiment may have had negative results, too. The equally dramatic recent rise in Attention Deficit Disorder may be the flip side of the same coin. Some people were probably always better than others at paying sustained attention to just one thing. But these variations would have made no difference throughout most of human history—that kind of sustained, focused attention isn't especially important for a hunter or a farmer, and it may even be a disadvantage.

However, paying attention makes a very big difference in the environment of a schoolroom. In school, children who are good at paying attention to begin with will develop even more impressively focused attention skills. So the genetic differences become exaggerated, and being bad at attention becomes a problem, even a kind of disease.

Sometimes our ability to create our own environment can completely overcome our genetic risks—the PKU story is a triumph of human ingenuity—but, equally, this ability can multiply those risks. This is particularly true when we interact with other people. As we've seen, we act on the social world even more effectively than we act on the physical world. And, in turn, our social environment shapes us.

For example, we know that stressful events—like death, divorce, loss, humiliation—can make anybody depressed. In fact, sadness and grief are normal and appropriate responses to these events. But people with a genetic risk for depression are much more vulnerable to these stresses. Some people bounce back after a loss, while other people spiral into deepening grief.

To make things worse, people with a genetic risk for depression are actually more likely to experience stressful events. Remember that we influence our own social environment. Depressed people are more likely to act in ways that lead to rejection and humiliation than cheerful and resilient people are, which makes them more depressed. Angry people are more likely to provoke anger in others, which, of course, makes them more angry. Think of the sad woman in the bar who pours out the tearful true story of her unhappy love life to the guy beside her, or the angry man in the bar who thinks the guy beside him is trying to pick a fight. The guy on the next stool is almost certain to react in a way that makes the woman sadder and the man angrier.

HOW BABIES RAISE THEIR PARENTS

These cycles of interaction between people and their surroundings begin in early childhood, in fact, even in infancy. Children shape their world—and then that world shapes them. In the past thirty years we've discovered that children influence their parents as much as parents influence their children. Individual differences in the ways that children act lead to differences in the ways that parents act.

The very same parent may treat two siblings very differently. You can see this in extreme cases, such as cases of abuse. Very often only one child in a family ends up being abused. Sickly or irritable children seem especially vulnerable. But it seems to happen in more ordinary cases too. Parents respond to different children in different ways and two siblings may, literally, grow up with very different parents. The demanding, difficult child (parenting books euphemistically describe them as "spirited") will literally have a different mother than the cuddly, warm, easy baby. My two oldest children are only a year apart and were inseparable in childhood. But Alexei, my passionate, emotional, outgoing oldest son, had a much more Mediterranean and less Anglo-Saxon mom than Nicholas, his calm, shy, intellectual brother.

It's not just that it's impossible to interact with very different children in the same way. In fact, even if you did exactly the same thing with each of your children, your actions would mean something different. Put the wriggly, active, thrill-seeking sister in a bouncy swing and she's overjoyed. Put the timid, shy, stay-close-to-home sister in the swing and she's terrified.

We can see these interactive effects in other kinds of studies. Psychologists have done adoption and twin studies of "antisocial behavior" or "neuroticism" or "substance abuse susceptibility" or a list of other ills. (I'll use "miserable" as an everyday synonym for the assorted technical terms, since it conveys the general picture of people who are unhappy themselves and make other people unhappy too.) Children of miserable birth parents who are raised by OK adoptive parents are slightly more at risk of becoming miserable themselves than other children. The same is true for children of OK birth parents who are raised by miserable adoptive parents. But if you combine the two effects, if you are unlucky enough to have been born to one set of miserable parents and to be raised by another set, you get a *much* higher risk for adult misery, far greater than just adding the two factors together would imply. Genetic risk and environmental risk don't just add up—one multiplies the other.

Even worse, much of the time genetic risk and environmental risk go together. Most children share both genes and environment with their parents: Depressed impoverished children are raised by depressed impoverished parents, children with a susceptibility to alcohol are raised by parents with the same vulnerabilities. And, of course, the opposite is true too: cheerful, well-supported babies are likely to be born to equally cheerful and well-supported parents.

Sometimes babies can transform their parents. After all, babies are a source of enormous intimacy and joy and meaning, and more than one poor single mother has been saved by a warm, affectionate baby. But, more often, the environmental and genetic risks multiply—the depressed mom has a depressed baby, which makes her more depressed, which makes the baby more depressed, and so on.

Vicious or benign cycles are the rule in development just because of our capacities for learning and intervention. Babies learn about the world based on what they see their parents do, and they act based on that knowledge. Those actions influence what their parents do, which influences what the babies do and how they act, and so forth. A naturally sad baby observes a sad mother, concludes that sadness is the human condition, acts sadly, and makes her mother even more sad. These capacities mean that genetic differences can be magnified, or can disappear altogether.

This may sound like a pessimistic conclusion, and in some ways it is. But, as the Romanian orphans demonstrate, it is also optimistic. If our genes or, for that matter, our early experiences simply determined our fate, the story would indeed be a bitter one. But while cycles are self-perpetuating they can also be interrupted. The same capacities that let children shape their worlds also let us intervene to influence the cycles of development.

Programs like the Perry Preschool Project in Michigan and the Carolina Abecedarian Project radically altered poor children's early experiences. Children in these programs spent their days in well-designed preschools with toys and books and sandboxes and water tables and, most of all, dedicated adults looking after them. Then the researchers compared them with other children in the community who did not get to go to these preschools. The scientific evidence is crystal clear: these interventions had lasting effects. Twenty or thirty years later the children in these programs were more prosperous, better educated, healthier, and less likely to go to jail than the children in the control group. Economic analyses show that the return on investment in these programs is staggering—a lot better than the stock market.

This might seem like a vindication of the simple view that early experience directly influences later life. But those programs didn't just influence the children, they influenced their parents, too. These programs gave poor parents, as well as poor children, a sense of autonomy and connection. The children in these programs didn't just have different early experiences, they had different parents, and they had those different parents for life. And making the children different, more confident and more curious, influenced the way that their parents and others treated them. Programs like the Perry Preschool Project don't work just by giving children particular enriched early experiences. They also work because those changes lead to cascading changes in the child's environment later on—all the way up to adulthood.

So when we think about the influence of early experience on adult life, we need to consider our human capacity for intervention. Even young children influence their own environments and imagine and create new environments. Those environments influence the children in turn. This creates a characteristically human cycle of development. It also means that parents, or other people more generally, can intervene in a way that alters, interrupts, or reinforces those cycles.

7.

Learning to Love

ATTACHMENT AND IDENTITY

*

THEORIES OF LOVE

In the last chapter I outlined one way that early experience can influence our later lives. Since we shape our own environments, early experiences can lead to vicious or benign cycles. But early experience can affect later life in other ways. Our causal maps of the world, our theories, change as we learn more, as we observe and experiment. As a result the counterfactuals we can consider and the interventions we can perform will change too. What we learn about the world early on can influence the way that we interpret new events, and help determine what we will learn next. That, in turn, can influence our further theories about the world, right up to adulthood. And those particular adult theories, those ideas about how the world works, will determine what we think and do.

The clearest case of this sort of theory change through life involves what psychologists call "attachment" and the rest of us call love. Babies and toddlers learn about beliefs and desires, but they also learn about love. It's particularly important for babies to learn about the people who nurture, protect, and take care of them—who love them—and to figure out how love works.

All children want and need love. The craving for protection and nurturance is innate and universal—it's a necessary part of the evolutionary scheme of protected immaturity. But care can take many different forms, and babies' ideas about love vary dramatically.

To find out how babies understand love we can watch what they do when their caregivers leave them and then return. Very young babies already are able to recognize familiar people—newborns can quickly recognize and prefer their mother's face and voice—but at first they greet all grown-ups, familiar or strange, with the same blissful smiles and engaging coos.

By the time babies are about a year old, though, they have discovered that some people treat them in a special way and that these people are the ones they should turn to for love. After about a year, affection and trust become centered on a few familiar people, not just mothers but also fathers, babysitters, and siblings. Many children this age become anxious when strangers approach and retreat to the safety of a parent's arms. Similarly, many become distressed when their caregivers leave. But they are swiftly comforted when they are reunited with their loved ones, and quickly turn their attention to other things.

This is a rather abstract way of putting it. Alexei, my emotional and intense child, "demonstrated a pattern of distress at separation" by hurling himself at the window as I was leaving, sobbing, "Mama! Mama!" and clawing at the glass. On the other hand, he "demonstrated comfort with reunion" by running at lightning speed from the other side of the house when I came home, literally throwing himself into my arms and hugging me passionately. The storms of misery and joy dissipated equally quickly five minutes after I left the house or returned to it.

Why does this happen? We know that even very young babies are paying careful attention to other people. They pay particularly close attention to the contingencies between their own actions and emotions and those of others—the statistics of love. The baby notices that when he smiles, Mom smiles back. When he cries, she looks sad and then comforts him. Or suppose the pattern is different: the baby might learn that when he smiles at Mom she's as likely to be sad or distracted as she is to smile back. Or that when he cries Mom goes on smiling anyway, or, worse, gets angry and intensifies his misery.

By the time they're a year old babies have learned these patterns. They also learn that some people respond differently than others. A parent will respond quickly to joy or sadness while a stranger will not. Babies have noticed that some people are more responsive than others, so they come to rely more on those people.

One of the most striking things about the Romanian orphans is that, understandably, they didn't learn this. In the bleak orphanages, a succession of constantly changing strangers looked after their basic physical needs and nobody looked after their emotional needs. Instead of looking to particular people to take care of them they made random bids for affection from everyone they met. When they were hurt or scared they were as likely to run to a total stranger as to someone they knew. They developed particular attachments only after they had been adopted.

But, even in less extreme circumstances, not all babies learn the same things about love. My intense baby's pattern is called "secure" attachment. The baby believes that this particular person is a reliable source of love, and so is unhappy when she leaves and comforted when she returns. But other babies don't react in this way.

Some "avoidant" babies actively avoid interacting with the caregiver both when she leaves and when she returns. Rather than crying or celebrating, these babies simply look at their toys with extrastudious interest. You might think that these babies are simply less distressed than the secure babies. But it turns out that if you measure their heart rate during the separation the physiological signs indicate that inside the babies are miserable—one of the saddest research findings I know. These babies do notice that the caregivers are gone and are unhappy as a result, but they seem to have learned that expressing that unhappiness just makes things worse. They've learned that crying is more likely to lead to misery than to comfort, and so even at this very early age they've learned to tamp down their emotions rather than express them.

Still other "anxious" babies not only become very distressed when a caregiver leaves—they are also inconsolable when she returns. Instead of a quick return to calm happiness they continue to cry and cling to their caregiver. They may get mad, too, throwing away their toys and crying angrily at Mom even as they cling to her.

It's hard to keep from feeling that secure babies are better off than avoidant or anxious babies, but we should remember that this depends at least partly on the environment these babies will find themselves in later on. There are cultural differences in the preponderance of different attachment styles, which should give us pause.

In Germany there are more avoidant babies than in America, and in Japan there are more anxious babies. We could think of the avoidant babies as tough, stiff-upper-lip types, and argue that the anxious babies simply need and expect a greater degree of closeness than other babies. Those patterns might be sensible and adaptive in a world where lots of other people share the same patterns. An avoidant baby might do well on the playing fields of Eton, where hardly anyone expresses much closeness, and an anxious baby might thrive in a small African village where hardly anyone is ever alone.

"Disorganized" babies are the worst off. These babies never develop a consistent set of expectations at all. Instead, they veer unpredictably from one pattern of behavior to another. These babies are particularly vulnerable to later problems and difficulties.

Why do babies behave in these different ways? Some of it may reflect differences in babies' temperaments, but most psychologists think that babies also develop "internal working models" of how other people will respond to them. These models are like the theories and causal maps I described earlier, but they are theories of love rather than theories of physics or biology or psychology. They are causal maps of care. Secure babies conclude that caregivers will quickly make them feel better. Avoidant babies think that expressing distress will only cause more misery. Anxious babies are unsure that comfort will be effective.

Although in the great scheme of things this may seem like a rather parochial theme for theorizing, from the baby's point of view there are few more important theories. Since babies depend entirely on caregiving for survival, figuring out how that caregiving works is even more important than understanding everyday physics or biology.

The internal working models of attachment, like other theories, are based on the evidence babies have about the people around them. Mothers who respond quickly to babies' signals—who return to babies after they leave and comfort babies when they are unhappy—are more likely to have "secure" babies. Mothers who don't react with comfort when babies are distressed are more likely to have avoidant babies. Mothers who express a great deal of distress themselves are more likely to have anxious babies.

Of course, some of this might reflect genetic or temperamental similarities between mothers and babies. But remember that babies develop attachments to all the people who care for them, not just to Mom. The same baby can develop different consistent attachment patterns to different people, depending on how those people act. Some babies learn that Dad is responsive though Mom is not, for example, and they are secure with Dad but avoidant with Mom. That means that these patterns can't just be due to the baby's temperament.

Most striking of all, a very recent study actually shows that secure and insecure babies have different theories of love. Susan Johnson tested one-year-olds to see if they had secure or insecure attachments. Then she did the sort of habituation experiment I described earlier. First the babies saw an animated film of a "mother," a big circle moving up a sloped hill, and a "baby," a small circle at the foot of the hill. The circles interacted like people, and at one point the "baby" began to pulsate and a terrible real baby's cry accompanied the film. Then the babies saw one of two outcomes. Either the mother moved down toward the baby or else she moved away from him up the slope. The secure babies expected that she would return to the baby; they looked longer at the puzzlingly unresponsive mother. The insecure babies, heartbreakingly, had just the opposite theory—they looked longer when the mother changed course and returned. In another study Johnson found that these babies also made different predictions about what the baby circle in the video would do—secure babies predicted that he would move toward the mom, insecure babies didn't. These babies, some only twelve months old, had already learned to make predictions about love.

There are also relationships between the way children act early on and the way they explicitly talk and think about love later, at five or six. When children get a little older you can ask them to make predictions and produce counterfactuals about love. Suppose another child had a parent who had to go away on a trip—how would he feel and what should he do? Children who had been secure as babies could predict how the other child would feel and could also suggest good interventions (call up, look at her picture, and so on). The children who had been avoidant also recognized that the child would feel sad but couldn't suggest anything that would help. (This is especially poignant when you remember that these are the children who don't express sadness themselves.)

But there is an important difference between a theory of love and other kinds of theories. When the baby is making up a theory of the physical or biological world she has a large and consistent data set. Most balls do fall down rather than up; most seeds, fortunately, quickly grow to be plants; most pet fish, unfortunately, quickly die. But when it comes to love, children have to draw conclusions based on a very small and very variable sample, the mothers and fathers, siblings, grandparents, and babysitters who care for them.

And while balls and seeds and plants all act pretty much the same way, caregivers may act in very different ways. Mothers, after all, are just particular women at a particular time with all their particular burdens and strengths and weaknesses. Some may respond immediately to a baby's joy and comfort his distress. But all mothers are distracted or angry or sad some of the time, and some may be distracted or angry or sad almost all the time. The poet Robert Hass captures this beautifully:

> When we say "mother" in poems,
> we usually mean some woman in her late twenties
> or early thirties, trying to raise a child.
> We use this particular noun
> to secure the pathos of the child's point of view,
> and to hold her responsible.

There *is* a terrible pathos about this basic asymmetry between caregivers and children. From an objective perspective caregivers are just individual people with complicated lives doing the best they can. But from the baby's perspective caregivers loom large; this handful of frail human beings may define a baby's conception of love and care.

This can be rough on parents and children, but it's a boon to psychologists. It's hard to test the continuity between early theories of the physical world and adult theories, because all adults seem to converge on pretty much the same theory. But there is a lot of recent evidence that adults, like babies, have different theories of love.

Psychologists can get at these theories in many ways—they can interview people about their relationships with their parents, or get them to list adjectives that describe the people who are important to them, or ask them to answer a questionnaire about their romances. Or they can even just watch how people act when they say good-bye to their loved ones at the airport. (I have watched my now thirty-year-old baby reproduce something very like his one-year-old separation behavior with a beautiful young woman in the departure lounge.)

Like babies, some adults seem to confidently, if not always accurately, believe that they have been loved in the past and will be loved in the future. Others tend to avoid even thinking about love past and future. They say, for example, that they just can't remember much about how their parents treated them, and in times of romantic stress they turn to computers and spreadsheets. Still others fear that they will always need love more than they will receive it, that their love is far more likely to be rejected than returned. In the departure lounge, some people cling to their beloved till the last moment when they disappear through the gate—others try to make the farewells as brief and painless as they can.

Our experiences of love influence us in far-reaching and often subtle and unconscious ways. In one striking experiment, Serena Chen and her colleagues asked undergraduates to write down a detailed list of the particular characteristics of a significant other, a person they loved (often a parent). They also wrote a similar list of the characteristics of someone they knew well but didn't love. Several weeks later they participated in what they thought was a completely different study. They read thumbnail sketches of other students and were asked to remember what the descriptions said and to say how they'd feel about meeting that particular person.

They didn't know that some of the sketches in the new study were designed to include a lot of the characteristics of the significant other they had described in the earlier study. If they had said that Mom was funny and short and made great lasagna, an amusing, petite gourmet might appear. The students reacted very differently to these sketches than to other sketches. For one thing, they tended to assume that these people would be like the significant other in additional ways. They might remember that the amusing, petite gourmet was also, like Mom, quick-tempered and untidy, even though nothing like that actually showed up in the description.

In addition, their attitudes toward the person in the sketch reflected their feelings about the significant other. If they had a good relationship with Mom they were more likely to want to meet the girl who resembled her. If they said that Mom often criticized them they felt anxious about meeting her fictional doppelganger. None of these effects showed up when the new person resembled someone they knew well but didn't care much about. (These studies, rather depressingly, confirm all our female suspicions that deep down inside he really does think I'm his mom.)

So these internalized theories of love influence our expectations about other grown-ups. They also seem to influence the way that we treat our own children. In one study, psychologists interviewed people who were expecting their first baby. They asked the prospective parents to talk about their own childhood and especially about their experiences of love. After the babies were born, the psychologists looked at how they reacted to separation. The parents' stories about their own childhood predicted the babies' behaviors. (Again confirming all our worst fears that deep down inside I really am my mom.)

There are several interesting insights that come out of these studies. The form of our knowledge turns out to be as important as the content. As you might expect, parents who talked at length about how much their own parents loved them were more likely to have secure babies. But, in addition, some people who reported difficult childhoods had worked-out, thoughtful, reflective ideas about their past, while other people had much more fragmentary and confused ideas.

There are some people who say they had very unhappy relationships with their parents but recounted those experiences in a thoughtful, organized way. They could tell a coherent story about how those early experiences had led to their present state. One of the advantages of a coherent causal picture of the world is that it allows you to entertain counterfactuals—to imagine ways that the world might be different. This was what had happened for these adults: they understood how their own parents had behaved and could imagine ways that they might act differently themselves. Those people, hearteningly, were more likely to have secure relationships with their own children. Other people said perfunctorily that they had been loved but couldn't remember anything more or give any details. Those parents were less likely to have secure children.

The obvious, and great, and difficult question, of course, is how early theories of love affect later ones. What's the relationship between the baby's implicit ideas about his particular mom and the grown-up's much more explicit ideas about love in general? There have been a number of heroic studies that tracked babies into adulthood for twenty or sometimes even thirty or forty years. In most of the studies there was a fairly good correlation between early and late attachment styles.

But there are also lots of exceptions—there are many babies who start out anxious or avoidant and then become secure and loving parents themselves, and some who start out secure and then grow up to be insecure. Remember the parents who gave thoughtful accounts of their own childhood unhappiness, and then went on to remedy this when it came to their own children.

Often, the crucial factor is a new experience that changes the child's ideas about love. A newly discovered adoptive parent or a dedicated teacher or a friend's welcoming family can transform an insecure baby. On the other hand, the unavoidable loss of love that comes when parents grow sick or die or divorce can make a once-secure baby more reluctant to believe in love.

Theories of love are like other theories—they show both continuity and change. Early beliefs shape the way we see the world later on. (Think about the undergraduates mistakenly attributing all of Mom's virtues and vices to the girl who just had a few of her quirks.) Having a particular early theory may make us more likely to adopt a similar theory later, but theories can also be overturned if we encounter sufficient counterevidence.

This is a cognitive version of the risk-and-resilience picture. Our early experiences affect our beliefs, which affect our actions, which affect our experiences, and so on. Negative early experiences put us at risk for negative experiences later on. But there is also resilience. With enough new experiences of love, even deep-seated theories can change. The Romanian orphans demonstrate this.

Many of these ideas sound Freudian and, indeed, John Bowlby, the founder of attachment theory, was heavily influenced by Freud. Clearly, like Piaget, Freud had many deep and genuine insights about childhood. Like Freud the attachment researchers suggest that very early experiences, especially our experience of our parents, may shape our emotions much later. They also suggest that much of this shaping is unconscious—we don't consciously know the way that our theory of Mom is influencing our reaction to that girl we met last night. And they make the same still-startling equation between the early love of parents and children and the later sexual love we feel for our romantic partners.

But there are also differences. Contemporary developmental psychologists don't just rely on their interpretation of what a patient says on the couch. They do careful, painstaking, and time-consuming empirical studies. And while the phenomena may look Freudian, the theoretical explanations are different. For Freud the fundamental forces that shape our nature are psychic drives, bubbling sources of psychological energy that are supposed to be distributed or redirected through repression and transference. In this picture, our beliefs about the world are determined, and often distorted, by these unconscious drives.

Psychology has always been influenced by technological metaphors, and in cognitive science and neuroscience the mind appears to be more like a computer than an engine. Our brains are designed to arrive at an accurate picture of the world, and to use that accurate picture to act on the world effectively, at least overall and in the long run. The same computational and neurological capacities that let us make discoveries about physics or biology also let us make discoveries about love.

And rather than saying, like Freud, that children want to have sex with their mothers, it's more true to say that grown-ups want mothering from the people they have sex with. We love the children we care for; the children we care for love us. In fact, as we'll see, we love the people who help us care for our children. Recent work suggests that there is an evolutionary as well as developmental link between the fact that we love our children and the fact that we love our mates. That love allows childhood to take place. It's as evolutionarily important and as deep as sex. But that love also goes way beyond just the relation between biological mothers and their children, or between sexual partners. Theories of love aren't just important for mothers, or fathers, or children, but for everyone.

BEYOND MOTHERS: SOCIAL MONOGAMY AND ALLOMOTHERING

Work on attachment shows that human babies can become attached to many different people—not just their mothers. This reflects a broader evolutionary fact. Our human concern for and about children isn't restricted to our own immediate genetic descendants but extends much more widely. For most of human history caregiving went way beyond just mothers, or even fathers, to include grandparents, older brothers and sisters, aunts, cousins, friends—the community at large. In fact, contemporary middle-class American society is very unusual in that so few people are involved in raising children. (This may also explain why those who do sometimes seem to make such a fuss about it. At most times and places parenting is something everybody takes for granted, but many modern parents seem to think it's another specialized profession to study for. There's nothing like the prospect of an exam to make you anxious and miserable.)

The particular human evolutionary trick of extended immaturity means that both parents and other adult members of human groups must make a particularly strong investment in their children for a particularly long time. The return on that investment goes not only to the individual parents but to the entire group.

Certainly, human beings, to a greater extent than even our closest primate relatives, go in for what evolutionary biologists call social monogamy and allomothering. Both are common in species that, for whatever reason, demand a large parental investment in their offspring—more of an investment than just a mother can afford. Social monogamy, which is very common in birds, though less so among mammals, means that people develop close social bonds to particular other people (or penguins or swans or voles) and they jointly raise children. Males and females are more than just sexual partners—they become social allies, too; they are mates.

Socially monogamous fathers, to be sure, are often actually the fathers of the children they raise, and so they have a genetic interest in their offspring. But socially monogamous species are almost never sexually monogamous. Recent DNA studies, rather startlingly, show that even swans mess around. There is a great deal of sexual activity between animals who are not mates, and many fathers raise children that are not their own. Socially monogamous species will sometimes even bond with a member of their own sex to raise the young, like the famous gay penguins at the Central Park Zoo. Birds seem especially likely to be socially monogamous because of the long period when eggs both demand warmth and are vulnerable to predators and accidents.

Alloparenting is found in many species of primates as well as in dolphins and elephants and some birds. In allomothering female members of the group who are not actually direct genetic parents of the young play a major role in childrearing. Lemurs and langurs have teenage babysitters. Mother lemurs leave their babies with other young lemurs while they go looking for food. Elephants even share nursing duties. There are also allofathers and allopaternal behavior, particularly in birds, though this is less common in primates.

Alloparenting is interesting from an evolutionary perspective because, like many altruistic behaviors, it seems paradoxical. Why expend all that energy to protect someone else's genes? Alloparenting species turn out to have a number of distinctive characteristics. Alloparenting shows up when mothers produce only one baby at a time, and only a limited number of babies across their lifetime. Alloparenting animals live in relatively small related groups with complex social and cooperative behaviors, and particularly intense parenting demands. Like social monogamy in birds, allomothering helps when babies are just too much for a single mother to manage. For example, you see extensive allomothering in monkeys who travel long distances but aren't strong enough to carry their babies entirely by themselves.

Biologists argue that for these species alloparenting has a wide variety of broader benefits. For some species, babies literally couldn't be raised without help. Helping your kin ensures that your genes will be more widely preserved. Reciprocal altruism means that I'll get help with my babies in exchange for my help with yours and we'll both benefit. Allomothers get to practice and learn how to mother themselves. Probably all these factors interact in different ways in different species.

Human beings are way out on the end of the distribution on all these ecological measures—we usually have only one baby at a time and, at most, a dozen or so in a liftetime; we have complex close social networks with a great deal of cooperative behavior; and, of course, we have especially needy children. The extended immaturity of our children that allows them to learn so much also demands especially intense and prolonged parenting. We engage in significantly more alloparenting and social monogamy than our closest primate relatives, the great apes.

In some ways, we are more like penguins than chimps, though our babies face the perils of our long human apprenticeship instead of the long Antarctic winter. Like penguins, we share caregiving with a few particular mates, and other people will dive in and take over caregiving duties when they are needed. (Though, like penguins, we may sometimes feel as if we spend an awfully long time in the cold and dark before the reinforcements show up.)

Our strategy of extended immaturity may even have extended our life span. Human females have both a longer period of childhood before they become fertile, and an unprecedented ability to survive after fertility is over. We live longer than chimps do, and historically, *Homo sapiens* seems to have lived longer than other hominids. There may have been a coevolutionary double whammy. A small change in the human developmental timetable gave us babies with a longer time to learn, and grandmothers, and even sweet old ladies in general, to help take care of them.

Understanding love, and extending it to children, isn't just a parochial concern of parents, but a much wider part of what it means to be human. Of course, the human capacity for change makes it hard to know which aspects of our beliefs and emotions are built in and which are the results of learning and imagination. We humans can actually figure out that babysitting is a really good idea even if it isn't in our genes. But even at the most basic evolutionary level, we humans seem to care about children in a particularly wide-ranging and general way.

That care reflects a deep truth about us. For human beings children serve a much broader function than just reproducing their parents' genes. Having children also lets us accumulate knowledge, adjust to new environments, and create our own environments. Those capacities benefit everybody in the human community.

LIFE'S WEATHER

So there are at least two important ways that early experience can influence later life. As we saw in the last chapter, a child's early experiences can lead to a cascade of causal interactions that result in an adult with a particular character. And, as we saw in this chapter, those early experiences can lead to a cascade of successive theories that result in an adult with a particular view of the world. None of these relations are deterministic.

Scientists are starting to untangle some of these complicated interactions. We are starting to learn some of the principles that govern these causal cascades. However, it is extremely unlikely that scientific knowledge will ever allow us to predict how a particular parent's actions will influence a particular child's life twenty years later—which is, of course, the question all those parents want answered.

Songwriters have always compared life and the weather (all those blue skies and April showers). This analogy may capture the way that childhood influences later life, as opposed to the way we think it does when we obsessively consult the parenting books. We can't tell for sure whether a particular storm like Hurricane Katrina was caused by carbon dioxide emissions. We can't predict whether or not another hurricane will hit New Orleans this year.

But, by analyzing the complex statistical relationships between emissions and weather patterns, we can discover that those emissions do affect the weather. The same kind of analysis tells us that early experiences do affect later life. We can predict that legislating for enriched preschools will lead to fewer crimes, just as we can predict that legislating for controls on carbon dioxide emissions will lead to fewer hurricanes.

But for each individual day in each individual place the weather remains the stuff of narrative and autobiography. The great diarists, Virginia Woolf or Sir Walter Scott or everyday journal keepers, begin by tracking the particularities of sun and cloud, rain and wind. And our children's real individual lives are much more like that kind of unique, irreplaceable narrative than like solutions to some general equation, or the application of some formula for happiness and success.

THE CHILD INSIDE

There is also another, more philosophical way of thinking about the relation between early experience and later life. I described the way that both young children and adults unify their changing lives. From the time we are four or five we think that we have a single, constant, unchanging identity. No matter how much I change, if I go from rags to riches, from radical to conservative, from libertine to prude and back again, I still think that all those changes happened to *me*. That past history is an essential part of who I am. Without that history I would no longer be myself.

It's interesting that even severe brain injuries can't disrupt this sense of identity. Brain damage can make it impossible to form new memories, and it can make people forget what happened just before they were injured, but brain damage never makes people forget their whole former life. In Alzheimer's disease distant memories may be the only thing left, even when the current person seems to have faded away almost completely. The absolute past amnesia of soap operas and melodramas is a myth. Ronald Colman could get knocked on the head and forget who he is only in a movie like *Random Harvest*.

In fact, the only time people show symptoms of this kind of soap-opera amnesia is when they are intentionally trying to escape from themselves. Sometimes people appear to lose their memory when they are terribly unhappy and are fleeing from their current life. The detective-novel writer Agatha Christie once turned up in a hotel room claiming, apparently sincerely, not to know who she was. The mystery was simple: she had just discovered that her beloved husband had been unfaithful. Agatha Christie didn't have brain damage—instead, she no longer wanted to be herself.

The experience of autobiographical memory obviously plays a role in this sense of a continuous identity. But as we saw, autobiographical memory is often inaccurate and is always constructed. In fact, we experience autobiographical memory because we have a unified sense of identity rather than the other way around.

Our relation to our past goes beyond autobiographical memory; there is something deeper and more metaphysical about it. Take the premise of the great Philip K. Dick story "We Can Remember It for You Wholesale," on which the movie *Total Recall* was based. An entrepreneur offers to implant detailed happy memories in your brain—a trip to Paris, a blissful love affair, a triumphant adventure—and also, of course, to erase any memory of the operation itself. Outside of science fiction such a business would go broke. We don't just want to have the memory of Paris; at some deeper level, we want to have that memory because we actually were in Paris. We need our past to be real.

Or consider the similar premise of *Eternal Sunshine of the Spotless Mind*, in which a similarly creepy entrepreneur offers to erase the memory of unhappy love affairs. That business would go broke too. Few of us would want to erase the knowledge of even the most unhappy events in our past, though we might try to blunt the vividness of those memories. The truth and reconciliation tribunals in places such as South Africa are a collective version of the same philosophical truth. Acknowledging the truth about the past, good or bad, individually or collectively, is deeply important to us, even when it will have no immediate effect on the present.

From an evolutionary point of view our investment in the past is rather puzzling, just as our investment in backwards counterfactuals is puzzling. Why do we care about the past so much when we can't change it? The answer may be the same in both cases. Owning our past is so important because it allows us to own our future. In order to plan and act, to envision alternate futures and to intervene to realize them, I need to care deeply about the fate of my future self.

This is true even when, perhaps especially when, that future self will be significantly different from my current self. The four-year-old wants the self of ten minutes from now to get both cookies, and he wants the self of tomorrow's trip to the beach to bring his sunglasses. The teenager wants her future self to be able to leave home, or to have children, even though she very definitely does not want to leave home or have children now. When teenagers feel they have no future selves, they seem strongly inclined to destroy their current ones. Even as a fifty-year-old I want my future self to have enough retirement money to live well, and I want her to be able to give up teaching, even though I wouldn't want to give up teaching now. Most tellingly, if my future self has changed so profoundly that she no longer has a life worth living, I want her to be able to end that life. My current self may make substantial sacrifices for the sake of the future self.

But since my future is always turning into my past, this commitment to my entire history goes both ways. The same psychological devices that dictate the importance of the future also dictate the importance of the past. In fact, there is even good neurological evidence for this link between our autobiographical memories and our capacity to imagine the future. The same brain regions light up when we reconstruct the past and project the future.

Whatever its evolutionary or neurological origins may be, this commitment to the past has a deep influence on our current lives. In this way childhood really does determine our adult life, not just in terms of complex causal interactions or sequences of probabilities, but in a strict and literal sense.

My memory and knowledge of my childhood is a part of my knowledge of myself. That memory and knowledge may be painful. The happy prewar childhood idyll may only make the darkness that followed more bleak. Memories of an abusive alcoholic mother may still haunt the successful, loving husband and father. But being without those memories would mean being a different person.

The significance of the past takes on a special moral depth and poignancy when it comes to childhood memories. We have some control over our adult experiences. We consider counterfactual possibilities, and we take freely willed actions to realize those possibilities, and those actions lead to the immutable events of our past. We look back on those events with pride or guilt, satisfaction or regret, because we know that we were the ones in charge.

Children have far less control over what happens to them. Parents and other caregivers are far more responsible for what actually happens to children than children are themselves. Of course, this is a good thing. It frees children to explore in the playful and unconstrained way that is so important for knowledge and imagination. But it also means that caregivers have a unique kind of responsibility for their children's childhood.

I can't determine what will happen to my son when he grows up. I can't tell whether he will get to go to Berkeley, or whether he will have a good wife. But I can determine what will happen to him when he is a child. I can determine that he will get to go to a leafy playground and a preschool full of sandboxes and pet fish and toys. I can determine that he will have a picnic by the beach and hot chocolate in front of the fire. And, at least to some extent, I can determine that he will have a good mother (though this is tougher than the picnics and hot chocolate).

We can control one very important aspect of our children's adult lives. We can determine whether they grow up to be adults who remember leafy playgrounds and picnics and affectionate parents. We can't ensure that our children will have a happy future— there, all we can do is move the odds around. But we can at least try to ensure that they will have a happy past.

This applies to the collective we, as well as the individual I. Of course, there are many mothers and fathers, at least 20 percent according to the latest numbers, who have so few resources they can't ensure that their children have any of these things, no matter how much they may want to. We have a collective responsibility to give these children, who are just as helpless as any other human children, a happy past as well.

When policy makers make arguments for early intervention, for universal high-quality preschool and medical care, or for programs such as Head Start and the Abecedarian Project, they think in terms of the direct causal effects of early experience on later life. And, indeed, when I talk about these programs to journalists and policy makers I bring out the statistics about changing the odds, about increased worker productivity and decreased prison bills. Like everyone else I use the language of current investment and future returns, of children as a present means to a future end.

But surely there is something a little crazy about thinking that children should be healthy so that adults will be more productive, or that children should be happy so that adults will be less violent. You would think that if there is anything in the world that we can all agree is an unequivocal good, a moral absolute, an end in itself, it is the happiness and health of children. You would think everyone would agree that a sick, or miserable, or abused child is an unequivocal evil if anything is.

And let's suppose we are thinking about the kinds of adults we would like to bring into the world. Surely it is as important to have adults who go through life with the ineradicable gift of a happy childhood as it is to have adults who are a little smarter or richer or less neurotic.

Parents often feel a kind of existential anxiety as they watch their children grow up—as we say, it goes by so fast. We watch that infinitely flexible, contingent, malleable future swiftly harden into the irretrievable, unchangeable past. Japanese poets have a phrase, *mono no aware*, for the bittersweetness inherent in ephemeral beauty—a falling blossom or a leaf in the wind. Children are a great source of *mono no aware*.

But there is another side to the ephemerality of childhood. There is a kind of immunity about a happy childhood, not an immunity from the disasters and catastrophes that may, that almost certainly do, lie ahead, but an intrinsic immunity. Change and transience are at the heart of the human condition. But as parents we can at least give our children a happy childhood, a gift that is as certain, as unchanging, as rock solid, as any human good.

8.

Love and Law

THE ORIGINS OF MORALITY

*

Empirical science can help answer many philosophical questions. However, moral questions look like an exception. Moral questions are about the way the world should be and what we ought to do. Scientific questions are about the way the world actually is and what we really do do. And it might seem especially unlikely that scientific studies of young children could answer moral questions.

In fact, until recently, the idea that young children can tell us anything at all about morality would have seemed crazy to most philosophers and psychologists. Surely, babies are quintessentially amoral creatures. The developmental psychologists Jean Piaget and Lawrence Kohlberg argued that even older children didn't understand morality, that truly moral ideas develop only in adolescence. Until then children's conceptions of good and bad, wrong and right, are just a matter of rewards, punishments, and social conventions. What your parents tell you to do is right, what you are punished for is wrong. In fact, Kohlberg thought that only some adults reached the stage of genuinely moral reasoning.

In the past few years, some psychologists have suggested that, on the contrary, morality is innate. This picture of morality is like Chomsky's picture of language. Back in the Pleistocene, universal moral intuitions evolved, and those intuitions constrain our moral thinking throughout our lives. There is a sort of universal moral grammar, despite superficial cultural differences, just as there is supposed to be a universal grammar that underlies superficially different languages. We might see signs of these moral intuitions even in young children.

Still others argue for a different version of this innatist picture. They say that morality comes from what we feel rather than what we know. Morality is rooted in innate, hardwired emotional responses that are only slightly modified by self-conscious adult reasoning. Like Chomsky's view of language, these views don't have much room for changes in moral thinking or for the moral discovery and growth that is so characteristically human.

New developmental research shows that children do have something to tell us about morality, but what they tell us is different from either the Piagetian or the Chomskyan story. We've seen that children's knowledge does have an innate basis, but children also have powerful abilities to learn about the world and transform it and themselves. We've seen that understanding the world and imagining how it could change go hand in hand.

The new research shows that children have some of the foundations of morality from the time they're very young, even from the time they're born. But these foundations aren't just an innate, unchanging "moral grammar" or a hardwired set of emotional reactions. Instead, children's moral thinking, and so our own, changes as we learn more about the world and ourselves. Just as children are born with theories about the world, but also with powerful capacities for changing those theories, they seem to be born with certain fundamental moral ideas, but also with powerful capacities to change their moral judgments and actions.

Morality depends on some basic underlying ideas about other people and ourselves. The "golden rule"—"do unto others as you would have others do unto you," or "love your neighbor as yourself"—assumes that you can take the perspective of others. Blame and responsibility depend on distinguishing between intentional and accidental actions, as in the legal doctrine of mens rea. The legal system also assumes that there are rules that we are morally obligated to follow. Piaget thought that children didn't have genuine moral knowledge because he thought that they couldn't take the perspective of others, infer intentions, and follow abstract rules.

Modern science shows that this just isn't true. Literally from the time they're born children are empathic. They identify with other people and recognize that their own feelings are shared by others. In fact, they literally take on the feelings of others. One-year-olds understand the difference between intentional and unintentional actions, and behave in genuinely altruistic ways. Three-year-olds have already developed a basic ethic of care and compassion.

At the same time, three-year-olds also understand rules and try to follow them. Understanding and using rules lets us go beyond our innate empathic instincts. But those empathic reactions also allow us to modify the rules we follow. Empathy and rule following, love and law, combine to give us our distinctively human morality.

Studying young children can help explain why we usually treat one another so well. But studying children can also explain why we often treat one another so badly. Looking at young children can help illuminate our moral failures and vulnerabilities as well as our successes. When they are still very young, children show some of the same impulses to anger and revenge that adults do, they start to divide people into social groups and to prefer their own group to others, and they accept even absurd and arbitrary rules.

IMITATION AND EMPATHY

Newborns imitate facial expressions. At first, this might seem interesting but not very important. We don't usually think of imitation as a powerful and deep cognitive capacity. Instead, we think it's a more superficial matter of mere mimicry. But in fact, early imitation points to a deeper, innate empathic link between babies and other people.

Newborns have never seen their own faces. To imitate facial expressions in particular, newborns must somehow map expressions to feelings. They have to link the way it looks when that pink thing comes in and out of the face of another person and the way it feels inside them when they stick out their own tongues. Somehow newborns know that their tongue feeling is like Mom's tongue action. Babies are born knowing that particular facial expressions reflect particular kinesthetic feelings.

In particular, facial expressions also reflect emotions. From Boston to Borneo, happiness leads to a particular constellation of upturned lip corners and crinkled eyes while anger causes bared teeth and furrowed brows. Babies imitate emotional expressions as well as simple gestures like sticking out your tongue. If babies automatically link facial expressions to the internal feelings that accompany them, they should link expressions to emotions.

Moreover, just making an emotional facial expression can itself lead you to feel the accompanying emotion. Smiling really does make you feel happy. So imitation can act as a kind of tutorial on emotion. I see someone smile, so I smile myself. Then I feel happy inside and I assume that they do too. This means that for babies imitation is both a symptom of innate empathy and a tool to extend and elaborate that empathy. Young babies know that Mom's joy or pain is the same as their own joy or pain. And they can also learn that their pride is like Mom's pride, or that their disgust mirrors hers.

As babies learn more about how minds work they automatically extend those discoveries both to themselves and to others. They assume that their own minds work the way that other people's do and vice versa. One-year-olds go beyond just emotion. As we saw earlier, they start to understand desires and intentions. They will imitate what other people want as well as what they feel. If the experimenter wants to bang his head on the box to make it light up, well, weird as it seems, so do they. Eighteen-month-olds will even imitate an unfulfilled goal. If they see you unsuccessfully try to pull apart a tube they will try to pull the tube apart themselves. They understand that the desires and goals of others are like their own desires and goals. By two or three, children have an explicit theory of mind that says that other people work the same way they do—that they're happy when they get what they want, for example, and sad when they don't.

Empathy requires that you recognize the similarity between the feelings of others and your own feelings, but it also requires that you take on those feelings as your own. When you imitate an emotional expression or an action or an intention you make that feeling or action or intention your own—you act as if you were experiencing that mental state rather than just observing it. When children see another person express sadness, or make the box light up, or try to pull apart the tube, they themselves will act and feel sad, make the box light up, or try to pull the tube apart.

Some neuroscientists, and many popular-science writers, have suggested that empathy, and other human abilities from altruism to art to language, are rooted in particular kinds of neurons—the so-called mirror neurons. These are cells that fire both when an animal performs an action itself and when it sees another animal perform that action. This is almost certainly not true. For one thing, mirror neurons have been studied in monkeys—who don't actually imitate what other monkeys do. So the ubiquitous and powerful imitation we see in human babies can't just be there because they have mirror neurons. For another, mirror neurons in monkeys are probably the result rather than the cause of actions. When a monkey moves his own hand, he will also see that hand move. So over time the feeling of moving a hand will be associated with seeing a hand move, and we know that these associations are reflected in the ways that neurons fire. Third, we really do know how some areas of the brain allow us to do things like detect shapes. And even the simplest abilities are the result of complex interactions among hundreds of different kinds of neurons. Something in the brain allows babies to imitate, but it isn't just that they have mirror neurons.

Wherever empathy comes from neurologically, you can imagine how it might motivate moral behavior. If witnessing another person's pain literally feels painful to a baby, he might act to try to alleviate that pain as he would act to alleviate his own misery. If witnessing joy makes him joyful, he might try to bring about that joy in others. This might seem like a rather selfish though effective basis for altruism—I ease another's pain because it makes me feel better.

But there is another way that empathy might motivate altruism. It's possible that babies literally don't see a difference between their own pain and the pain of others. Maybe babies want to end all suffering, no matter where it happens to be located. For them, pain is pain and joy is joy. Moral thinkers from Buddha to David Hume to Martin Buber have suggested that erasing the boundaries between yourself and others in this way can underpin morality. We know that children's conception of a continuous separate self develops slowly in the first five years.

Of course, as adults, parents do have a strong separate sense of self—a sense that usually distances us from others. But that sense dissolves in our interactions with babies. Parents are on the other side of those intimate early face-to-face interactions. And it sure doesn't feel as if we react to our baby's pain simply because we want to feel better ourselves. Instead, the pain just pulls on our heartstrings directly. I literally feel my baby's pain with as much intensity as I feel my own pain. The impulse to soothe my baby is just as automatic and immediate as my impulse to soothe myself. The immediate, intimate, loving interactions between babies and adults dissolve the boundaries between the self and others. It may feel that way for the babies, too.

Empathy is intertwined with attachment. It emerges first in intimate face-to-face interactions between babies and the people they love. There is a special moral intensity to the love between parents and children. Just deciding to care for this one particular, special, individual child automatically makes that child the focus of our deepest moral concern. Parents routinely sacrifice their sleep, their time, their happiness, even their lives for their children. And attachment research shows that babies develop a deep connection to a few particular, special, beloved caregivers.

My immediate, deep, selfless, uncalculating care for this particular baby, and the baby's love and care for me, are rooted in evolutionary imperatives. The helpless baby depends on the unconditional love of her close kin for her very survival. But no matter where it comes from, this intimate care is a model for moral concern at its most profound. It is no coincidence that so many of the great moral teachers talk about love.

ANGER AND VENGEANCE

Sometimes imitation and empathy can make us behave badly instead of well. Joy inspires joy and sadness leads to sadness, but seeing anger can also make us angry. If mutual joy is a natural route to benevolence, the cycle of anger upon anger is a natural route to violence. Most of the aggression we see in young children is this sort of "reactive aggression"—aggression, anger, and even violence that are a response to a threat from someone else.

In fact, aggressive children are particularly quick to perceive anger in others. Say one child bumps into another child on a crowded playground. The typical child thinks it was just an accident, but the reactively aggressive child is much more likely to think that the other child was intentionally trying to hurt him. These children assume that other people are angry and threatening and react with anger and threat of their own. From the child's perspective he's not being a mean kid, he's just reacting to all those other mean kids.

Vicious cycles of social interaction can quickly develop. The early empathic reactions that respond to anger with anger can be reinforced by our developing theories. Other studies show that school-age children make judgments about whether another child is mean extremely quickly, within minutes. They are more likely to treat these children badly themselves. This, of course, confirms the aggressive child's theory that everybody treats him badly, and makes him act more aggressively and so forth. In childhood, people can't do each other much real physical harm, but by adolescence this cycle of reactive aggression, combined with physical maturity, roiling hormones, unfinished frontal lobes, and easily available weapons, can lead to the self-destructive violence that plagues American high schools.

It is not a large leap from these playground tragedies to the intractable patterns of grievance and revenge that we see in the Balkans or the Middle East. If emotional imitation underpins some of our best impulses it may also underpin some of our worst failings.

BEYOND EMPATHY

Empathy grounds morality, but morality goes beyond empathy. After all, crying yourself when someone else is hurt doesn't actually help them any—sheer empathy can just be morally self-indulgent. The real secret of altruism is to try to allay the pain of others even when you don't feel it yourself. We saw earlier that fourteen-month-olds empathically assume that you'll like the same things they like—given a choice between broccoli and crackers they'll always give you the crackers. Eighteen-month-olds realize that you might feel differently or want something different from what they want—they give you broccoli if you like broccoli and crackers if you like crackers. These older children know that you may *not* want the same thing they do.

But once these children understood what someone else wanted, they took it for granted that they should try to help them get it. As soon as they could interpret the expressions of the other person they spontaneously handed them the food they liked. Now the golden rule operates at a higher level. Just as I try to get what I want, I will try to help you get what you want, even if you want something as peculiar as broccoli.

Other studies also show that these young children are genuinely altruistic. In one striking recent series of studies Felix Warneken showed that even fourteen-month-olds will try hard to help someone else. If they see an experimenter straining for a pen that is out of reach, for example, they will obligingly help him to get it. In fact, they'll toddle all the way across the room and clamber over a couple of cushions to get there to help. They will not only get upset when they see someone in pain, they will also try to help, petting and kissing and trying to make it better. When I once came home and burst into tears over the stress of work, my two-year-old ran to get a box of Band-Aids. It's immensely touching to suddenly realize that the baby you love and care for so deeply wants to take care of you, too.

These older babies can use their capacities for causal and counterfactual reasoning to make other people happy. The eighteen-month-old in our experiment understands that, for you, broccoli leads to happiness and Goldfish crackers lead to disgust. So if he wants to make you happy, he'd better go with the broccoli. He knows that if you reach for the pen you must want it, and he knows that to get you the pen, he'll have to get across those cushions and all the way over to the other side of the room. He even knows that Band-Aids make you feel better and that they're over there in the bathroom. Two-year-olds can imagine what to do to give other people pleasure or to soothe their pain.

Such children not only act in a genuinely moral way, they also make genuinely moral judgments. In a groundbreaking study, Judith Smetana presented children as young as two and a half with simple, everyday scenarios. In some of the stories children broke a preschool rule—they didn't put their clothes in the cubby or they talked at naptime. In others, they caused real physical or psychological harm to another child, by hitting, teasing, or stealing a snack. Smetana asked the children how bad the transgressions were, and whether they deserved punishment. But, most important, she asked whether the actions would be OK if the rules were different or if they took place in a school with different rules. Would it be OK to talk at naptime if the teachers all said so? Would it be OK to hit another child if the teachers all said so?

Even the youngest children differentiated between rules and harm. Children thought that breaking rules and causing harm were both bad, but that causing harm was a lot worse. They also said that the rules could be changed or might not apply at a different school, but they insisted that causing harm would always be wrong, no matter what the rules said or where you were.

Children made similar judgments about actual incidents that had happened in the preschool, not just hypothetical cases. And when you looked at the natural interactions in the playground you saw much the same pattern. Children reacted differently to harm and rulebreaking. Children in the Virgin Islands, South Korea, and Colombia behaved like American children. Poignantly, even abused children thought that hurting someone was intrinsically wrong. These children had seen their own parents cause harm, but they knew how much it hurt, and thought it was wrong.

Although these results are startling, they're consistent with the early development of both empathy and altruism. Eighteen-month-olds are both empathic and altruistic—they feel the pain of others and they try to ameliorate it. So it's easy for them to judge that hurting someone is always and necessarily wrong.

PSYCHOPATHS

There is one group of people, however, who don't distinguish between breaking rules and causing harm. They also don't have immediate empathic reactions to others. They are psychopaths. The neuroscientist James Blair studied people who were imprisoned in maximum-security prisons for horrific crimes. He has the most chilling methods section I've ever read. Even among these murderers and rapists there were important differences. Some criminals acted impulsively, in reaction to passions and temptations. Another group, the psychopaths, felt no remorse about their crimes at all. They were often superficially charming and articulate and they were good at manipulating other people, but they just didn't understand that other people were worth caring about.

Blair discovered that both psychopathic adults and children with psychopathic tendencies behaved very differently than typical preschoolers. They were unperturbed by facial expressions of fear and sadness—expressions that are deeply disturbing even to young children. In fact, the psychopaths even had difficulty recognizing those expressions, though they had little difficulty with expressions of anger and disgust.

Even their brain responses were different. When most people see facial expressions of fear and sadness, the expressions that indicate harm, a particular part of the brain called the amygdala is activated. The amygdala didn't respond in the same way in the psychopaths. And the children with psychopathic tendencies didn't just show the reactive aggression that we see in typical children. They didn't just lash out when they felt threatened. They would also cold-bloodedly use violence as a way of getting what they wanted. A child with psychopathic tendencies might threaten to kill the family pet if he wasn't allowed to watch TV.

Most striking, though, the fully adult and intelligent psychopaths didn't understand the difference between harm and rule-breaking. When you gave them problems like the ones that Smetana gave the children, they didn't think that hitting someone was any worse than breaking an arbitrary rule. Their reaction to these moral questions was not only unlike that of typical adults, even typical criminals, but was also unlike that of typical three-year-olds.

Even young babies emotionally identify with other people, but psychopaths apparently don't. It's not that they can't understand other people. They do just as well at "theory of mind" tasks such as predicting the desires or beliefs of others. Indeed, this sort of knowledge often helps them to be particularly effective manipulators. Instead they simply don't take on the fear or sadness of others and treat it like their own fear or sadness.

Psychopaths really do seem to be amoral, but babies aren't. Tiny babies recognize that their fear and sadness is your fear and sadness and that their joy is your joy. Even more profoundly, very young children feel that they should alleviate the fear and sadness of others, and help them get what they want. They use their causal understanding of the world and other people to do this effectively. And finally, and most profoundly of all, children treat this feeling as intrinsically moral. No matter what, it's never OK to hurt someone else. This kind of moral understanding inextricably mingles judgment and feeling, reason and emotion.

TROLLEYOLOGY

This early core moral understanding provides a foundation for both of the great ethical theories in philosophy. There is a classic philosophical distinction between "utilitarian" and "deontological" ethics. Utilitarians, like Jeremy Bentham or John Stuart Mill, say that the basic moral principle is to obtain the greatest good for the greatest number of people, whatever that takes. Deontologists, like Immanuel Kant, say that certain acts are right or wrong intrinsically, regardless of their consequences.

The "trolley problem" is a classic example of the contrast between these views. You see a trolley about to head toward a barrier—if it crashes, all five people on board will die. You can turn a switch that will put the trolley on another track, where it will run over one person, but save the rest. What should you do? Most people say you should pull the switch—the utilitarian answer. Now suppose you give people a different version of the problem. You notice that a large man is standing on the footbridge over the track. If you push him off the footbridge onto the track you will stop the trolley and save the passengers (he's large enough to stop the trolley though you aren't—you couldn't save anyone by jumping off the bridge yourself). What should you do? Here people seem to have the Kantian intuition. It's just wrong to push a stranger off the bridge to his death, no matter what.

There is a classic debate between these two views in philosophy. And there is an enormous body of work on these problems both in philosophy and psychology and even neuroscience—sometimes it's called "trolleyology." Ordinary people, unlike philosophers, seem to want to have it both ways—sometimes they act like utilitarians and sometimes like deontologists. And the factors that push them in one direction or the other can be quite subtle—as in the trolley problem.

From the perspective of childhood, though, the similarity between the two views is more striking than the differences. Our instinctive deontological reaction that harming another person is just wrong is rooted in early empathy. But the baby's basic identification with others also underpins the utilitarian response. After all, why should we care about the good of others at all? Why worry about the five lives on the trolley? Even the "rational" utilitarian is rooted in an emotional identification with other people. The utilitarian wants to make other people happy just as much as the deontologist does. The utilitarian slogan of "the greatest good for the greatest number" and the deontological slogan of "do no harm" are two sides of the same coin. Both are elaborations on the golden rule. This fundamental moral attitude is in place even in the youngest children.

NOT LIKE ME

Empathy is rooted in intimacy, but genuine moral reasoning requires us to go beyond these intuitive and immediate responses to those we love. Early empathy depends on close personal contact—the kind of contact that lets us actually see the grief or joy on someone's face. It's part of the intense intimacy of caregivers and babies—as close and profound an intimacy as we humans ever feel. However, human beings can't even keep track of more than about 150 people, let alone love them all. Moral decisions, decisions about global warming, for example, may involve the welfare of millions of people thousands of miles away. So simply relying on immediate emotion isn't going to work. Somehow we need to extend that emotion to people we aren't close enough to see and touch. We need to care about people we don't even know.

Counterfactual and hypothetical thinking can help children care about strangers. After all, the children in Smetana's studies were no longer reacting to real emotions, like the infants. Nevertheless, like little utilitarians, they could extend their moral concern to those hypothetical children in hypothetical schoolyards.

Another way to extend empathy is to define a category of persons, beings worthy of moral concern. Recall that babies *don't* imitate an action performed by a mere machine—they don't ascribe intentions to a pair of pincers, or try to help the pincers to fulfill their goals—but they will imitate when the machine shows other signs of personhood, even if they are rather odd. They will imitate a strange brown blob if it beeps back at them consistently when they talk to it, and they will treat that strange being as if it's human in other ways, too.

When I was a visitor at the California Institute of Technology I met some of the scientists at Sony who were inventing human-like robots. The machines looked like typical robots, all metal and wiring, but they beeped at you when you talked to them, like the responsive brown blobs in the imitation experiments. The Sony engineers had placed one of these robots in a preschool classroom for several months and videotaped what had happened. When the preschoolers saw the robot tip over and fall, which it often did, they treated it like another child. They carefully picked the robot up, brushed it off, and even kissed it to make it feel better.

There is a great deal of research showing that babies already differentiate people, even strange brown blob people or electronic robotic people, from other objects. By creating a general, identifiable category of "persons" children can generalize the empathy they feel toward Mom or Dad to a much greater range of beings. They imitate the robot or the blob, taking on its desires and intentions in the same way that they take on the desires and intentions of other people. And, at least anecdotally, they also show concern and altruism for the robot. You should care about the strange child or the blob or the robot even if you aren't intimate with them.

So we extend moral concern to people we decide are like us. But this has a darker side. We can refuse to put someone in the "person" category too. Human beings also deny moral concern to people that they decide are not like them. They can treat a mere machine like a person but they can also treat a person like a mere machine. The most disturbing evidence for this human tendency to dehumanize comes from social psychology studies of "minimal groups." When you divide people into arbitrary groups the "in-group" will start to dehumanize and dislike the "out-group." Give a bunch of undergraduates red feathers and blue feathers to wear, and very quickly the red feathers will start to prefer the company of other red feathers, and decide that the blue feathers just aren't their type. You don't need a long history of conflict or oppression to hate another group. Just giving them a different name is enough. And indeed some of the most notorious examples of intimate cruelty, of people willing to slaughter their close neighbors, involve divisions that are just about as arbitrary as red feather and blue feather—Hutu and Tutsi, Catholic and Protestant, Serb and Croat.

The most chilling example of this is the famous Stanford Prison Experiment. Philip Zimbardo, an ambitious young social psychologist, set up an experiment in which perfectly normal Stanford undergraduates were arbitrarily assigned the role of prisoners or guards. Within a staggeringly brief time the guards were brutally persecuting the prisoners. Zimbardo's girlfriend at the time, Christina Maslach, is a professor in my department at Berkeley. She says that when she looked at the films of the experiment she was horrified by just how terribly the "guards" behaved. She insisted that Zimbardo stop the experiment, and he immediately realized that he had to end it. (Then she married him, and they are still together forty years later.)

Very young children already classify their fellow human beings into groups. By the time they are three, and quite possibly even in infancy, children recognize that people can be divided into different races, genders, and even language groups. And these young children already show preferences, both explicit and implicit, for the people they think are most like them. They do this even when adults insist that it's wrong to treat African Americans or girls or Spanish-speakers (or white people or boys or Anglos) differently.

A couple of recent experiments suggest that this may even be true for completely arbitrary groups—the three-year-old equivalent of the red feathers and blue feathers. Three-year-olds said they would prefer to play with a child who had the same color of hair and the same color of T-shirt that they did, rather than one with a different color of shirt. In another experiment, the experimenter would arbitrarily put a red T-shirt or a blue T-shirt on a particular child. Then the child saw pictures of other children in red or blue T-shirts. The children characteristically said that the kids with their own color of T-shirt were nicer, and that they'd prefer to play with them.

Children already seem to be sensitive to signals, like different ways of looking or dressing, talking or acting, that might signal that someone is a member of another group. Ironically, a small difference, a different T-shirt, accent, or skin color, may weigh more heavily than a large difference like being a robot. But this is consistent with our adult behavior, too—small differences in religion or race may be more significant than large ones.

Classifying other people into groups gives us a way of deciding how to extend our empathy. People who are like me, in this more abstract sense, as well as the more immediate intimate sense, are the subjects of moral concern. I can extend my concern to a robot, but I can also withdraw it from those awful blue T-shirt guys.

WIDENING THE CIRCLE

Is it wrong to feel more moral concern for people who are more like you? Cases such as the Hutu genocide may make you think so. The classic philosophical traditions, both utilitarian and deontological, insist that moral concern should be universal. For the utilitarian, the good of the greatest number includes everyone. For the deontologist, it is wrong to intentionally harm anyone, even a stranger.

But other philosophers point out the particularity of our moral life. After all, we do feel that we have a particularly strong responsibility to keep our own children or parents from harm and to promote their happiness. I might feel obligated to give up a kidney for my sick brother but not for a stranger. We disapprove of people who are moral reformers but treat their own families badly, and we extend this sense of particular concern to communities or nations. You could argue, at least, that I have a special obligation to pay taxes to support my fellow Americans or Californians or Berkeley-ans. Sometimes this impulse to differentiate between intimates—my people—and strangers seems right.

Still, historically, most moral advances widen the circle of our moral concern. Within the United States the legal system has gradually evolved to give full moral status to women, African Americans, and most recently gays and lesbians. Internationally, the human rights movement attempts to widen the legal circle to everyone in the world. The animal rights movement is on the current cutting edge of this widening of concern, arguing that moral status should be extended beyond human beings themselves.

The great moral teachers try to widen the sphere of concern by invoking the emotions of intimacy. In Buddhist *metta* meditation you begin by practicing compassion and sympathy for someone you love, then extend it to someone you don't know, and finally imagine feeling it for someone who is your enemy. In the Bible, the injunction to "love thy neighbor" is followed by the more difficult "love the stranger" and finally the even more difficult "love thy enemy as thyself"—one of Christ's most emphatic injunctions. Caring about our children or parents is practically automatic, caring about our neighbors is a little harder, caring about strangers is even more difficult, and caring about those guys in the blue T-shirts is the hardest of all.

FOLLOWING THE RULES

Some philosophers think that morality is a matter of judgment—beliefs about what is good or bad. Others think that morality is about emotion—sentiments of indignation, guilt, and disgust, or pride, admiration, and awe. The altruism we see in babies does have a strong emotional element. But another way of looking at it is that morality is first and foremost about what we should do. Morality is about choices.

For human beings, including young children, understanding the world is inextricably connected to changing it. Our theories let us think about all the possible ways that the world might be. That's true whether we're thinking about the physical world or the psychological world—whether we're changing the world or other people or even ourselves.

If knowledge is linked to change then we need to ask which changes we should make. Counterfactual thinking inevitably leads to choices—deciding to do one thing rather than others, realize some worlds rather than others, become one type of person rather than another. Once you can think counterfactually, even doing nothing becomes a choice—you choose to forgo that other world you could create if you were just a little less lazy. And as soon as we make choices, deciding that some options are better or worse than others, we are getting close to moral reasoning. We are deciding what we ought to do. Philosophers call it "normative" reasoning.

Moral reasoning is normative, but other kinds of reasoning are normative too. The "oughts" of life may range from grave moral duties ("I ought to sacrifice myself for my child") to simple practical rationality ("I ought to choose the credit card with the lowest interest rate"), to mere etiquette ("I ought to put the forks on the left"). Causal thinking lets us know what will happen if we do one thing rather than another; normative thinking tells us which of those things we ought to do.

Normative reasoning depends on rules. Making choices is hard—it means weighing all the complex information about what we want and what might happen and then making a single decision. Following rules makes that decision-making process much easier. It also lets me coordinate my decisions right now with my past and future decisions. Instead of calculating each time whether the benefit of doing my exercises outweighs the pleasure of Web surfing on the couch, I have a rule—it's yoga every Monday, Wednesday, and Friday, and I don't get dressed until I'm done.

Rules also let us coordinate our own decisions with the decisions of other people. When all of us follow the same rule, I can predict how you will make choices and coordinate your choices with mine. At Berkeley, we have a rule that each faculty member must teach one big undergraduate course. This ensures that the courses get taught and the load is shared evenly, without a complicated power struggle each September.

Rules have other advantages. Often, it doesn't really matter what we do as long as we all do the same thing. It doesn't matter whether we drive on the left or the right or use red for stop or for go. But whatever we decide on, we need to make sure that everybody else makes the same decision. Rules allow for this sort of coordination too.

We might think that we follow rules because we are punished for breaking them or because we engage in a rational analysis that tells us that the rules will benefit us. But our impulse to follow rules runs much more deeply. It seems to be an innate part of our human nature. In fact, many rules don't involve explicit punishments or rewards, and many rules are at least superficially arbitrary and irrational. They are about how we do things here and now, in this particular place and time—forks on the left, cars on the right, jeans only on Friday. And yet we instinctively follow these rules. Even in Berkeley, I'd never eat with my hands at the chancellor's lunch or lecture in my nightgown, and I'd be shocked if anyone else did.

Rules are a particularly powerful way to extend our immediate emotional moral reactions. Our moral intuitions may tell us that hitting someone is wrong, and helping them is right—even very young babies seem to appreciate that. But what about all the more complex and subtle harms and goods that shape our lives, especially collective harms and goods? The events that lead to harm or good are usually much more complex than just the simple causal route from a fist to a jaw. How do we prevent the harm of global warming? How do we ensure the good of prenatal health care? Solving problems like these doesn't just depend on a single person acting but on dozens or hundreds or even millions of people acting in a coordinated way. The human ability to coordinate actions for the good of the larger group is one of our greatest evolutionary advantages. This ability depends on the distinctively human tendency to make and follow rules.

BABY RULES

Imitation studies show that babies implicitly adopt normative rules. Eighteen-month-olds will "over-imitate." Say a baby sees an adult make a machine go by acting in an unnecessarily convoluted way, turning around three times and moving the button twice before pressing a lever. The baby would imitate all his particular

wiggles and bells and whistles. Chimpanzees are more rational—
they solve the problem in the most efficient way, by going straight
for the lever, not the complicated way that the demonstrator
solved it. This particularly human impulse to imitate is a foundation for rule-following. You turn around three times and move the
button just because that is the way we do things around here.

By age three, children understand rules more explicitly and
they are surprisingly sophisticated. The Smetana studies are interesting because they show that children understand the difference between the morality of harm and the morality of rules, but
they are interesting also because they show that children understand the nature of rules themselves. Children did think that it
was wrong to break rules. They just recognized that it was a different kind of wrong than hurting somebody. They knew that rules
could be changed, but they also knew you had to follow the current rules.

Children also understand the basic structure of rules. Rules
involve obligation, prohibition, and permission. When rules specify obligations, then you have to act the way the rule says. When
they specify prohibitions, you can't ever act that way. When they
give you permission, you can decide on independent grounds
whether you will act that way. You have to wash your hands before
a snack, and you must never, ever blow bubbles in your milk, but
you can play on the swings after nap if you want to.

When Henry Wellman looked at CHILDES, the database of
children's spontaneous speech, he found that children as young as
two talked about rules, obligations, prohibitions, and permissions
appropriately. Three-year-olds said things like "If we go camping,
we should make a [our own] canoe. Then we won't have to pay,
and we can ride whenever we want to."

In fact, children understand normative rules better than they understand logic. Logical reasoning involves "if P then Q" deductions. Suppose Jane says, "When I go outside (P) I wear my hat (Q)." Then you show children four pictures: (1) Jane outside and wearing a hat (P, Q); (2) Jane outside and not wearing a hat (P, not Q); (3) Jane inside and wearing a hat (not P, Q); and (4) Jane inside and not wearing a hat (not P, not Q). You ask them to choose the picture where "Jane is not doing what she said." Logically, the correct answer is 2. But children are quite bad at this kind of reasoning—they tend to pick by chance.

However, children do much better if you ask them to reason about rules. Suppose Jane's mom says, "If you go outside you must wear your hat." Then the child sees the same four pictures as before. But this time she has to choose the picture where "Jane was being naughty and not doing what she is supposed to do." Once again the right answer is (2), Jane standing out there in the cold risking her death without a hat. Even three-year-olds are very good at picking out the rule violation. Moreover, young children in Nepal and in Colombia are as good at rule logic as children in the United States and Britain.

DOING IT ON PURPOSE

Young children understand that breaking a rule and causing harm are wrong. But do they understand that they're wrong because of what people think and intend as much as because of what they do? When we blame someone for breaking a rule, or directly causing harm, we need to know whether they acted intentionally. We may occasionally blame someone even when they didn't directly intend to cause harm. We may send the drunk driver to jail even though he didn't intentionally run over his victim. But some kind of intention seems to be crucial to moral judgment. The driver did, after all, intentionally drink and intentionally drive. This is the legal doctrine of mens rea.

We've seen that even one-year-olds already understand human intentions and differentiate intentional and unintentional actions. And even babies seem to blame people based on their intentions. In one experiment, an adult played a game with a baby in which he gave the baby toys across a table. Occasionally, the adult held up a toy but didn't give it to the baby. Sometimes he just refused to hand it over. But sometimes he seemed willing to hand it over but was held up by circumstances that were beyond his control—for example, the toy was in a transparent box that he couldn't open. Nine- to eighteen-month-olds were more impatient and fussy when the adult willfully kept the toy for himself than when he tried to give them the toy but just couldn't manage it.

By the time they're three, children consider intentions when they make basic moral judgments about good and harm. They say that intentionally pushing another child is bad, but it's OK if you just accidentally bump into them. They also differentiate between intentional and accidental rulebreaking. Remember the study that looked at children's early normative logic, where Mom said Jane had to wear a hat outside. The experimenters also asked whether the child was naughty if "she's outside and the wind's blown her hat off" and if "she's outside and she's taken her hat off." The youngest children they tested, who were only three, distinguished the two cases. They said the child who broke the rule on purpose was much naughtier than the child who broke the rule accidentally.

RULES AS CAUSES

The core of morality lies in our intimate emotional identification with others, and our resulting desire to help them and not harm them. Even babies want to help. But this desire is fruitless by itself. To be effective moral agents children need to combine that impulse with their causal understanding of the world and other people. Like little utilitarians they need to figure out the most effective method to bring about happiness and ameliorate harm. And they need to understand the causal power of rules.

Rules are an especially effective way to control choices. They are a particular and peculiar kind of psychological cause. Once a rule has been established, it becomes much simpler to make people do things, even very complicated and arbitrary things (think about doing your taxes). We don't have to persuade or coax or coerce them or directly change their desires and beliefs. All we need to do is remind them to follow the rule.

Most significantly, rules can be changed. The very youngest children already understand that we can change the rules, although we can't change the basic moral principles of harm and help. This gives us a characteristically human ability to implement new visions of reality. Changing the rules can make amazing new things happen.

For example, we use our powerful human learning abilities to discover the principles of internal combustion, and this lets us change the world. Normative reasoning tells us that cars would be a really good thing, and lo and behold, the twentieth century is the Age of the Automobile. But how can we possibly keep a thousand people each moving two thousand pounds of steel at sixty miles per hour on a fifty-foot strip of road from killing one another? Miraculous lifesaving traffic rules enter the universe. But then we use the same powerful learning capacities to discover something new—global warming. Driving, which once seemed unequivocally good, turns out to be harmful, too. We can change the rules about driving to reflect that new understanding. The same banal highway code that saved lives might save the planet, too.

We don't have any innate moral intuitions about driving. SUVs aren't innately disgusting, even if some people in Berkeley act as though they are. But we do have our ability to learn, our ability to make new rules, and our foundational instinct to help and not harm. Among them they let us make moral decisions about this unprecedented human activity.

In fact, sometimes we can use our rulemaking abilities to overturn evolutionarily determined, but harmful, moral intuitions. It's like the way that we use our learning abilities to overturn evolutionarily determined, but incorrect, intuitions about physics. It's at least plausible that impulses to sexual jealousy or revenge, the kind that justify "honor killings" of an adulterous wife or an insulting neighbor, have an evolutionary basis. These intuitions take a moral form and may even become part of the law. But, as we consider the harms and goods more carefully, we can revise even evolutionarily determined intuitions like these.

We govern the flexibility of rules by having metarules, rules about how to formulate new rules and change existing ones. These include the principles of democracy, one of the great moral and psychological inventions of our species. But at other times and places the rules might be determined by consensus, or negotiation. Or we may delegate rulemaking authority to people who are expert or knowledgeable or powerful or just plain cool.

For very young children, parents and teachers are natural rule givers. There is no categorical imperative more fearsome than Mommy's "Because I said so." But older children already start to learn to negotiate rules among themselves. Five-year-olds spontaneously invent games with rules. These aren't boring grown-up games but the ones that just emerge mysteriously in the playground like four square and wall ball and Chinese jump rope. These games teach children how to make rules. The endless negotiations about who is out and who is It are a forerunner of courts and legislatures.

THE PERILS OF RULES

Rule following, like imitation, and like our impulse to categorize people into social groups, has moral perils as well as moral benefits. People follow rules long after their original function has disappeared. There is a story about a woman who made her mother's favorite pot roast, carefully following the rules that had led to such a succulent outcome. The first step was always cutting off the end of the meat. It was only when her mother came to visit that she realized that Mom had always done it this way because her pan was too small for a whole roast. Many more obviously moral rules are passed on and followed this way.

Food taboos are a good example. When rats eat a food that makes them sick, even just once, they avoid it forever after—it's called the Garcia effect. Similarly, when people get food poisoning even once they may end up with a personal distaste for the food that caused it—one bad salad and they never eat lobster again. The anthropologist Daniel Fessler suggests that this may lead to food taboos. If the person who doesn't eat lobster is influential and important, the sort of person who makes rules, other people may unwittingly follow his example. The taboo becomes institutionalized, and may even become religious or moral.

Since rules are such a good way to make people do things, they can also be a source of power. People may enforce rules that serve their own individual ends or the ends of their own group rather than serving the general good. The human impulse to accept and follow rules means that rule-based injustices can easily be perpetuated. People who might resist individual bullying or oppression will accept it when it's just part of the rules. My shy intellectual middle son grew up to become an expert in mathematical finance. He told me the economist's version of the golden rule: "He who has the gold makes the rules."

THE WISDOM OF HUCK FINN

Making rules gives us a powerful mechanism for changing what we do and adjusting to new circumstances, but our basic empathic assumptions about good and harm govern those changes and protect us from moral relativism. In much the same way, the basic assumptions of learning allow us to make radical changes in our theories of the world, but they protect us from knowledge relativism. We choose theories that lead to good predictions, or rules that lead to good outcomes. This allows us to produce radically new kinds of theories and rules without saying that anything goes.

In both cases, of course, there's lots of room for argument. Figuring out what's a good outcome is no easier than figuring out what's a good prediction. Harm and help aren't straightforward. People may want things that are bad for them in the long run, or they may seem content because they don't realize that a better life is even possible. But, at the core, we rely on general principles that are in place even in very young babies. We may not agree whether a particular rule will make things better, or whether a particular theory will explain things better. But at least we can agree that it should.

Even two-year-olds have an immediate, intuitive, emotional, empathic understanding of help and harm, rooted in intimate interactions. They also understand that they should follow rules, but that rules can be changed. These two abilities, in concert, give us a very human capacity for moral innovation. Morality, like everything else that is human, is deeply rooted in our evolutionary history, but the most important feature of that evolutionary history is that it allows us to reflect on our own actions and to change them.

Rules allow us to perform complex, coordinated behaviors—they let us help other people in new and powerful ways. But intimate, emotional empathy is a force that can change even the most entrenched rules. If we discover that a rule leads to harm rather than good we can reject that rule. This is especially true if we experience that harm in the rich, intimate way that comes from interacting face-to-face with a real person in real life.

Often a return to the intimate empathy of infancy—that immediate sense of how other people feel—can be the most powerful way to change what people do. For example, we dehumanize people in the "out-group"—people who are not like us. This impulse is deep-seated and very difficult to overturn completely. One of the best ways to change it is to actually become intimate with the out-group—to recognize that those people are actually like me. People who come to know someone well who is openly gay are much more likely to support gay rights. Individual stories are powerful agents of moral change—often more powerful than rational arguments.

One of the greatest moral stories in all of literature is about the way that empathy changes rules. And it's a story about a child. Huckleberry Finn is only thirteen when he runs away from his abusive father and joins Jim, a runaway slave, on a raft on the Mississippi. Huck knows the rules about slavery, rules that have all the force of tradition, authority, law, and religion behind them. He knows that the rules say that protecting a runaway slave is an egregious theft. He knows that people who break the rules are condemned to hell. But he also knows Jim and he knows him intimately, face-to-face, with the intimacy of early childhood. In fact, Jim, unlike his real father, has been Huck's caregiver. At the crucial juncture of the novel Huck has to decide whether to give Jim up to the authorities.

> So I was full of trouble, full as I could be; and didn't know what to do. At last I had an idea; and I says, I'll go and write the letter—and then see if I can pray. Why, it was astonishing, the way I felt as light as a feather right straight off, and my troubles all gone. So I got a piece of paper and a pencil, all glad and excited, and set down and wrote:

> > Miss Watson, your runaway nigger Jim is down here two mile below Pikesville, and Mr. Phelps has got him and he will give him up for the reward if you send.
> >
> > HUCK FINN

> I felt good and all washed clean of sin for the first time I had ever felt so in my life, and I knowed I could pray now. But I didn't do it straight off, but laid the paper down and set there thinking—thinking how good it was all this happened so, and how near I come to being lost and going to hell. And went on thinking. And got to thinking over our trip down the river; and I see Jim before me all the time: in the day and in the night-time, sometimes moonlight, sometimes storms, and we a-floating along, talking and singing and laughing. But somehow I couldn't seem to strike no places to harden me against him, but only the other kind. I'd see him standing my watch on top of his'n, 'stead of calling me, so I could go on sleeping; and see him how glad he was when I come back out of the fog; and when I come to him again in the swamp, up there where the feud was; and such-like times; and would always call me honey, and pet me and do everything he could think

of for me, and how good he always was; and at last I struck the time I saved him by telling the men we had small-pox aboard, and he was so grateful, and said I was the best friend old Jim ever had in the world, and the ONLY one he's got now; and then I happened to look around and see that paper.

It was a close place. I took it up, and held it in my hand. I was a-trembling, because I'd got to decide, forever, betwixt two things, and I knowed it. I studied a minute, sort of holding my breath, and then says to myself:

"All right, then, I'll GO to hell"—and tore it up.

9.

Babies and the Meaning of Life

*

I love Christmas and have always celebrated it with particular fervor and intensity. Every year, neglecting final exams, faculty meetings, and grant submission deadlines, I decorate a big tree, put swags on the mantelpieces, bake gingerbread houses, roast geese, sing carols, and spend far too much on stocking stuffers—the works. For almost all my life I've had children at home and that has made Christmas especially rich, even if it came with the ambivalence of so much parenting. There was great egocentric pleasure in the doing itself, even more pleasure in thinking how much the children liked it, just a little edge of exhaustion at the effort and just a smidgen of doubt about whether the children really appreciated it enough.

I love Christmas so much in spite of the fact that my great-grandfather was a devout and distinguished rabbi, and I was raised as an equally devout atheist. I resolve the apparent contradiction by telling people that I love Christmas because, above all, it's a holiday that celebrates birth and children—the most moving

Christmas carols are both hymns and lullabies. I can't think of anything more worthy of celebration.

In this book, I've argued that thinking about children can help solve some deep and ancient philosophical questions—questions about imagination, truth, and consciousness, and also identity, love, and morality. But beyond even these questions are what we might call the meaning-of-life questions—more broadly philosophical or even spiritual and religious questions that academic philosophers like me rarely tackle. What makes life meaningful, beautiful, and morally significant? Is there something that we care about more than we care about ourselves? What endures beyond death?

For most parents, in day-to-day, simple, ordinary life, there is an obvious answer to these questions—even if it isn't the only answer. Our children give point and purpose to our lives. They are beautiful (with a small dispensation for chicken pox, scraped knees, and runny noses), and the words and images they create are beautiful too. They are at the root of our deepest moral dilemmas and greatest moral triumphs. We care more about our children than we do about ourselves. Our children live on after we are gone, and this gives us a kind of immortality.

Curiously, though these feelings are so pervasive, they're rarely even considered in philosophy and theology. In fact, it was thinking about immortality that first made me notice the missing children in philosophy. When I was ten, I read Plato for the first time and it changed my life. I still vividly remember the battered Penguin paperback that made me want to become a philosopher. But even in that very first encounter with philosophy there was a catch. The argument in the Penguin Plato that impressed me the most was Socrates' case for immortality in the *Phaedo*. Like many ten-year-olds—or fifty-year-olds, for that matter—I was existentially terrified by death and was certainly in the market for a good argument for immortality. Socrates argues that something as complex as the soul can't appear and vanish out of nowhere, and therefore it must exist, before and after our individual lives, in an abstract Platonic heaven.

What struck me about the argument was that there was no mention anywhere of children. It seemed obvious to me that your soul was created, at least in part, by the genes you inherited and the ideas you acquired from your parents, and that it continued after death in the genes and ideas you passed on to your children. Of course, this idea depended on scientific concepts that weren't available to Socrates. But even if Socrates didn't know about genes, he definitely knew about children. I'll admit that attaining immortality through your children isn't necessarily the answer to Socrates' question. But he could have at least mentioned it as a possibility.

Nor did children appear in the 2,500 years of philosophy to come. Many profound questions about human nature can be answered by thinking about children. And thinking about children raises new and profound questions itself. Most parents, and even alloparents, feel that children help give their lives meaning. Yet children have been almost invisible to the deepest thinkers in human history.

There is an obvious historical explanation for this—Socrates was a man, like nearly all the philosophers and theologians who followed him. Children have always been part of women's realm. Like most other aspects of life that are associated with women, they were not the sort of thing philosophers talked about.

But the problem may run deeper. Perhaps our intuitions about children really are too parochial and personal to be genuinely profound. My children are *mine*, after all. My feeling for them doesn't have the universal character that we expect from spiritual intuitions. They seem beautiful to me, but then mothers love even a face that only a mother could love. From an evolutionary point of view, too, those intuitions might just be an illusion. Of course, you feel that your own children are important—it's just another evolutionary trick that genes use to reproduce themselves. Your genes might make you really want to take care of the children who share those genes. But this doesn't have anything to do with the meaning of life.

This is part of the deeper question that haunts all scientists who think about spirituality. Human beings have characteristic emotions of awe and wonder, moral worth and aesthetic profundity. They have a sense of meaning and purpose, and an intuition that there is something larger than themselves. But do these emotions and intuitions capture something real about the world? From a scientific perspective, these emotions and beliefs, like all emotions and beliefs, are the result of activity in our brains and have an evolutionary history. Often this is taken to mean that they are illusory—or at least that they don't have the significance they appear to have.

In fact, my brain is designed to tell me the truth, at least most of the time. When I look at the desk in front of me, my belief that the desk is there is entirely due to activity in my brain—activity that has a long evolutionary history. But there really *is* a desk there and my brain activity accurately tells me about it. I can use that information as a guide to real actions in the real world—I can put my teacup down there without spilling it. When I look down from the edge of a cliff, I feel fear. I can tell you how my evolutionary history and the activity in my brain generate that feeling, but that doesn't mean the feeling is just an illusion. On the contrary, I *should* feel fear—my brain is telling me something terribly important about the world and my relation to it. The fact that a belief is the result of evolutionary processes that shaped my brain makes it more likely to be true, not less so. Evolution tracks the real world.

On the other hand, there are perceptions, emotions, and beliefs that really are just bits of faulty wiring, mind bugs. When the moon looks larger at the horizon than at the apex of the sky, or seems to be following my car, or appears to have a face, those really are illusions. We know something about how the brain creates those illusions. When I see a harmless garter snake and recoil in horror, that really is a mistake left over from my evolutionary past. So the great question isn't whether spiritual intuitions are in our brains—of course they are. The question is whether they're simply a bit of deceptive brain wiring or whether they tell us something important, valuable, and true about the world and ourselves. Are they like seeing the man in the moon or seeing the teacup on the desk?

I don't know about the spiritual intuitions that accompany mystical experiences or religious ceremonies. But I do think that the sense of significance that accompanies the experience of raising children isn't just an evolutionarily determined illusion, like the man in the moon or the terrifying garter snake. Children really do put us in touch with important, real, and universal aspects of the human condition.

AWE

Like most scientists, I doubt that there is some ultimate, transcendent, foundational purpose to our lives, or to the universe, whether we interpret this in terms of a personal God or a mystical metaphysics. But certainly we can point to sources of real meaning in our actual human lives as we live them.

One classic kind of spiritual intuition is awe: our sense of the richness and complexity of the universe outside our own immediate concerns. It's the experience of standing outside on a dark night and gazing up at the infinite multitude of stars. This kind of awe is the scientific emotion par excellence. Many scientists who are otherwise atheists point to it as a profound, deep, and significant reward of their work. Scientists are certainly subject to ambition, the lust for fame, the desire for power, and other dubious motivations. Still, I think all scientists, even the most domineering Harvard silverbacks, are also moved by this kind of pure amazement at how much there is to learn about the world.

I've argued that babies and young children experience this kind of feeling, this lantern consciousness, all the time. They may feel this way gazing up at a Mickey Mouse mobile instead of at the Milky Way, but the experience is very much the same. And it's more than just a feeling for both the scientists and the children. The universe at every level, from Mickey Mouse to the Milky Way and beyond, is indeed wonderfully rich and complex and, well, just awesome. And our capacity to appreciate this richness is entirely genuine. Not everybody engages in science or even cares about it—but almost everybody shares in the learning of young children.

MAGIC

A second and rather different kind of spiritual intuition, what we might call our sense of magic, is our feeling that there are also possible worlds beyond the world we know. There are worlds of the imagination, worlds that are quite different from ours, magic, un-real worlds. The earliest recorded human stories are myths and legends, wild tales of faraway counterfactuals. Grey-eyed Athena, Pele the volcano goddess, and Thor the thunder hurler are as un-likely as Dunzer or Charlie Ravioli or Gawkin the Dinosaur. The restrained and realistic imaginary creatures of novels are relatively modern creations.

These stories—expressions of magic, myth, and metaphor—have always been closely connected to a different kind of spiritual sense, a different intuition that the world is wider than we are. Ex-plicitly religious writers such as C. S. Lewis and J. R. R. Tolkien link religion and magic. They point to the wonder and richness of the fairy tales we tell children, and children tell us. And, of course, both Lewis and Tolkien wrote stories that captured that sense of possibility, that sense that an alternate universe might lurk in every wardrobe. Those stories were aimed at children, but they speak equally to adults. In their pretend play, young children ex-plore the magic of human possibility in a particularly wide-ranging and creative way. Their liberation from mundane cares lets them move into the world of the possible with particular ease.

This sense of possibility isn't an illusion. The human world really is rich with magical potential in a very concrete and realistic way. I can watch *Beauty and the Beast*, the quintessentially magi-cal Jean Cocteau fairy tale, on my computer, Skyping with my dis-tant son at the same time. As Beauty looks into the magic mirror that sends her visions of her loved ones, I can stare into the real images in the real magic mirror of my laptop, images that once ex-isted only in the minds of imaginative geeks.

Stories can also create new ways for human beings to live, as well as new worlds for them to live in. Religious stories do this, in particular, whether they are parables or koans, tales of Valhalla or Chelm. By imagining alternative minds, alternative ways that people might think and act, human beings can transform themselves and their communities. The sense of magical possibility that is so vivid in children is also at the root of much that is real and important about our lives. And the space of human imaginative possibilities really is much wider than any individual mind can capture.

LOVE

Children can also tell us, more than anything else, about the spiritual intuitions that we might call love. Our love for our children, and our children's love for us, has a special quality. I said before that the particularity of our feelings about children might make them seem spiritually dubious. But the love we feel for children, not just mother love but the father love of social monogamy and the babysitter/sibling/grandmother/next-door-neighbor love of the alloparent, has a special quality of both particularity and universality. It is a powerful model for the love that underpins religious and moral intuitions.

One of the everyday but astonishing facts of life is that while we choose our friends and our mates, we don't choose our children. When we give birth to a baby, and even when, as an alloparent, we take on the care of a baby we haven't borne, we have no idea what that baby will be like. I may hope that my baby combines the best features of myself and my mate, while I fear that he actually combines the worst ones. Still, given the genetic lottery of human mating, and the contingencies of human nurturing, the most likely outcome is that the jumbled-up genes of each individual will come out looking like nothing else on earth. Even the most basic features of what a baby is like are beyond our control, a situation that becomes vivid for the parents of children with disabilities.

And yet, with some tragic exceptions, caregivers love the babies they care for. Sometimes they love the neediest babies, the babies with Down syndrome and cerebral palsy and cystic fibrosis, most of all. And even more oddly, when we care for a child we love *that* child, not some arbitrary notion of children in general. We love our children just for the particular characteristics that we couldn't possibly have anticipated—my oldest son's intensity, talent, and straight-backed confidence; my middle son's brown curls, wit, and intelligence; my youngest's luminous smile, warm blue eyes, and sensitivity. In fact, these lists don't capture it either—I just love *them*, not even because they are my children, but just because they are Alexei, Nicholas, and Andres.

Even more paradoxically, yet even more profoundly, our love for our children is inversely related to the benefits they provide us. Even with mates, and certainly with friends, we expect a certain reciprocity—I'll take care of your neuroses if you'll tolerate mine. The neediest of our intimates gives us something in return. But *every* child is needier than the most intolerably demanding friend or lover.

Imagine a novel in which a woman took in a stranger who was unable to walk or talk or even eat by himself. She fell completely in love with him at first sight, fed and clothed and washed him, gradually helped him to become competent and independent, spent more than half her income on him, nursed him through sickness, and thought about him more than about anything else. And after twenty years of this she helped him find a young wife and move far away. You couldn't bear the sappiness of it. But that, quite simply, is just about every mother's story. And it's also the story of every human community—every constellation of mothers and fathers and socially monagomous mates, every group of siblings and babysitters and alloparents. It's not so much that we care for children because we love them as that we love them because we care for them.

These moral intuitions about childrearing aren't captured in most philosophical traditions. The classic philosophical moral views—utilitarian or Kantian, libertarian or socialist—are rooted in intuitions about good and harm, autonomy and reciprocity, individuality and universality. Each individual person deserves to pursue happiness and avert harm, and by cooperating reciprocally we can maximize the good of everyone—the basic idea of the social contract. But individualist, universalist, and contractual moral systems just don't seem to capture our intuitions about raising kids.

On the other hand, this combination of particularity and selflessness is much like the love and concern that are part of our spiritual intuitions. We capture it in stories of saints and bodhisattvas and tzaddikim. They are supposed to feel that combination of singular, transparent, particular affection and selfless concern for *everybody*. No real human can do that. And, of course, there are many ways to approach that ideal and to care for others—ways that don't involve children. Still, caring for children is an awfully fast and efficient way to experience at least a little saintliness.

CONCLUSION

We can return to the questions we started at the beginning of this book. How is it possible for human beings to change? What does this tell us about children and childhood, especially very young children and very early childhood? There are three intertwined strands in the answer—learning, counterfactuals, and caregiving, or more poetically, truth, imagination, and love. In science and philosophy these three aspects of human experience are often treated as if they were quite separate from one another—epistemology, aesthetics, and ethics all have very different traditions. But for young children truth, imagination, and love are inextricably intertwined.

Truth, first. We change what we do as we learn more about what the world is like. Human beings can learn more than any other animal and that's one reason they can change more than any other animal. Children are born knowing a lot about the world and other people. That knowledge gives them a head start in learning new things about the particular world they live in and the particular set of people they share it with. But, at the end of the day, they may even learn to overthrow the assumptions they started with.

Babies love to learn. They learn by simply observing the unfolding statistics of the events around them. They are open to all the richness of the wide world. They pay attention to anything new and unexpected—anything they might learn from—but they also actively do things to learn. When they play, children actively experiment on the world and they use the results of those experiments to change what they think. The statistics they observe and the experiments they perform help them to make new causal maps of the world around them.

Children don't just learn about the physical world. They also learn about the psychological world. They learn what the people around them are like. Since human cultures can change, this means that what children learn about people can also change. Children learn the psychology of those around them—their particular combination of beliefs, desires, and feelings, personality traits, motivations, and interests. But they also learn the normative aspects of human psychology. They rapidly learn the rules that those around them follow, both the arbitrary conventions and the moral principles.

And children don't just learn about other people—they learn about themselves. Literally, from the time they are born they link their own feelings to those of others. They use what they learn about other people to learn about themselves and vice versa. Children begin to see how understanding your own mind can help you to change what you do—how, for example, closing your eyes can help you resist that cookie. They also start to use their psychological understanding to make a unified and coherent story of their own experiences, a story that continues through all the twists and turns of human life.

This remarkable ability to find the truth, in turn, depends on the capacity to imagine and to love. The Bayesian theory of learning depends on the idea that children can imagine alternatives to their current picture of the world. Children construct alternative hypotheses about what the world is like, they compare and contrast different possible causal maps of the world. And a fundamental principle of this kind of learning is that even the most unlikely possibilities may eventually turn out to be true.

And babies can devote their attention and action to learning because they depend on the care of the people around them. Because we love babies, they can learn. Even more significantly, one of the central ways that babies and children learn is by watching what the people they love do and listening to what they say. This kind of learning allows children to take advantage of the discoveries of the previous generations. Caregivers implicitly and unconsciously teach babies at the same time that they care for them.

If imagination helps children to find the truth, finding the truth also increases the power of the imagination. Very young children can use their causal maps of the world—their theories—to imagine different ways that the world might be. They can think about counterfactual possibilities. As those theories change, as children learn and their ideas about the world become more and more accurate, the counterfactuals they can produce and the possibilities they can envision become richer and richer. These counterfactuals let children create different worlds and they underpin the great flowering of pretend play in early childhood. Eventually, they enable even adults to imagine alternative ways the world could be and make those alternatives real.

Causal maps also apply to minds as well as things. And that means that children can imagine counterfactual people, like imaginary companions, as well as counterfactual worlds. This lets children interact with people in new and more complex ways. And it lets them, and us, create new social conventions and moral rules that will bring about better outcomes.

So imagination depends on knowledge, but it also depends on love and care. Just as children can learn so freely because they are protected by adults, they can imagine so freely because they are loved. More, counterfactual thinking necessarily has a normative element—imagining the future also means evaluating which futures you should bring about. From the time they are very young children root these decisions in moral responses. They try to do good and avoid harm. And those responses are themselves rooted in the deeply empathic, intimate, and literally selfless interactions between babies and caregivers.

Finally, love itself depends on knowledge and imagination. For babies, who are so utterly helpless and dependent, no theory is as important as a theory of love. From the time they are very small babies are figuring out these theories of love, based on what they see the caregivers around them do and say. And these theories in turn shape the way these babies will care for their own children when they grow up.

Knowledge about love, like other kinds of knowledge, leads babies to imagine how their caregivers will act and how they should act themselves. These predictions and actions lead to the vicious and benign cycles that are so characteristically human. But imagination also gives babies, and the rest of us, a way to escape those cycles. Even a little evidence lets children imagine other, better ways that love might work.

"But what about immortality?" ten-year-old Alison asks. I suspect that she, like Woody Allen, would have said that she didn't want to achieve immortality through her children, she wanted to achieve it through not dying. Failing that, though, children aren't bad. One of the worst things about writing about the importance of children is that practically everything you say turns out to sound like a greeting card. Still, clichés often get to be clichés because they're true, and the cliché that children are our future is no more than simple, literal truth.

For human children the cliché runs particularly deep. Children are not just our future because they carry on our genes. For human beings, in particular, our sense of who we are, both as individuals and as a group, is intimately tied to where we come from and where we're going, to our past and our future. The human capacity for change means that we can't figure out what it is to be human just by looking at the way we are now. We need instead to peer forward into the vast ramifying space of human possibilities. The explorers we see out there at the farthest edge look very much like our children.

Notes

*

Science and philosophy rest on the achievements of thousands of precursors, and for a book as wide-ranging as this one, a really complete list of references would go on for hundreds of pages. Since most readers of this book will not be professional philosophers or scientists, I've used a different approach. In the notes, I've directed the reader to at least one source for each empirical fact I've talked about in the book. I've also tried to refer to review articles that will give the reader a big picture of lots of experiments and data. And I've tried to flag books that I think are particularly significant or helpful.

INTRODUCTION

6   Encyclopedia of Philosophy: Edwards 1967; Craig 1998.
7   *"evolutionary psychology"*: Pinker 1997; Barkow et al. 1994.
11 *Babies' brains seem to have*: For some reviews of brain development findings see Huttenlocher 2002a, b; Johnson et al. 2002; Dawson and Fischer 1994.
12 *They involve the prefrontal cortex*: For a review of prefrontal cortex development see Krasnegor et al. 1997.
13 *"inhibition"*: Diamond 2002.
13 *plastic frontal lobes*: Shaw et al. 2006.

1: POSSIBLE WORLDS

19   *"counterfactuals"*: Lewis 1986.
22   *Who is more upset?*: Tversky and Kahneman 1973.
22   *bronze medalist or the silver?*: Medvec et al. 1995.
24   *standard baby toy*: This ring task, and the rake task that follows, were adapted from Uzgiris and Hunt 1975. See Gopnik 1982; Gopnik and Meltzoff 1986.
25   *right kinds of information*: Willatts 1999.
25   *little evidence that chimpanzees*: Povinelli et al. 2000.
25   *smart birds like crows*: Bluff et al. 2007.
25   *success of* Homo sapiens: Byrne 2002.
26   *psychologist Paul Harris*: Harris's book (Harris 2000) is by far the best review and discussion of children's pretense and imagination.
26   *English countryside story*: Harris et al. 1996.
26   *if you put them in order*: Sobel 2002, 2004.
27   *eighteen months old or even younger*: Belsky and Most 1981; Lillard 2002; Leslie 1987.
29   *use tools in an insightful way*: Gopnik 1982; Gopnik and Meltzoff 1986.
29   *you'll need a broom*: Harris 2000.
30   *"just pretend"*: Lillard and Witherington 2004.
30   *not the pretend one*: Woolley and Wellman 1990, 1993.
31   *cat just by thinking about it*: Wellman and Estes 1986.
31   *gingerly moved away from the box*: Harris 2000.
31   *they still wouldn't drink it*: Rozin et al. 1990.
32   *causal knowledge and counterfactual thinking*: Lewis 1986.
33   *make that future real*: The idea that causality can be understood in terms of interventions has been articulated most persuasively and extensively by James Woodward in Woodward 2003.
35   *Piaget*: Piaget 1954.
36   *good logical explanations all the same*: Hickling and Wellman 2001.
36   *invisible germs make you ill*: Gelman 2003.
36   *their understanding of life and death*: Inagaki and Hatano 2006.
38   *knowledge to discriminate possibilities*: Schult and Wellman 1997.
39   *"cognitive maps"*: Tolman 1948; O'Keefe and Nadel 1979.
41   *complex causal relations among events*: Gopnik et al. 2004.
41   *draw all these consequences*: Inagaki and Hatano 2006; Gelman 2003.
42   *give a mathematical account*: Spirtes et al. 1993.
42   *that scientific experts make*: Pearl 2000.
44   *counterfactual predictions*: Gopnik et al. 2001.
45   *same experiment in a different way*: Schulz and Gopnik 2004.

2: IMAGINARY COMPANIONS

48   *"Machiavellian intelligence"*: Byrne and Whiten 1988.
49   *psychologist Marjorie Taylor*: Marjorie Taylor's wonderful book (Taylor 1999) is the source for much of this chapter.

51 *imaginary friend was Charlie Ravioli*: Gopnik 2002.
55 *theory of the mind*: This has become an enormous area of research. For good reviews see Astington 1993; Flavell 1999; and Wellman 2002.
55 *broccoli and Goldfish crackers*: Repacholi and Gopnik 1997.
56 *raw broccoli or Cheerios*: Wellman et al. 2000.
56 *there are pencils in there!*: Wimmer and Perner 1983. For a meta-analysis see Wellman et al. 2001. Some recent work may show that even younger children can do this.
56 *children's everyday explanations*: Bartsch and Wellman 1995.
58 *they are also better liars*: LaLonde and Chandler 1995.
58 *the same thing in experiments*: Sodian et al. 1991; Talwar and Lee 2002.
59 *"executive control"*: Carlson and Moses 2001; Carlson et al. 2004.
59 *"delay of gratification" experiments*: Mischel et al. 1989.
62 *people with autism*: Grandin 1995; Gopnik et al. 2005.
62 the Dog in the Night-Time: Haddon 2004.
62 *theory of other people's minds*: Baron-Cohen 1995; Baron-Cohen et al. 2005.
63 *what pretend play is all about*: Baron-Cohen et al. 2005.
63 *Henry James*: James 1909.
69 *engineers of human souls*: Škvorecký 1999.
70 Lord of the Rings: Auden 1956.
72 *changes in inhibition*: e.g., Diamond 2002.

3: ESCAPING PLATO'S CAVE

75 *Plato's* Republic: Plato translated by Jowett 1888.
76 *learning techniques that scientists use*: Carey 1985; Gopnik 1988; Wellman and Gelman 1992.
76 *David Hume*: Hume 2007. Originally published 1748.
77 *actually learn about the world*: Spirtes et al. 1993; Glymour et al. 1988; Scheines et al. 1998.
78 *Reverend Thomas Bayes*: Bayes 1963; Griffiths et al. 2008. Also see Wikipedia on Bayes for a good brief explanation of Bayesianism.
79 *The famous Turing test*: Turing 1950.
80 *rocks on Mars*: Ramsey et al. 2002.
80 *turns a genome into an organism*: e.g., Helman et al. 2004 (there are many more).
80 *causes monsoons in India*: Steinbach et al. 2003.
81 *sensitive to statistical patterns*: Saffran et al. 1996.
83 *the beginning of music appreciation*: Saffran et al. 1999.
83 *often see a window nearby*: Kirkham et al. 2002; Aslin et al. 1998.
83 *some important statistical ideas*: Xu and Garcia 2008.
83 *two and a half, and probably earlier*: Sobel and Kirkham 2006.
83 *make genuinely causal inferences*: Gopnik et al. 2001; Sobel et al. 2004.
85 *the detector than the first one*: Kushnir and Gopnik 2005.
85 *probability of causes and effects*: Sobel et al. 2004.
87 *results than observation alone*: Eberhardt and Scheines 2007.

87 *happy because the experiment succeeds*: Papousek et al. 1987.
88 *to make the mobile move*: For a review of many of these mobile studies see Rovee-Collier and Barr 2001.
88 *Piaget described this kind*: Piaget 1952a, b.
88 *the gear toy*: Schulz et al. 2007.
90 *to figure out causal problems*: Schulz and Bonawitz 2007.
90 *Christine Legare*: Legare et al. 2008.
93 *directed toward particular goals*: Woodward 1998.
94 *and actions of other people*: Meltzoff and Moore 1977, 1983.
94 *results of those actions*: Meltzoff 1988.
94 *using your head instead*: Gergely et al. 2002.
94 *dumbbell, as Meltzoff did*: Meltzoff 1995.
95 *perform the experiments themselves*: Schulz et al. 2007.
95 *Barbara Rogoff studied Mayan*: Rogoff 1990.
98 *to differentiate people and things*: Watson 1972.
98 *psychologist Susan Johnson*: Johnson et al. 2007a, b, 2008; Shimizu and Johnson 2004.
98 *the blicket detector*: Schulz and Gopnik 2004.
100 *act similarly in those situations*: Zimbardo 2007.
100 *to test what was wrong*: Weinberg and Tronick 1996; Gusella et al. 1988.
100 *mimicking everything that the baby did*: Meltzoff 2007.
101 *IQ and verbal tests*: Ruffman et al. 1998; Sulloway 1996.
101 *the minds of others*: For a review and meta-analysis see Milligan et al. 2007.
102 *until they are eight or nine*: Peterson and Siegal 1995.
102 *Jennie Pyers*: Pyers 2005.

4: WHAT IS IT LIKE TO BE A BABY?

107 *Thomas Nagel*: Nagel 1974.
108 *"blindsight"*: Christensen et al. 2008; Weizkrantz 2007.
109 *smooth, unbroken visual field*: Dennett 1992.
110 *Peter Singer*: Singer 1976.
111 *endogenous attention*: Posner 2004.
111 *associated with attention*: e.g., Polich 2003; Knight and Scabini 1998.
112 *"inattentional blindness"*: Mack and Rock 1998; Simons and Chabris 1999.
113 *particular kind of chemical*: For a review of the role of neurotransmitters in attention see Robbins et al. 2004.
114 *Merzenich and his colleagues*: e.g., Polley et al. 2006; Recanzone et al. 1992a, b.
114 *cholinergic transmitters*: e.g., Metherate and Weinberger 1989; Blake et al. 2002.
116 *their capacity for attention*: For reviews on infant attention see Ruff and Rothbart 1996; Colombo 2004; Richards 2004. John Colombo provided very helpful information for this discussion.
118 *give children a memory task*: Hagen and Hale 1972.

120 *anesthetics act on these neurotransmitters*: Taylor and Lerman 1991; Lerman et al. 1983.

120 *young animals' cells changed*: Zhang et al. 2001; de Villers-Sidani et al. 2007.

120 *quite early in infancy*: Colombo 2004.

121 *Rafael Malach*: Goldberg et al. 2006; Golland et al. 2007.

122 *prune more connections*: Huttenlocher 2002a, b; Johnson et al. 2002.

124 *philosophically intriguing results*: Flavell et al. 1995a, b, 1997, 1999, 2000.

129 *"flow"*: Csíkszentmihályi 1992.

130 *"beginner's mind"*: Suzuki and Brown 2002.

130 *meteoric showers of images*: James 2001.

5: WHO AM I?

134 *sea slugs have that kind*: Rankin et al. 1987.

135 *episodic or autobiographical memory*: For a review see Tulving 2002.

135 *his initials as H.M.*: Scoville and Milner 1957; Corkin 2002.

136 Challenger *disaster shortly after*: Neisser and Harsch 1992.

136 *creating false memories*: Loftus 1997a, b.

137 *abducted by aliens*: Clancy 2005.

138 *occurred to them in the past*: Fivush et al. 1987.

138 *into a continuous narrative*: Nelson and Fivush 2004.

140 *free recall*: Ornstein et al. 2006.

141 *trouble with sources*: Shimamura and Squire 1987.

141 *where their beliefs come from*: Gopnik and Graf 1988; O'Neill and Gopnik 1991.

142 *their understanding of sources*: Giles et al. 2002.

143 *"false belief" experiment*: Gopnik and Astington 1988; Gopnik and Slaughter 1991.

145 *philosopher John Campbell*: Campbell 1994.

145 *recognize themselves in the mirror*: Brooks-Gunn and Lewis 1984.

145 *Teresa McCormack*: McCormack and Hoerl 2005, 2007.

146 *more dramatic experiment*: Povinelli et al. 1999.

147 *Cristina Atance*: Atance and Meltzoff 2005; Atance and O'Neill 2005.

149 *philosopher Jerry Fodor*: Fodor 1998.

150 *what the Flavells did*: Flavell et al. 1997.

159 *couldn't tolerate the delay*: Mischel et al. 1989.

159 *aboriginal communities in Canada*: Chandler and Proulx 2006.

161 *irrational unconscious bias*: Wegner 2002.

161 *notably Daniel Dennett*: Dennett and Weiner 1991.

161 *Paul and Patricia Churchland*: Churchland 1995, 2002.

161 *John Searle and David Chalmers*: Searle 1992; Chalmers 1996.

163 *experience those changes themselves*: For a more extended philosophical discussion of this point see Gopnik 1993.

6: HERACLITUS' RIVER AND THE ROMANIAN ORPHANS

165 *What should she do?*: Parfit 1984, p. 145.
168 *Romanian orphanages*: The most extensive, exhaustive, and masterful work
     on the fate of the Romanian orphans has been done by Michael Rutter
     and his colleagues. See, e.g., Rutter et al. 2004, 2007; Beckett et al. 2006.
     Also see Rutter 2006 for an excellent review of the interplay of genes and
     environments.
170 *"heritability"*: For heritability and twin and adoption studies see Plomin
     1994.
171 *alcoholism is heritable*: Dick and Beirut 2006.
172 *Eric Turkheimer*: Turkheimer et al. 2003.
172 The Bell Curve: Herrnstein and Murray 1994.
173 *although our genes have remained the same*: This is known as the "Flynn ef-
     fect." See Flynn 1987; Dickens and Flynn 2001.
174 *experience stressful events*: Kendler and Prescott 2006.
175 *cases of abuse*: For a recent review see Cicchetti and Valentino 2006.
175 *list of other ills*: For good reviews of this literature see Rutter 2006; Kendler
     and Prescott 2006.
177 *poor children's early experiences*: For a readable recent review of the effects
     of early preschool interventions see Kirp 2007.

7: LEARNING TO LOVE

180 *leave them and then return*: The classic reference is Ainsworth et al. 1978.
     There have been hundreds of other studies since.
180 *mother's face and voice*: DeCasper and Fifer 1980; Field et al. 1984.
181 *the statistics of love*: Ainsworth 1993.
181 *Romanian orphans*: Rutter et al. 2004, 2007.
181 *not all babies learn the same things*: Ainsworth et al. 1978.
182 *inside the babies are miserable*: Spangler and Grossman 1993.
182 *cultural differences*: Van Ijzendoorn and Kroonenberg 1988.
183 *"Disorganized" babies*: Main and Solomon 1986.
183 *"internal working models"*: Bowlby 1980; Main et al. 1985.
183 *based on the evidence*: Ainsworth 1993; Blehar et al. 1977.
184 *different theories of love*: Johnson et al. 2007a.
184 *at five or six*: Main et al. 1985.
185 *poet Robert Hass*: From "Dragonflies Mating," Hass 1996.
186 *theories in many ways*: For a recent review of adult attachment see
     Mikulincer and Shaver 2007.
186 *loved ones at the airport*: Fraley and Shaver 1998.
187 *Serena Chen*: Chen et al. 1999; Chen 2003.
188 *expecting their first baby*: Benoit and Parker 1994.
189 *thirty or forty years*: For a good review of these studies see Grossman et al.
     2005.
192 *social monogamy*: See, e.g., Reichard and Boesche 2003.

192 *allomothering*: See Sarah Hrdy's magisterial book for a full account of allomothers (Hrdy 2000).
194 *extended our life span*: Hawkes et al. 2003.
199 *imagine the future*: Schacter and Addis 2007.

8: LOVE AND LAW

202 *Piaget and Lawrence Kohlberg*: Piaget 1965; Colby and Kohlberg 1987.
203 *morality is innate*: Mikhail 2007; Hauser 2006.
203 *hardwired emotional responses*: Haidt 2007.
205 *Newborns imitate facial expressions*: Meltzoff and Moore 1983.
205 *imitate emotional expressions*: Field et al. 1982.
205 *feel the accompanying emotion*: Levenson et al. 1990.
207 *so-called mirror neurons*: See, e.g., Iacoboni and Dapretto 2006; for rebuttals of the mirror neuron idea see Gopnik 2007.
209 *perceive anger in others*: Dodge and Cole 1987.
211 *to help someone else*: Warneken and Tomasello 2006, 2007.
211 *Judith Smetana*: Smetana 1981, 1984, 1985, 1989; Smetana et al. 1984, 1993; Song et al. 1987; Smetana and Braeges 1990. For a theoretical review see Turiel 1983.
213 *psychopaths*: Blair et al. 2005.
215 *"trolley problem"*: Foot 2002; Thomson 1976; Greene 2003.
216 *about 150 people*: Dunbar 1996.
217 *"minimal groups"*: Tajfel 1982 and many studies since then.
218 *Zimbardo*: Zimbardo 2007.
218 *are most like them*: Dunham et al. in press.
219 *completely arbitrary groups*: Dunham 2007; Fawcett 2008.
220 *particularity of our moral life*: Williams 1985.
223 *"over-imitate"*: Lyons et al. 2007.
224 *the way we do things around here*: Gergely and Csibra 2004.
224 *understand the basic structure of rules*: Wellman and Miller in press; Núñez and Harris 1998; Harris and Núñez 1996.
226 *based on their intentions*: Kuhlmeier et al. 2003; Behne et al. 2005.
226 *about good and harm*: Núñez and Harris 1998; Harris and Núñez 1996.
229 *too small for a whole roast*: Gergely and Csibra 2004.
229 *the Garcia effect*: Garcia and Koelling 1966.
229 *may lead to food taboos*: Fessler and Navarrete 2003.

Bibliography

*

Ainsworth, Mary S. 1993. "Attachment as Related to Mother-Infant Interaction." *Advances in Infancy Research* 8: 1–50.

Ainsworth, Mary S., Mary C. Blehar, Everett Waters, and Sally Wall. 1978. *Patterns of Attachment: A Psychological Study of the Strange Situation.* Oxford, England: Lawrence Erlbaum.

Aslin, Richard N., Jenny R. Saffran, and Elissa L. Newport. 1998. "Computation of Conditional Probability Statistics by 8-month-old Infants." *Psychological Science* 9 (4) (July): 321–24.

Astington, Janet Wilde. 1993. *The Child's Discovery of the Mind.* Cambridge, Mass.: Harvard University Press.

Atance, C. M., and A. N. Meltzoff. 2005. "My Future Self: Young Children's Ability to Anticipate and Explain Future States." *Cognitive Development* 20 (3) (July–Sept.): 341–61.

Atance, C. M., and D. K. O'Neill. 2005. "The Emergence of Episodic Future Thinking in Humans." *Learning and Motivation* 36 (2) (May): 126–44.

Auden, W. H. 1956. "At the End of the Quest, Victory." *The New York Times,* Jan. 26.

Barkow, Jerome H., Leda Cosmides, and John Tooby, eds. 1992. *The Adapted Mind: Evolutionary Psychology and the Generation of Culture.* New York: Oxford University Press.

Baron-Cohen, Simon. 1995. *Mindblindness: An Essay on Autism and Theory of Mind.* Cambridge, Mass.: MIT Press.

Baron-Cohen, Simon, Helen Tager-Flusberg, and Donald J. Cohen, eds. 2005. *Understanding Other Minds: Perspectives from Developmental Cognitive Neuroscience.* 2nd ed. New York: Oxford University Press.

Bartsch, Karen, and Henry M. Wellman. 1995. *Children Talk About the Mind.* New York: Oxford University Press.

Bayes, Thomas. 1963. Facsimiles of two papers by Bayes. I. An essay toward solving a problem in the doctrine of chances, with Richard Price's foreword and discussion; *Phil. Trans. Royal Soc.*, pp. 370–418, 1763. with a commentary by Edward C. Molina. II. A letter on asymptotic series from Bayes to John Canton; pp. 269–71 of the same volume, with a commentary by W. Edwards Deming. New York: Hafner Publishing Co.

Beckett, Celia, Barbara Maughan, Michael Rutter, Jenny Castle, Emma Colvert, Christine Groothues, Jana Kreppner, Suzanne Stevens, Thomas G. O'Connor, and Edmund J. S. Sonuga-Barke. 2006. "Do the Effects of Early Severe Deprivation on Cognition Persist into Early Adolescence? Findings from the English and Romanian Adoptees Study." *Child Development* 77 (3) (May–June): 696–711.

Behne, Tanya, Malinda Carpenter, Josep Call, and Michael Tomasello. 2005. "Unwilling Versus Unable: Infants' Understanding of Intentional Action." *Developmental Psychology* 41 (2) (Mar.): 328–37.

Belsky, Jay, and Robert K. Most. 1981. "From Exploration to Play: A Cross-sectional Study of Infant Free Play Behavior." *Developmental Psychology* 17 (5) (Sept.): 630–39.

Benoit, Diane, and Kevin C. H. Parker. 1994. "Stability and Transmission of Attachment Across Three Generations." *Child Development* 65 (5) (Oct.): 1444–56.

Blair, James, Derek Mitchell, and Karina Blair. 2005. *The Psychopath: Emotion and the Brain.* Malden, Mass.: Blackwell Publishing.

Blake, D. T., N. N. Byl, and M. M. Merzenich. 2002. "Representation of the Hand in the Cerebral Cortex." *Behavioural Brain Research* 135 (1–2) (Sept. 20): 179–84.

Blehar, Mary C., Alicia F. Lieberman, and Mary D. Ainsworth. 1977. "Early Face-to-Face Interaction and Its Relation to Later Infant-Mother Attachment." *Child Development* 48 (1) (Mar.): 182–94.

Bluff, Lucas A., Alex A. S. Weir, Christian Rutz, Joanna H. Wimpenny, and Alex Kacelnik. 2007. "Tool-related Cognition in New Caledonian Crows." *Comparative Cognition & Behavior Review* 2 (1): 1–25.

Bowlby, John. 1980. *Attachment and Loss.* New York: Basic Books.

Brooks-Gunn, Jeanne, and Michael Lewis. 1984. "The Development of Early Visual Self-recognition." *Developmental Review* 4 (3) (Sept.): 215–39.

Byrne, Richard W. 2002. "Social and Technical Forms of Primate Intelligence." In *Tree of Origin: What Primate Behavior Can Tell Us About Human Social Evolution*, ed. Frans B. M. de Waal, 145–72. Cambridge, Mass.: Harvard University Press.

Byrne, Richard W., and Andrew Whiten, eds. 1988. *Machiavellian Intelligence: Social Expertise and the Evolution of Intellect in Monkeys, Apes, and Humans.* New York: Oxford University Press.

Campbell, John. 1994. *Past, Space, and Self.* Cambridge, Mass.: MIT Press.

Carey, Susan. 1985. *Conceptual Change in Childhood.* MIT press series in learning, development, and conceptual change. Cambridge, Mass.: MIT Press.

Carlson, Stephanie M., and Louis J. Moses. 2001. "Individual Differences in Inhibitory Control and Children's Theory of Mind." *Child Development* 72 (4) (July–Aug.): 1032–53.

Carlson, Stephanie M., Dorothy J. Mandell, and Luke Williams. 2004. "Executive Function and Theory of Mind: Stability and Prediction from Ages 2 to 3." *Developmental Psychology* 40 (6) (Nov.): 1105–22.

Chalmers, David John. 1996. *The Conscious Mind: In Search of a Fundamental Theory.* New York: Oxford University Press.

Chandler, Michael, and Travis Proulx. 2006. "Changing Selves in Changing Worlds: Youth Suicide on the Fault-lines of Colliding Cultures." *Archives of Suicide Research. Special Issue: Suicide Among Indigenous Peoples: The Research* 10 (2) (Mar.): 125–40.

Chen, Serena. 2003. "Psychological-state Theories About Significant Others: Implications for the Content and Structure of Significant-other Representations." *Personality and Social Psychology* Bulletin 29 (10) (Oct.): 1285–1302.

Chen, Serena, Susan M. Andersen, and Katrina Hinkley. 1999. "Triggering Transference: Examining the Role of Applicability in the Activation and Use of Significant-other Representations in Social Perception." *Social Cognition* 17 (3) (Fall): 332–65.

Christensen, Mark Schram, Lasse Kristiansen, James B. Rowe, and Jens Bo Nielsen. 2008. "Action-blindsight in Healthy Subjects After Transcranial Magnetic Stimulation." *Proceedings of the National Academy of Sciences of the United States of America* 105 (4) (Jan.): 1353–57.

Churchland, Patricia Smith. 2002. *Brain-wise: Studies in Neurophilosophy.* Cambridge, Mass.: MIT Press.

Churchland, Paul M. 1995. *The Engine of Reason, the Seat of the Soul: A Philosophical Journey into the Brain.* Cambridge, Mass.: MIT Press.

Cicchetti, Dante, and Kristin Valentino. 2006. "An Ecological-Transactional Perspective on Child Maltreatment: Failure of the Average Expectable Environment and Its Influence on Child Development." In *Developmental Psychopathology*, vol. 3: *Risk, Disorder, and Adaptation.* 2nd ed., eds. Dante Cicchetti, Donald J. Cohen, 129–201. Hoboken, N.J.: John Wiley and Sons.

Clancy, Susan A. 2005. *Abducted: How People Come to Believe They Were Abducted by Aliens.* Cambridge, Mass.: Harvard University Press.

Colby, Anne, and Lawrence Kohlberg. 1987. *The Measurement of Moral Judgment*, vol. 1: *Theoretical Foundations and Research Validation*; vol. 2: *Standard Issue Scoring Manual.* New York: Cambridge University Press.

Colombo, John. 2004. "Visual Attention in Infancy: Process and Product in Early Cognitive Development." In *Cognitive Neuroscience of Attention.* Michael I. Posner. New York: Guilford Press.

Corkin, S. 2002. "What's New with the Amnesic Patient H.M.?" *Nature Reviews Neuroscience* 3 (2) (Feb.): 153–60.

Craig, Edward. 1998. *Routledge Encyclopedia of Philosophy*, 10 vols. London: Routledge.

Csíkszentmihályi, Mihaly. 1992. *Flow: The Psychology of Optimal Experience.* New York: HarperPerennial.

Dawson, Geraldine, and Kurt W. Fischer, eds. 1994. *Human Behavior and the Developing Brain.* New York: Guilford Press.

de Villers-Sidani, E., E. F. Chang, S. Bao, and M. M. Merzenich. 2007. "Critical Period Window for Spectral Tuning Defined in the Primary Auditory Cortex (A1) in the Rat." *The Journal of Neuroscience: The Official Journal of the Society for Neuroscience* 27 (1) (Jan. 3): 180–89.

DeCasper, Anthony J., and William P. Fifer. 1980. "Of Human Bonding: Newborns Prefer Their Mothers' Voices." *Science* 208 (4448) (June): 1174–76.

Dennett, Daniel C. 1991. *Consciousness Explained.* New York: Little, Brown and Co.

———. 1992. "'Filling In' Versus Finding Out: A Ubiquitous Confusion in Cognitive Science." In *Cognition: Conceptual and Methodological Issues,* eds. Herbert L. Pick Jr., Paulus Willem van den Broek, and David C. Knill, 33–49. Washington, D.C.: American Psychological Association.

Diamond, Adele. 2002. "Normal Development of Prefrontal Cortex from Birth to Young Adulthood: Cognitive Functions, Anatomy, and Biochemistry." *Principles of Frontal Lobe Function.* New York: Oxford University Press.

Dick, D. M., and L. J. Bierut. 2006. "The Genetics of Alcohol Dependence." *Current Psychiatry Reports* 8 (2) (Apr.): 151–57.

Dickens, William T., and James R. Flynn. 2001. "Heritability Estimates Versus Large Environmental Effects: The IQ Paradox Resolved." *Psychological Review* 108 (2) (Apr.): 346–69.

Dodge, Kenneth A., and John D. Cole. 1987. "Social-information-processing Factors in Reactive and Proactive Aggression in Children's Peer Groups." *Journal of Personality and Social Psychology. Special Issue: Integrating Personality and Social Psychology* 53 (6) (Dec.): 1146–58.

Dunbar, Robin. 1996. *Grooming, Gossip, and the Evolution of Language.* Cambridge, Mass.: Harvard University Press.

Dunham, Yarrow, Andrew Baron, and Mahzarin Banaji. In press. "The Development of Implicit Intergroup Cognition." *Trends in Cognitive Science.*

Dunham, Yarrow. 2007. "Assessing the Automaticity of Intergroup Bias." Unpublished Ph.D. dissertation, Harvard University.

Eberhardt, F., and R. Scheines. 2007. "Interventions and Causal Inference." *Philosophy of Science* 74: 981.

Edwards, Paul. 1967. *The Encyclopedia of Philosophy.* New York: Macmillan.

Fawcett, Christine. 2008. "Children's Understanding of Preference." Unpublished Ph.D. dissertation, University of California at Berkeley.

Fessler, Daniel M. T., and Carlos David Navarrete. 2003. "Meat Is Good to Taboo: Dietary Proscriptions as a Product of the Interaction of Psychological Mechanisms and Social Processes." *Journal of Cognition and Culture* 3 (1): 1–40.

Field, Tiffany M., Robert Woodson, Reena Greenberg, and Debra Cohen. 1982. "Discrimination and Imitation of Facial Expressions by Neonates." *Science* 218 (4568) (Oct.): 179–81.

Fivush, Robyn, Jacquelyn T. Gray, and Fayne A. Fromhoff. 1987. "Two-year-olds Talk About the Past." *Cognitive Development* 2 (4) (Oct.): 393–409.

Flavell, John H. 1999. "Cognitive Development: Children's Knowledge About the Mind." *Annual Review of Psychology* 50: 21–45.

Flavell, John H., Frances L. Green, and Eleanor R. Flavell. 1995a. "The Development of Children's Knowledge About Attentional Focus." *Developmental Psychology* 31 (4) (July): 706–12.

———. 1995b. "Young Children's Knowledge About Thinking." *Monographs of the Society for Research in Child Development* 60 (1): v–96.

———. 2000. "Development of Children's Awareness of Their Own Thoughts." *Journal of Cognition and Development* 1 (1) 97–112.

Flavell, John H., Frances L. Green, Eleanor R. Flavell, and James B. Grossman. 1997. "The Development of Children's Knowledge About Inner Speech." *Child Development* 68 (1) (Feb.): 39–47.

Flavell, John H., Frances L. Green, Eleanor R. Flavell, and Nancy T. Lin. 1999. "Development of Children's Knowledge About Unconsciousness." *Child Development* 70 (2) (Mar.–Apr.): 396–412.

Flynn, James R. 1987. "Massive IQ Gains in 14 Nations: What IQ Tests Really Measure." *Psychological Bulletin* 101 (2) (Mar.): 171–91.

Fodor, Jerry. 1998. "The Trouble with Psychological Darwinism." *The London Review of Books.* Jan. 22.

Foot, Philippa. 2002. *Moral Dilemmas and Other Topics in Moral Philosophy.* Oxford, England: Oxford University Press.

Fraley, R. Chris, and Phillip R. Shaver. 1998. "Airport Separations: A Naturalistic Study of Adult Attachment Dynamics in Separating Couples." *Journal of Personality and Social Psychology* 75 (5) (Nov.): 1198–1212.

Garcia, John, and Robert A. Koelling. 1966. "Relation of Cue to Consequence in Avoidance Learning." *Psychonomic Science* 4 (3): 123–24.

Gelman, Susan A. 2003. *The Essential Child: Origins of Essentialism in Everyday Thought.* New York: Oxford University Press.

Gergely, György, Harold Bekkering, and Ildikó Király. 2002. "Rational Imitation in Preverbal Infants." *Nature* 415 (6873) (Feb.): 755.

Gergely, György, and Csibra Gergely. 2004. "The Social Construction of the Cultural Mind: Imitative Learning as a Mechanism of Human Pedagogy." *Interaction Studies: Social Behaviour and Communication in Biological and Artificial Systems. Special Issue: Making Minds II* 6 (3): 463–81.

Giles, Jessica W., Alison Gopnik, and Gail D. Heyman. 2002. "Source Monitoring Reduces the Suggestibility of Preschool Children." *Psychological Science* 13 (3) (May): 288–91.

Glymour, C., R. Scheines, P. Spirtes, and K. Kelly. 1988. "TETRAD: Discovering Causal Structure." *Multivariate Behavioral Research* 23 (2) (Apr.): 279–80.

Goldberg, I. I., M. Harel, and R. Malach. 2006. "When the Brain Loses Its Self: Prefrontal Inactivation During Sensorimotor Processing." *Neuron* 50 (2) (Apr. 20): 329–39.

Golland, Y., S. Bentin, H. Gelbard, Y. Benjamini, R. Heller, Y. Nir, U. Hasson, and R. Malach. 2007. "Extrinsic and Intrinsic Systems in the Posterior

Cortex of the Human Brain Revealed During Natural Sensory Stimulation." *Cerebral Cortex* 17 (4) (Apr.): 766–77.

Gopnik, Adam. 2002. "Bumping into Mr. Ravioli." *The New Yorker* 78 (29) (Sept. 30): 80.

Gopnik, Alison. 1982. "Words and Plans: Early Language and the Development of Intelligent Action." *Journal of Child Language* 9 (2) (June): 303–18.

———. 1988. "Conceptual and Semantic Development as Theory Change." *Mind and Language* 3 (Autumn): 197–216.

———. 1993. "How We Know Our Minds: The Illusion of First-person Knowledge of Intentionality." *Behavioral and Brain Sciences* 16 (1) (Mar.): 1, 14, 29–113.

———. 2007. "Cells That Read Minds? What the Myth of Mirror Neurons Gets Wrong About the Human Brain." *Slate* (Thurs., Apr. 26).

Gopnik, Alison, and Andrew N. Meltzoff. 1986. "Relations Between Semantic and Cognitive Development in the One-Word Stage: The Specificity Hypothesis." *Child Development* 57 (4) (Aug.): 1040–53.

Gopnik, Alison, and Janet W. Astington. 1988. "Children's Understanding of Representational Change and Its Relation to the Understanding of False Belief and the Appearance-Reality Distinction." *Child Development* 59 (1) (Feb.): 26–37.

Gopnik, Alison, and Peter Graf. 1988. "Knowing How You Know: Young Children's Ability to Identify and Remember the Sources of Their Beliefs." *Child Development* 59 (5) (Oct.): 1366–71.

Gopnik, Alison, and Virginia Slaughter. 1991. "Young Children's Understanding of Changes in Their Mental States." *Child Development* 62 (1) (Feb.): 98–110.

Gopnik, Alison, Clark Glymour, David M. Sobel, Laura E. Schulz, Tamar Kushnir, and David Danks. 2004. "A Theory of Causal Learning in Children: Causal Maps and Bayes Nets." *Psychological Review* 111 (1) (Jan.): 3–32.

Gopnik, Alison, David M. Sobel, Laura E. Schulz, and Clark Glymour. 2001. "Causal Learning Mechanisms in Very Young Children: Two-, Three-, and Four-Year-Olds Infer Causal Relations from Patterns of Variation and Covariation." *Developmental Psychology* 37 (5) (Sept.): 620–29.

Grandin, Temple. 1995. "How People with Autism Think." In *Learning and Cognition in Autism*, eds. Eric Schopler, Gary B. Mesibov, 137–56. New York: Plenum Press.

Greene, Joshua. 2003. "From Neural 'Is' to Moral 'Ought': What Are the Moral Implications of Neuroscientific Moral Psychology?" *Nature Reviews Neuroscience* 4 (10) (Oct.): 846–49.

Griffiths, T. L., C. Kemp, and J. B. Tenenbaum. 2008. "Bayesian Models of Cognition." In *The Cambridge Handbook of Computational Cognitive Modeling*, ed. Ron Sun. New York: Cambridge University Press.

Grossmann, Klaus E., Karin Grossmann, and Everett Waters, eds. 2005. *Attachment from Infancy to Adulthood: The Major Longitudinal Studies*. New York: Guilford Publications.

Gusella, Joanne L., Darwin Muir, and Edward A. Tronick. 1988. "The Effect of Manipulating Maternal Behavior During an Interaction on Three- and Six-Month-Olds' Affect and Attention." *Child Development* 59 (4) (Aug.): 1111–24.

Haddon, Mark. 2004. *The Curious Incident of the Dog in the Night-Time*. New York: Vintage Contemporaries.

Hagen, John W., and Gordon H. Hale. 1972. "The Development of Attention in Children." In *Minnesota Symposia on Child Psychology*. Minneapolis, Minnesota: University of Minnesota Press.

Haidt, Jonathan. 2007. "The New Synthesis in Moral Psychology." *Science* 316 (5827) (May): 998–1002.

Harris, Paul L. 2000. *The Work of the Imagination*. Malden, Mass.: Blackwell Publishing.

Harris, Paul L., Tim German, and Patrick Mills. 1996. "Children's Use of Counterfactual Thinking in Causal Reasoning." *Cognition* 61 (3) (Dec.): 233–59.

Harris, Paul L., and María Núñez. 1996. "Understanding of Permission Rules by Preschool Children." *Child Development* 67 (4) (Aug.): 1572–91.

Hass, Robert. 1996. *Sun Under Wood: New Poems*. Hopewell, N.J.: Ecco Press.

Hauser, Marc. 2006. *Moral Minds: How Nature Designed Our Universal Sense of Right and Wrong*. New York: Ecco/HarperCollins.

Hawkes, Kristen, James F. O'Connell, and Nicholas G. Blurton Jones. 2003. "Human Life Histories: Primate Trade-offs, Grandmothering Socioecology, and the Fossil Record." In *Primate Life Histories and Socioecology*, eds. Peter M. Kappeler, Michael E. Pereira, 204–27. Chicago: University of Chicago Press.

Helman, P., R. Veroff, S. R. Atlas, and C. Willman. 2004. "A Bayesian Network Classification Methodology for Gene Expression Data." *Journal of Computational Biology: A Journal of Computational Molecular Cell Biology* 11 (4): 581–615.

Herrnstein, Richard J., and Charles A. Murray. 1994. *The Bell Curve: Intelligence and Class Structure in American Life*. New York: Free Press.

Hickling, Anne K., and Henry M. Wellman. 2001. "The Emergence of Children's Causal Explanations and Theories: Evidence from Everyday Conversation." *Developmental Psychology* 37 (5) (Sept.): 668–83.

Hrdy, Sarah Blaffer. 2000. *Mother Nature: Maternal Instincts and How They Shape the Human Species*. New York: Ballantine Books.

Hume, David. 2007. *An Enquiry Concerning Human Understanding*. New York: Oxford University Press.

Huttenlocher, Peter R. 2002a. "Morphometric Study of Human Cerebral Cortex Development." In *Brain Development and Cognition: A Reader*. 2nd ed. Malden, Mass.: Blackwell Publishing.

———. 2002b. *Neural Plasticity: The Effects of Environment on the Development of the Cerebral Cortex*. Cambridge, Mass.: Harvard University Press.

Iacoboni, Marco, and Mirella Dapretto. 2006. "The Mirror Neuron System and the Consequences of Its Dysfunction." *Nature Reviews Neuroscience* 7 (12) (Dec.): 942–51.

Inagaki, Kayoko, and Giyoo Hatano. 2006. "Young Children's Conception of the Biological World." *Current Directions in Psychological Science* 15 (4) (Aug.): 177–81.

James, Henry. 1909. *The Ambassadors*. In *Novels and Tales of Henry James*, vols. 21–22. New York: Charles Scribner's Sons.

James, William. 2001. *Talks to Teachers on Psychology and to Students on Some of Life's Ideals*. Mineola, N.Y.: Dover Publications.

Johnson, Mark H., Yuko Munakata, and Rick O. Gilmore, eds. 2002. *Brain Development and Cognition: A Reader*. 2nd ed. Malden, Mass.: Blackwell Publishing.

Johnson, Susan C., Carol S. Dweck, and Frances S. Chen. 2007a. "Evidence for Infants' Internal Working Models of Attachment." *Psychological Science* 18 (6) (June): 501–502.

Johnson, Susan C., Matthias Bolz, Erin Carter, John Mandsanger, Alisha Teichner, and Patricia Zettler. 2008. "Calculating the Attentional Orientation of an Unfamiliar Agent in Infancy." *Cognitive Development* 23 (1) (Jan.): 24–37.

Johnson, Susan C., Y. Alpha Shimizu, and Su-Jeong Ok. 2007b. "Actors and Actions: The Role of Agent Behavior in Infants' Attribution of Goals." *Cognitive Development* 22 (3) (July): 310–22.

Kendler, Kenneth S., and Carol A. Prescott. 2006. *Genes, Environment, and Psychopathology: Understanding the Causes of Psychiatric and Substance Use Disorders*. New York: Guilford Press.

Kirkham, Natasha Z., Jonathan A. Slemmer, and Scott P. Johnson. 2002. "Visual Statistical Learning in Infancy: Evidence for a Domain General Learning Mechanism." *Cognition* 83 (2) (Mar.): B35–42.

Kirp, David L. 2007. *The Sandbox Investment: The Preschool Movement and Kids-First Politics*. Cambridge, Mass.: Harvard University Press.

Knight, R. T., and D. Scabini. 1998. "Anatomic Bases of Event-Related Potentials and Their Relationship to Novelty Detection in Humans." *Journal of Clinical Neurophysiology* 15: 3–13.

Krasnegor, Norman A., G. Reid Lyon, and Patricia S. Goldman-Rakic, eds. 1997. "Development of the Prefrontal Cortex: Evolution, Neurobiology, and Behavior." *Human Learning and Behavior Branch of National Institute of Child Health and Human Development*, Sept. 1994. Baltimore: Paul H. Brookes Publishing.

Kuhlmeier, Valerie, Karen Wynn, and Paul Bloom. 2003. "Attribution of Dispositional States by 12-month-olds." *Psychological Science* 14 (5) (Sept.): 402–408.

Kushnir, Tamar, and Alison Gopnik. 2005. "Young Children Infer Causal Strength from Probabilities and Interventions." *Psychological Science* 16 (9) (Sept.): 678–83.

Lalonde, Chris E., and Michael J. Chandler. 1995. "False Belief Understanding Goes to School: On the Social-Emotional Consequences of Coming Early or Late to a First Theory of Mind." *Cognition and Emotion* 9 (2–3) (Mar.–May): 167–85.

Legare, C. H., S. A. Gelman, H. M. Wellman, and T. Kushnir. 2008. "The

Function of Causal Explanatory Reasoning in Children." *Proceedings of the 30th Annual Meeting of the Cognitive Science Society.*

Lerman, J., S. Robinson, M. M. Willis, and G. A. Gregory. 1983. "Anesthetic Requirements for Halothane in Young Children 0–1 Month and 1–6 Months of Age." *Anesthesiology* 59 (5) (Nov.): 421–24.

Leslie, Alan M. 1987. "Pretense and Representation: The Origins of 'Theory of-Mind.'" *Psychological Review* 94 (4) (Oct.): 412–26.

Levenson, Robert W., Paul Ekman, and Wallace V. Friesen. 1990. "Voluntary Facial Action Generates Emotion-Specific Autonomic Nervous System Activity." *Psychophysiology* 274 (4) (July): 363–84.

Lewis, David. 1986. *Counterfactuals.* Cambridge, Mass.: Harvard University Press.

Lillard, Angeline. 2002. "Pretend Play and Cognitive Development." In *Blackwell Handbook of Childhood Cognitive Development*, ed. Usha Goswami, 189–205. Malden, Mass.: Blackwell Publishing.

Lillard, Angeline S., and David C. Witherington. 2004. "Mothers' Behavior Modifications During Pretense and Their Possible Signal Value for Toddlers." *Developmental Psychology* 40 (1) (Jan.): 95–113.

Loftus, Elizabeth F. 1997a. "Creating False Memories." *Scientific American* 277 (3) (Sept.): 70–75.

———. 1997b. "Memories for a Past That Never Was." *Current Directions in Psychological Science. Special Issue: Memory as the Theater of the Past: The Psychology of False Memories* 6 (3) (June): 60–65.

Lyons, Derek, Andrew Young, and Frank Keil. 2007. "The Hidden Structure of Over-imitation." *Proceedings of the National Academy of Sciences* 104 (50): 19751.

Mack, Arien, and Irvin Rock. 1998. *Inattentional Blindness.* Cambridge, Mass.: MIT Press.

Main, Mary, Nancy Kaplan, and Jude Cassidy. 1985. "Security in Infancy, Childhood, and Adulthood: A Move to the Level of Representation." *Monographs of the Society for Research in Child Development* 50 (1–2): 66–104.

Main, Mary, and Judith Solomon. 1986. "Discovery of an Insecure-Disorganized/ Disoriented Attachment Pattern." In *Affective Development in Infancy*, eds. T. Berry Brazelton and Michael W. Yogman, 95–124. Westport, Conn.: Ablex Publishing.

McCormack, Teresa, and Christoph Hoerl. 2005. "Children's Reasoning About the Causal Significance of the Temporal Order of Events." *Developmental Psychology* 41 (1) (Jan.): 54–63.

———. 2007. "Young Children's Reasoning About the Order of Past Events." *Journal of Experimental Child Psychology* 98 (3) (Nov.): 168–83.

Medvec, Victoria Husted, Scott F. Madey, and Thomas Gilovich. 1995. "When Less Is More: Counterfactual Thinking and Satisfaction Among Olympic Medalists." *Journal of Personality and Social Psychology* 69 (4) (Oct.): 603–10.

Meltzoff, Andrew N. 1995. "Understanding the Intentions of Others: Reenactment of Intended Acts by 18-month-old Children." *Developmental Psychology* 31 (5) (Sept.): 838–50.

————. 2007. "'Like Me': A Foundation for Social Cognition." *Developmental Science* 10 (1) (Jan.): 126–34.

Meltzoff, Andrew N., and M. Keith Moore. 1977. "Imitation of Facial and Manual Gestures by Human Neonates." *Science* 198 (4312) (Oct.): 75–78.

————. 1983. "Newborn Infants Imitate Adult Facial Gestures." *Child Development* 54 (3) (June): 702–709.

————. 1988. "Infant Imitation and Memory: Nine-month-olds in Immediate and Deferred Tests." *Child Development* 59 (1) (Feb.): 217–25.

Metherate, R., and N. M. Weinberger. 1989. "Acetylcholine Produces Stimulus-Specific Receptive Field Alterations in Cat Auditory Cortex." *Brain Research* 480 (1–2) (Feb. 20): 372–77.

Mikhail, John. 2007. "Universal Moral Grammar: Theory, Evidence and the Future." *Trends in Cognitive Sciences* 11 (4) (Apr.): 143–52.

Mikulincer, Mario, and Phillip R. Shaver. 2007. *Attachment in Adulthood: Structure, Dynamics, and Change.* New York: Guilford Press.

Milligan, Karen, Janet Wilde Astington, and Lisa Ain Dack. 2007. "Language and Theory of Mind: Meta-analysis of the Relation Between Language Ability and False-Belief Understanding." *Child Development* 78 (2) (Mar.–Apr.): 622–46.

Mischel, Walter, Yuichi Shoda, and Monica L. Rodriguez. 1989. "Delay of Gratification in Children." *Science* 244 (4907) (May): 933–38.

Nagel, Thomas. 1974. "What Is It Like to Be a Bat?" *Philosophical Review* 83 (Oct.): 435–50.

Neisser, Ulric, and Nicole Harsch. 1992. "Phantom Flashbulbs: False Recollections of Hearing the News About *Challenger.*" In *Affect and Accuracy in Recall: Studies of "Flashbulb" Memories*, eds. Eugene Winograd, Ulric Neisser, 9–31. New York: Cambridge University Press.

Nelson, Katherine, and Robyn Fivush. 2004. "The Emergence of Autobiographical Memory: A Social Cultural Developmental Theory." *Psychological Review* 111 (2): 486–511.

Núñez, María, and Paul L. Harris. 1998. "Psychological and Deontic Concepts: Separate Domains or Intimate Connection?" *Mind & Language* 13 (2) (June): 153–70.

O'Keefe, John, and Lynn Nadel. 1979. "Précis of O'Keefe and Nadel's 'The Hippocampus as a Cognitive Map.'" *Behavioral and Brain Sciences* 2 (4) (Dec.): 487–533.

O'Neill, Daniela K., and Alison Gopnik. 1991. "Young Children's Ability to Identify the Sources of Their Beliefs." *Developmental Psychology* 27 (3) (May): 390–97.

Ornstein, Peter A., Catherine A. Haden, and Holger B. Elischberger. 2006. "Children's Memory Development: Remembering the Past and Preparing for the Future." In *Lifespan Cognition: Mechanisms of Change*, eds. Ellen Bialystok and Fergus I. M. Craik. New York: Oxford University Press.

Papoušek, Mechthild, Hanus Papoušek, and Betty J. Harris. 1987. "The Emergence of Play in Parent-Infant Interactions." In *Curiosity, Imagination, and Play: On the Development of Spontaneous Cognitive Motivational Processes,* eds. Dietmar Görlitz, Joachim F. Wohlwill, 214–46. Hillsdale, N.J.: Lawrence Erlbaum Associates.

Parfit, Derek. 1984. *Reasons and Persons*. Oxford, England: Oxford University Press.

Pearl, Judea. 2000. *Causality: Models, Reasoning, and Inference*. New York: Cambridge University Press.

Peterson, Candida C., and Michael Siegal. 1995. "Deafness, Conversation and Theory of Mind." *Journal of Child Psychology and Psychiatry* 36 (3) (Mar.): 459–74.

Piaget, Jean. 1952a. *Play, Dreams and Imitation in Childhood*. New York: W. W. Norton.

———. 1952b. *The Origins of Intelligence in Children*. Oxford, England: International Universities Press.

———. 1954. *The Construction of Reality in the Child*. Oxford, England: Basic Books.

———. 1965. *The Moral Judgment of the Child*. New York: Free Press.

Pinker, Steven. 1997. *How the Mind Works*. New York: W. W. Norton.

Plato. 1888. *The Republic of Plato*. 3d ed. Translated by Benjamin Jowett. Revised and corrected throughout. Oxford, England: Oxford University Press.

Plomin, Robert. 1994. "Genetics and Experience: The Interplay Between Nature and Nurture." *Sage Series on Individual Differences and Development*, vol. 6. Thousand Oaks, Calif.: Sage Publications.

Polich, John, ed. 2003. *Detection of Change: Event-related Potential and fMRI Findings*. Dordrecht, Netherlands: Kluwer Academic Publishers.

Polley, Daniel B., Elizabeth E. Steinberg, and Michael M. Merzenich. 2006. "Perceptual Learning Directs Auditory Cortical Map Reorganization Through Top-down Influences." *Journal of Neuroscience* 26 (18) (May): 4970–82.

Posner, Michael I., ed. 2004. *Cognitive Neuroscience of Attention*. New York: Guilford Press.

Povinelli, Daniel J., Anita M. Landry, Laura A. Theall, Britten R. Clark, and Conni M. Castille. 1999. "Development of Young Children's Understanding That the Recent Past Is Causally Bound to the Present." *Developmental Psychology* 35 (6) (Nov.): 1426–39.

Povinelli, Daniel J., James E. Reaux, and Laura A. Theall, et al. 2000. *Folk Physics for Apes: The Chimpanzee's Theory of How the World Works*. Oxford, England: Oxford University Press.

Pyers, Jennie Emma. 2005. "The Relationship Between Language and False-Belief Understanding: Evidence from Learners of an Emerging Sign Language in Nicaragua." Unpublished Ph.D. dissertation, University of California at Berkeley.

Ramsey, Joseph, Paul Gazis, Ted Roush, Peter Spirtes, and Clark Glymour. 2002. "Automated Remote Sensing with Near Infrared Reflectance Spectra: Carbonate Recognition." *Data Mining and Knowledge Discovery* 6 (3) (July): 277–93.

Rankin, C. H., M. Stopfer, E. A. Marcus, and T. J. Carew. 1987. "Development of Learning and Memory in Aplysia. I. Functional Assembly of Gill and Siphon Withdrawal." *The Journal of Neuroscience: The Official Journal of the Society for Neuroscience* 7 (1) (Jan.): 120–32.

Recanzone, Gregg H., Michael M. Merzenich, and Christoph E. Schreiner. 1992a. "Changes in the Distributed Temporal Response Properties of SI Cortical Neurons Reflect Improvements in Performance on a Temporally Based Tactile Discrimination Task." *Journal of Neurophysiology* 67 (5) (May): 1071–91.

Recanzone, Gregg H., Michael M. Merzenich, and William M. Jenkins. 1992b. "Frequency Discrimination Training Engaging a Restricted Skin Surface Results in an Emergence of a Cutaneous Response Zone in Cortical Area 3a." *Journal of Neurophysiology* 67 (5) (May): 1057–70.

Reichard, Ulrich, and Christophe Boesche. 2003. *Monogamy: Mating Strategies and Partnerships in Birds, Humans and Other Mammals*. New York: Cambridge University Press.

Repacholi, Betty M., and Alison Gopnik. 1997. "Early Reasoning About Desires: Evidence from 14- and 18-month-olds." *Developmental Psychology* 33 (1) (Jan.): 12–21.

Richards, John E. 2004. "The Development of Sustained Attention in Infants." In *Cognitive Neuroscience of Attention*, ed. Michael I. Posner, 342–56. New York: Guilford Press.

Robbins, Trevor W., Jean A. Milstein, and Jeffrey W. Dalley. 2004. "Neuropharmacology of Attention." In *Cognitive Neuroscience of Attention*, ed. Michael I. Posner, 283–93. New York: Guilford Press.

Rogoff, Barbara. 1990. *Apprenticeship in Thinking: Cognitive Development in Social Context*. New York: Oxford University Press.

Rovee-Collier, Carolyn, and Rachel Barr. 2001. "Infant Learning and Memory." In *Blackwell Handbook of Infant Development*, eds. Gavin Bremner, Alan Fogel, 139–68. Malden, Mass.: Blackwell Publishing.

Rozin, Paul, Maureen Markwith, and Bonnie Ross. 1990. "The Sympathetic Magical Law of Similarity, Nominal Realism and Neglect of Negatives in Response to Negative Labels." *Psychological Science* 1 (6) (Nov.): 383–84.

Ruff, Holly Alliger, and Mary Klevjord Rothbart. 1996. *Attention in Early Development: Themes and Variations*. New York: Oxford University Press.

Ruffman, Ted, Josef Perner, Mika Naito, Lindsay Parkin, and Wendy A. Clements. 1998. "Older (but Not Younger) Siblings Facilitate False Belief Understanding." *Developmental Psychology* 34 (1) (Jan.): 161–74.

Rutter, Michael. 2006. *Genes and Behavior: Nature-Nurture Interplay Explained*. Malden, Mass.: Blackwell Publishing.

Rutter, Michael, Celia Beckett, Jenny Castle, Emma Colvert, Jana Kreppner, Mitul Mehta, Suzanne Stevens, and Edmund Sonuga-Barke. 2007. "Effects of Profound Early Institutional Deprivation: An Overview of Findings from a UK Longitudinal Study of Romanian Adoptees." *European Journal of Developmental Psychology* 4 (3) (Sept.): 332–50.

Rutter, Michael, Thomas G. O'Connor, and English and Romanian Adoptees (ERA) Study Team. 2004. "Are There Biological Programming Effects for

Psychological Development? Findings from a Study of Romanian Adoptees."
  Developmental Psychology 40 (1) (Jan.): 81–94.
Saffran, Jenny R., Elizabeth K. Johnson, Richard N. Aslin, and Elissa L. New-
  port. 1999. "Statistical Learning of Tone Sequences by Human Infants and
  Adults." *Cognition* 70 (1) (Feb.): 27–52.
Saffran, Jenny R., Richard N. Aslin, and Elissa L. Newport. 1996. "Statistical
  Learning by 8-month-old Infants." *Science* 274 (5294) (Dec.): 1926–28.
Schacter, Daniel L., Donna Rose Addis, and Randy L. Buckner. 2007. "Re-
  membering the Past to Imagine the Future: The Prospective Brain." *Nature
  Reviews Neuroscience* 8 (9) (Sept.): 657–61.
Scheines, R., P. Spirtes, C. Glymour, C. Meek, and T. Richardson. 1998. "The
  TETRAD Project: Constraint Based Aids to Causal Model Specification."
  Multivariate Behavioral Research 33 (1): 65–117.
Schult, Carolyn A., and Henry M. Wellman. 1997. "Explaining Human Move-
  ments and Actions: Children's Understanding of the Limits of Psychologi-
  cal Explanation." *Cognition* 62 (3) (Mar.): 291–324.
Schulz, Laura E., Alison Gopnik, and Clark Glymour. 2007. "Preschool Children
  Learn About Causal Structure from Conditional Interventions." *Develop-
  mental Science* 10 (3) (May): 322–32.
Schulz, Laura E., and Alison Gopnik. 2004. "Causal Learning Across Domains."
  Developmental Psychology 40 (2) (Mar.): 162–76.
Schulz, Laura E., and Elizabeth Baraff Bonawitz. 2007. "Serious Fun: Pre-
  schoolers Engage in More Exploratory Play When Evidence Is Con-
  founded." *Developmental Psychology* 43 (4): 1045–50.
Scoville, William Beecher, and Brenda Milner. 1957. "Loss of Recent Memory
  After Bilateral Hippocampal Lesions." *Journal of Neurology, Neurosurgery &
  Psychiatry* 20: 11–21.
Searle, John R. 1992. *The Rediscovery of the Mind*. Cambridge, Mass.: MIT Press.
Shaw, P., D. Greenstein, J. Lerch, L. Clasen, R. Lenroot, N. Gogtay, A. Evans,
  J. Rapoport, and J. Giedd. 2006. "Intellectual Ability and Cortical Develop-
  ment in Children and Adolescents." *Nature* 440 (7084) (Mar.): 676–79.
Shimamura, Arthur P., and Larry R. Squire. 1987. "A Neuropsychological Study
  of Fact Memory and Source Amnesia." *Journal of Experimental Psychology:
  Learning, Memory, and Cognition* 13 (3) (July): 464–73.
Shimizu, Y. Alpha, and Susan C. Johnson. 2004. "Infants' Attribution of a Goal
  to a Morphologically Unfamiliar Agent." *Developmental Science* 7 (4)
  (Sept.): 425–30.
Simons, Daniel J., and Christopher F. Chabris. 1999. "Gorillas in Our Midst:
  Sustained Inattentional Blindness for Dynamic Events." *Perception* 28 (9):
  1059–74.
Singer, Peter. 1976. *Animal Liberation: A New Ethics for Our Treatment of Ani-
  mals*. London: Cape.
Škvorecký, Josef. 1999. *The Engineer of Human Souls*. Normal, Ill.: Dalkey
  Archive Press.
Smetana, Judith G. 1981. "Preschool Children's Conceptions of Moral and So-
  cial Rules." *Child Development* 52 (4) (Dec.): 1333–36.

————. 1984. "Toddlers' Social Interactions Regarding Moral and Conventional Transgressions." *Child Development* 55 (5) (Oct.): 1767–76.

————. 1985. "Preschool Children's Conceptions of Transgressions: Effects of Varying Moral and Conventional Domain-Related Attributes." *Developmental Psychology* 21 (1) (Jan.): 18–29.

————. 1989. "Toddlers' Social Interactions in the Context of Moral and Conventional Transgressions in the Home." *Developmental Psychology* 25 (4) (July): 499–508.

Smetana, Judith G., and Judith L. Braeges. 1990. "The Development of Toddlers' Moral and Conventional Judgments." *Merrill-Palmer Quarterly* 36 (3) (July): 329–46.

Smetana, Judith G., Mario Kelly, and Craig T. Twentyman. 1984. "Abused, Neglected, and Nonmaltreated Children's Conceptions of Moral and Social-Conventional Transgressions." *Child Development* 55 (1) (Feb.): 277–87.

Smetana, Judith G., Naomi Schlagman, and Patricia W. Adams. 1993. "Preschool Children's Judgments About Hypothetical and Actual Transgressions." *Child Development* 64 (1) (Feb.): 202–14.

Sobel, David M. 2002. "Examining the Coherence of Young Children's Understanding of Causality: Evidence from Inference, Explanation, and Counterfactual Reasoning." Unpublished Ph.D. dissertation, University of California at Berkeley.

————. 2004. "Exploring the Coherence of Young Children's Explanatory Abilities: Evidence from Generating Counterfactuals." *British Journal of Developmental Psychology* 22 (1) (Mar.): 37–58.

Sobel, David M., and Natasha Z. Kirkham. 2006. "Blickets and Babies: The Development of Causal Reasoning in Toddlers and Infants." *Developmental Psychology* 42 (6) (Nov.): 1103–15.

Sobel, David M., Joshua B. Tenenbaum, and Alison Gopnik. 2004. "Children's Causal Inferences from Indirect Evidence: Backwards Blocking and Bayesian Reasoning in Preschoolers." *Cognitive Science: A Multidisciplinary Journal* 28 (3) (May–June): 303–33.

Sodian, Beate, Catherine Taylor, Paul L. Harris, and Josef Perner. 1991. "Early Deception and the Child's Theory of Mind: False Trails and Genuine Markers." *Child Development* 62 (3) (June): 468–83.

Song, Myung-ja, Judith G. Smetana, and Sang Yoon Kim. 1987. "Korean Children's Conceptions of Moral and Conventional Transgressions." *Developmental Psychology* 23 (4) (July): 577–82.

Spangler, G., and K. E. Grossmann. 1993. "Biobehavioral Organization in Securely and Insecurely Attached Infants." *Child Development* 64 (5) (Oct.): 1439–50.

Spirtes, Peter, Clark N. Glymour, and Richard Scheines. 1993. *Causation, Prediction, and Search.* New York: Springer-Verlag.

Steinbach, M., Pang-Ning Tan, Vipin Kumar, Steven Klooster, and Christopher Potter. 2003. "Discovery of Climate Indices Using Clustering." *Proceedings of 2003 Conference on Knowledge, Discovery, and Data Mining.*

Sulloway, Frank J. 1996. *Born to Rebel: Birth Order, Family Dynamics, and Creative Lives.* New York: Pantheon Books.

Suzuki, Shunryu, and Edward Espe Brown. 2002. *Not Always So: Practicing the True Spirit of Zen.* New York: HarperCollins.

Tajfel, Henri. 1982. "Social Psychology of Intergroup Relations." *Annual Review of Psychology* 33: 1–39.

Talwar, Victoria, and Kang Lee. 2002. "Development of Lying to Conceal a Transgression: Children's Control of Expressive Behaviour During Verbal Deception." *International Journal of Behavioral Development* 26 (5) (Sept.): 436–44.

Taylor, Marjorie. 1999. *Imaginary Companions and the Children Who Create Them.* New York: Oxford University Press.

Taylor, R. H., and J. Lerman. 1991. "Minimum Alveolar Concentration of Desflurane and Hemodynamic Responses in Neonates, Infants, and Children." *Anesthesiology* 75 (6) (Dec.): 975–79.

Thomson, Judith Jarvis. 1976. "Killing, Letting Die, and the Trolley Problem." *Monist: An International Quarterly Journal of General Philosophical Inquiry* 59 (Apr.): 204–17.

Tolman, Edward C. 1948. "Cognitive Maps in Rats and Men." *Psychological Review* 55 (4) (July): 189–208.

Tulving, Endel. 2002. "Episodic Memory: From Mind to Brain." *Annual Review of Psychology* 53 (1): 1–25.

Turiel, Elliot. 1983. *The Development of Social Knowledge: Morality and Convention.* New York: Cambridge University Press.

Turing, Alan M. 1950. "I.—Computing Machinery and Intelligence." *Mind* 59 (236) (Oct. 1): 433–60.

Turkheimer, Eric, Andreana Haley, Mary Waldron, Brian D'Onofrio, and Irving I. Gottesman. 2003. "Socioeconomic Status Modifies Heritability of IQ in Young Children." *Psychological Science* 14 (6) (Nov.): 623–28.

Tversky, Amos, and Daniel Kahneman. 1973. *Judgment Under Uncertainty: Heuristics and Biases.* Oxford, England: Oregon Research Institute.

Uzgiris, Ina C., and J. McV. Hunt. 1975. *Assessment in Infancy: Ordinal Scales of Psychological Development.* Champaign: University of Illinois Press.

Van Ijzendoorn, Marinus H., and Pieter M. Kroonenberg. 1988. "Cross-Cultural Patterns of Attachment: A Meta-analysis of the Strange Situation." *Child Development* 59 (1) (Feb.): 147–56.

Warneken, Felix, and Michael Tomasello. 2006. "Altruistic Helping in Human Infants and Young Chimpanzees." *Science* 311 (5765) (Mar.): 1301–303.

————. 2007. "Helping and Cooperation at 14 Months of Age." *Infancy* 11 (3): 271–94.

Watson, John S. 1972. "Smiling, Cooing, and 'the Game.'" *Merrill-Palmer Quarterly* (10).

Wegner, Daniel M. 2002. *The Illusion of Conscious Will.* Cambridge, Mass.: MIT Press.

Weinberg, Katherine M., and Edward Z. Tronick. 1996. "Infant Affective Reactions to the Resumption of Maternal Interaction After the Still-face." *Child Development* 67 (3) (June): 905–14.

Weiskrantz, Lawrence. 2007. "The Case of Blindsight." In *The Blackwell Companion to Consciousness*, eds. Max Velmans, Susan Schneider, 175–80. Malden, Mass.: Blackwell Publishing.

Wellman, Henry M. 2002. "Understanding the Psychological World: Developing a Theory of Mind." In *Blackwell Handbook of Childhood Cognitive Development*, ed. Usha Goswami, 167–87. Malden, Mass.: Blackwell Publishing.

Wellman, Henry M., and David Estes. 1986. "Early Understanding of Mental Entities: A Reexamination of Childhood Realism." *Child Development* 57 (4) (Aug.): 910–23.

Wellman, Henry M., and Joan Miller. In press. "Including Deontic Reasoning as Fundamental to Theory of Mind." *Human Development*.

Wellman, Henry M., and Susan A. Gelman. 1992. "Cognitive Development: Foundational Theories of Core Domains." *Annual Review of Psychology* 43: 337–75.

Wellman, Henry M., Ann T. Phillips, and Thomas Rodriguez. 2000. "Young Children's Understanding of Perception, Desire, and Emotion." *Child Development* 71 (4) (July–Aug.): 895–912.

Wellman, Henry M., David Cross, and Julanne Watson. 2001. "Meta-analysis of Theory-of-Mind Development: The Truth About False Belief." *Child Development* 72 (3) (May–June): 655–84.

Willatts, Peter. 1999. "Development of Means-End Behavior in Young Infants: Pulling a Support to Retrieve a Distant Object." *Developmental Psychology* 35 (3) (May): 651–67.

Williams, Bernard. 1985. *Ethics and the Limits of Philosophy*. Cambridge, Mass.: Harvard University Press.

Wimmer, Heinz, and Josef Perner. 1983. "Beliefs About Beliefs: Representation and Constraining Function of Wrong Beliefs in Young Children's Understanding of Deception." *Cognition* 13 (1) (Jan.): 103–28.

Woodward, Amanda. 1998. "Infants Selectively Encode the Goal Object of an Actor's Reach." *Cognition* 69 (1), (Nov.): 1–34.

Woodward, James. 2003. *Making Things Happen: A Theory of Causal Explanation*. Oxford, England: Oxford University Press.

Woolley, Jacqueline D., and Henry M. Wellman. 1990. "Young Children's Understanding of Realities, Nonrealities, and Appearances." *Child Development* 61 (4) (Aug.): 946–61.

———. 1993. "Origin and Truth: Young Children's Understanding of Imaginary Mental Representations." *Child Development* 64 (1) (Feb.): 1–17.

Xu, Fei, and Vashti Garcia. 2008. "Intuitive Statistics by 8-Month-Old Infants." *Proceedings of the National Academy of Sciences* 105 (13) (Apr. 1): 5012–15.

Zhang, L. I., S. Bao, and M. M. Merzenich. 2001. "Persistent and Specific Influences of Early Acoustic Environments on Primary Auditory Cortex." *Nature Neuroscience* 4 (11) (Nov.): 1123–30.

Zimbardo, Philip. 2007. *The Lucifer Effect: Understanding How Good People Turn Evil*. New York: Random House.

Acknowledgments

*

This book took me five years to write and the number of people who helped grew steadily each year. The University of California at Berkeley has been my home and native land for many years, particularly the Department of Psychology, the Institute of Human Development, and the Institute of Cognitive and Brain Sciences; I have been deeply influenced by all my colleagues and students there. Among my colleagues, Steve Palmer, Lucia Jacobs, Tom Griffiths, Tania Lombrozo, and Mary Main all contributed ideas to this book. My graduate students and postdocs, past and present, have contributed greatly to this book and to all my work, including Frederick Eberhardt, Tamar Kushnir, Chris Lucas, David Sobel, Elizabeth Seiver, and especially Laura Schulz.

I began this book thanks to a fellowship at the Center for Advanced Study in the Behavioral Sciences at Stanford University. A year at the center is one of the few experiences in life that is actually even better than you think it will be, and I am deeply grateful to the staff at that magnificent institution and to my fellow fellows there, especially Thomas Richardson, Bas van Fraassen, and Webb

Keane. I finished *The Philosophical Baby* thanks to a Moore Distinguished Visiting Scholar fellowship at another magnificent institution, the California Institute of Technology. I am also very grateful to all the friends and colleagues at Caltech who read and commented on the manuscript, including Jim Woodward, Chris Hitchcock, Jiji Zhang, Dominic Murphy, Zoltan Nadasdy, and Fiona Cowie. Christof Koch was especially helpful in educating me about the neuroscience of consciousness.

The National Science Foundation funded my research for many years. This book, however, owes an especially large debt to the James S. McDonnell Foundation and its president, John Bruer, for helping fund the Causal Learning Collaborative, a unique joint venture among developmental psychologists, philosophers, and computer scientists. Being part of this collaboration has been the most stimulating and rewarding experience of my intellectual life, and all of its members have made central contributions to this book. But I must particularly thank four of these collaborators, who have also been long-standing and profound intellectual mentors and good friends. Andrew Meltzoff first taught me about Piaget thirty years ago at Oxford and has been a collaborator, coauthor, and cothinker ever since. Henry Wellman and I have exchanged thoughts about children, philosophy, morality, religion, and much else for nearly twenty years, and he read and commented on most of the manuscript with characteristic thoughtfulness and insight. John Campbell has been a philosophical guide for many years and was part of the causal learning group at the Center for Advanced Study in the Behavioral Sciences—working through the mathematics and philosophy of causal inference together was a pleasure. Clark Glymour, above all—the smartest guy I know—was the source of central ideas in this book, and bringing

"Baby Bayes Nets" into the world with him has been a great satisfaction and joy.

Other colleagues and friends read and advised on crucial parts of the manuscript. Michael Merzenich and John Colombo provided invaluable help for the consciousness chapter. Paul Harris provided special help with the chapters on imagination. Jane Hirshfield read several drafts and contributed her ex-monk's knowledge of Buddhism, her sage's sense of the numinous, and her poet's ear for language. I owe a great debt to Eric Chinski, my editor at Farrar, Straus and Giroux, who had faith in the book from the start and guided it through the finish. Katinka Matson, my agent, was invaluable in seeing the book through several rocky patches, and it simply would not have been finished without her help.

This book argues that, for all human beings, children and families are among the greatest sources of meaning, truth, and love. I may be accused of overgeneralizing from my own experience—my own family has unquestionably been the most important part of my life. My parents, Myrna and Irwin, and my siblings, Adam, Morgan, Hilary, Blake, and Melissa, are the foundation of everything I am and everything I do. Adam and Blake played an especially important role in this book. Adam read drafts, suggested titles, and gave invaluable literary advice. And, at a difficult time in my life, Blake consoled and counseled and talked and talked and talked. This book is dedicated to him with love and gratitude. Finally, my own children, Alexei, Nicholas, and Andres Gopnik-Lewinski, are, simply, the meaning of my life, and I am deeply grateful to them and their father, George Lewinski.

I am lucky that this book was written in beautiful places, in Stanford and Berkeley and Caltech. But the happiest writing was in the most beautiful place of all—Alvy Ray Smith's tranquil and serene beach house on Puget Sound. It is emblematic of the intelligence and art, happiness and peace, and love and companionship that he has brought to my life, not to mention the formatting skills. The bibliography of this book alone would justify endless gratitude; I can't possibly be thankful enough for all the rest.

Index

*

National Aeronautics and Space
Administration (NASA), 43, 80,
81
neuroscience, 5, 14, 114, 119,
131, 207, 213, 215; computer
metaphor for brain in, 190;
lantern consciousness and, 130;
mirror neurons in, 207; plasticity
in, 8–9, 12; "trolleyology" and,
215
neurotransmitters, cholinergic and
inhibitory, 113–15, 119–20, 125
New Yorker, The, 51
New York Times, The, 113
"No child left behind" testing
policies, 28
normative reasoning, 221–25, 227,
245

observational learning, 80–85, 92,
105, 244
occipital cortex, 120
Olympic Games, 22
open awareness meditative
practices, 127–28, 154, 155
orphans, see adopted children
Oxford University, 26, 28

paracosms, 53–54, 61
paradigm shifts, 158
Parfit, Derek, 165
parietal cortex, 120
past: reconstructing, 26–27; see
also early childhood experience
Pavlov, Ivan, 134

Pearl, Judea, 42
Perry, Anne, 54
Perry Preschool Project, 177, 178
personality traits, conclusions
about, 99–100
Phaedo (Plato), 235
phenylketonuria (PKU), 171–72,
174
Philadelphia Museum of Art, 135,
140
philosophy, 8–9, 14, 235–36; Asian,
160; ethical theories in, 214–16,
219–21; Greek, 15, 70, 74–75, 164,
235–36; of consciousness, 160–62;
of science, 16, 42
physics, 191; everyday ideas about,
38, 48, 183; intuitions about, 228
Piaget, Jean, 20, 30, 88, 163, 190,
202–204
Picasso, Pablo, 135
Pinker, Steven, 82
planning, 11–13, 20, 110, 152,
153; attention and, 127–29,
131; causal maps and, 96;
consciousness and, 110, 131–32,
155, 156; counterfactuals of,
23–25, 73; executive control
and, 148–49, 159; identity and,
133–34
plasticity, 8, 12–14, 106, 159;
attention and, 114–15, 120, 125
Plato, 47, 74–75, 104–105,
235–36
play, 14, 70–73, 244; experimental,
88–91, 105; imaginative, 27–31
(see also pretending;
companions, imaginary)
Pleistocene epoch, 7, 9, 203
poetry, 47; Romantic, 130, 131